HOMICIDAL PSYCHO
JUNGLE CAT

Other Books by Bill Watterson

Calvin and Hobbes
Something Under the Bed Is Drooling
Yukon Ho!
Weirdos from Another Planet
The Revenge of the Baby-Sat
Scientific Progress Goes "Boink"
Attack of the Deranged Mutant Killer Monster Snow Goons
The Days Are Just *Packed*

Treasury Collections

The Essential Calvin and Hobbes
The Calvin and Hobbes Lazy Sunday Book
The Authoritative Calvin and Hobbes
The Indispensable Calvin and Hobbes

HOMICIDAL PSYCHO JUNGLE CAT

A Calvin and Hobbes Collection by Bill Watterson

WARNER BOOKS

A *Warner* Book

First published in Great Britain by Warner Books in 1994

Homicidal Psycho Jungle Cat copyright © 1994 by Bill Watterson
All rights reserved

Calvin and Hobbes is a cartoon feature created by Bill Watterson, syndicated
internationally by Universal Press Syndicate and first published in the United States by
Andrews and McMeel

The moral right of the author has been asserted.

A CIP catalogue record for this book
is available from the British Library.

ISBN 0 7515 1127 7

Printed and bound in Great Britain by
BPC Hazell Books Ltd
A member of
The British Printing Company Ltd

Warner Books
A Division of
Little, Brown and Company (UK) Limited
Brettenham House
Lancaster Place
London WC2E 7EN

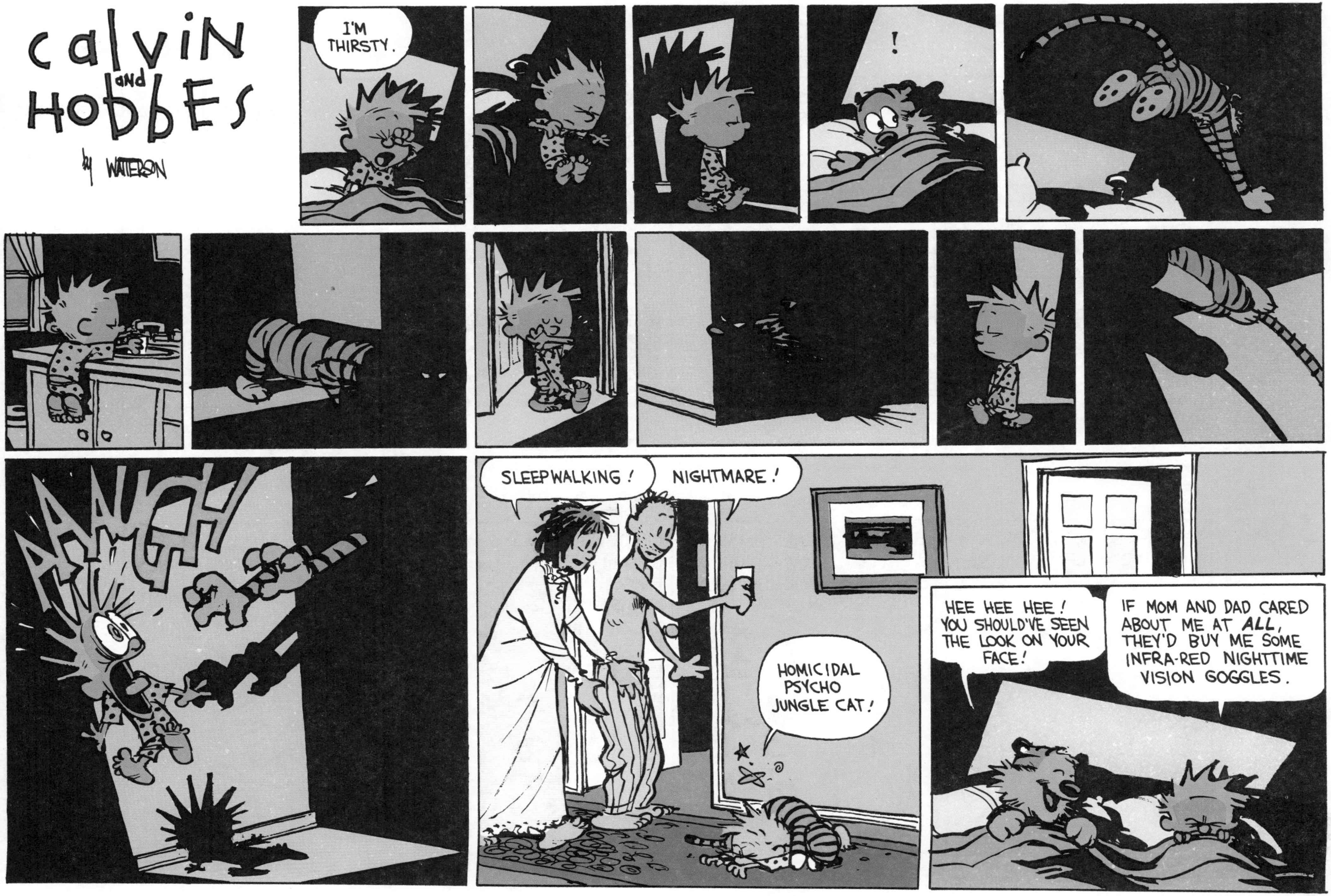
calvin and Hobbes
by WATTERSON
I'M THIRSTY.
!
AAAUGH
SLEEPWALKING!
NIGHTMARE!
HOMICIDAL PSYCHO JUNGLE CAT!
HEE HEE HEE! YOU SHOULD'VE SEEN THE LOOK ON YOUR FACE!
IF MOM AND DAD CARED ABOUT ME AT ALL, THEY'D BUY ME SOME INFRA-RED NIGHTTIME VISION GOGGLES.

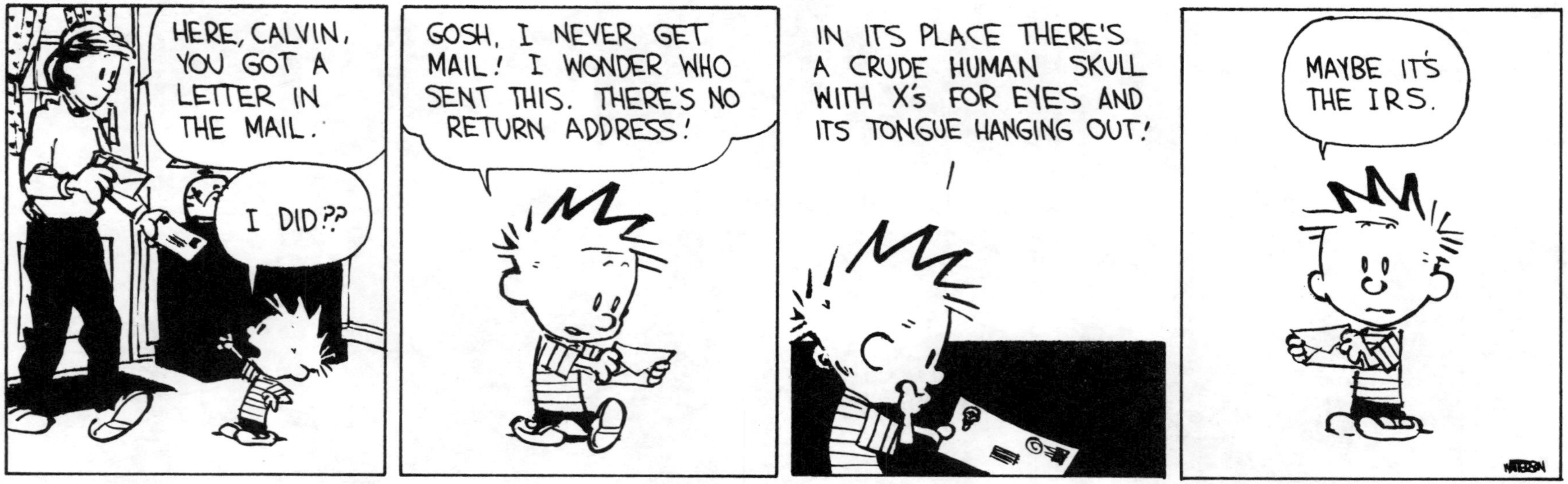
HERE, CALVIN, YOU GOT A LETTER IN THE MAIL.
I DID??
GOSH, I NEVER GET MAIL! I WONDER WHO SENT THIS. THERE'S NO RETURN ADDRESS!
IN ITS PLACE THERE'S A CRUDE HUMAN SKULL WITH X's FOR EYES AND ITS TONGUE HANGING OUT!
MAYBE IT'S THE IRS.

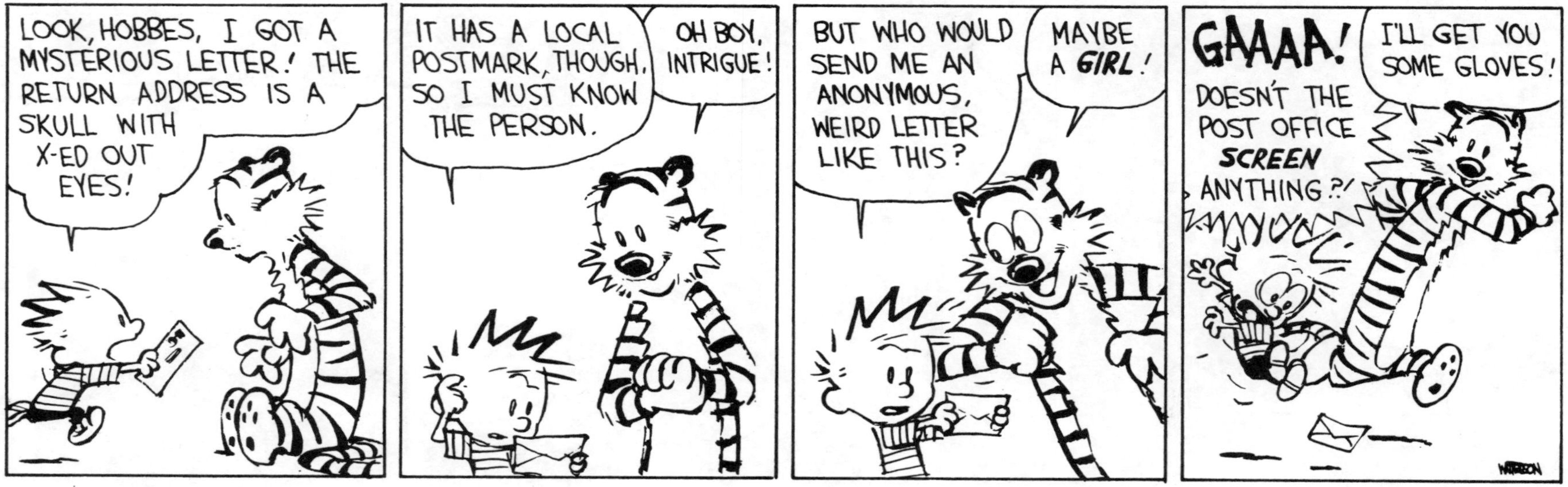
LOOK, HOBBES, I GOT A MYSTERIOUS LETTER! THE RETURN ADDRESS IS A SKULL WITH X-ED OUT EYES!
IT HAS A LOCAL POSTMARK, THOUGH, SO I MUST KNOW THE PERSON.
OH BOY, INTRIGUE!
BUT WHO WOULD SEND ME AN ANONYMOUS, WEIRD LETTER LIKE THIS?
MAYBE A GIRL!
GAAAA!
DOESN'T THE POST OFFICE SCREEN ANYTHING?!
I'LL GET YOU SOME GLOVES!

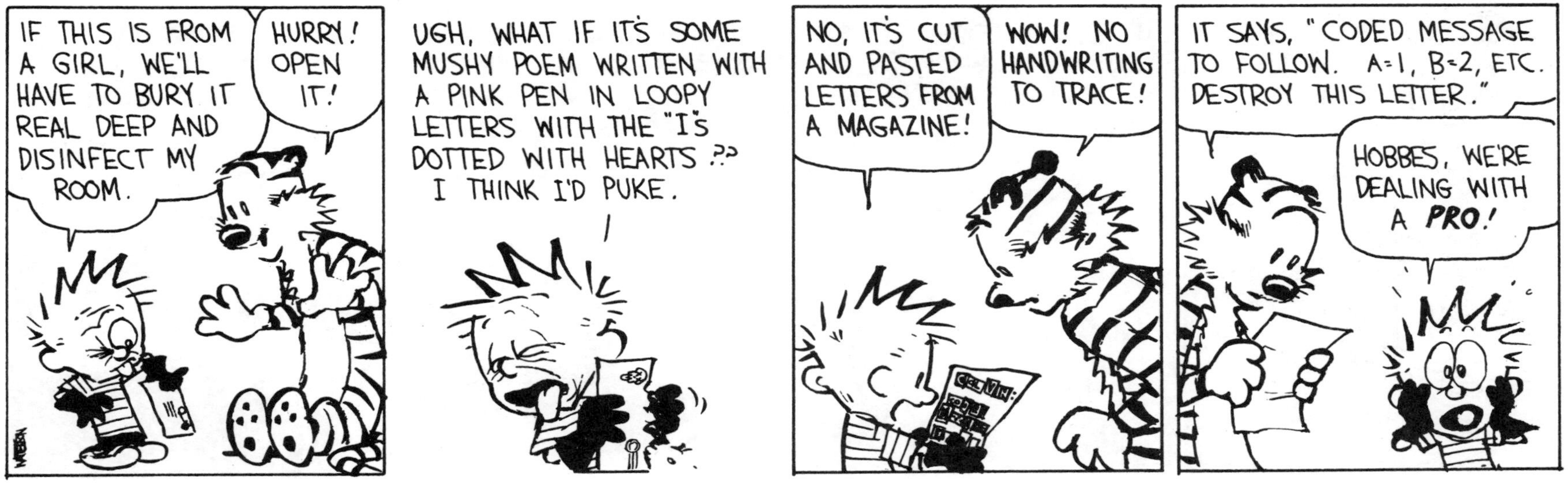
IF THIS IS FROM A GIRL, WE'LL HAVE TO BURY IT REAL DEEP AND DISINFECT MY ROOM.
HURRY! OPEN IT!
UGH, WHAT IF IT'S SOME MUSHY POEM WRITTEN WITH A PINK PEN IN LOOPY LETTERS WITH THE "I'S DOTTED WITH HEARTS ?? I THINK I'D PUKE.
NO, IT'S CUT AND PASTED LETTERS FROM A MAGAZINE!
WOW! NO HANDWRITING TO TRACE!
IT SAYS, "CODED MESSAGE TO FOLLOW. A=1, B=2, ETC. DESTROY THIS LETTER."
HOBBES, WE'RE DEALING WITH A **PRO**!

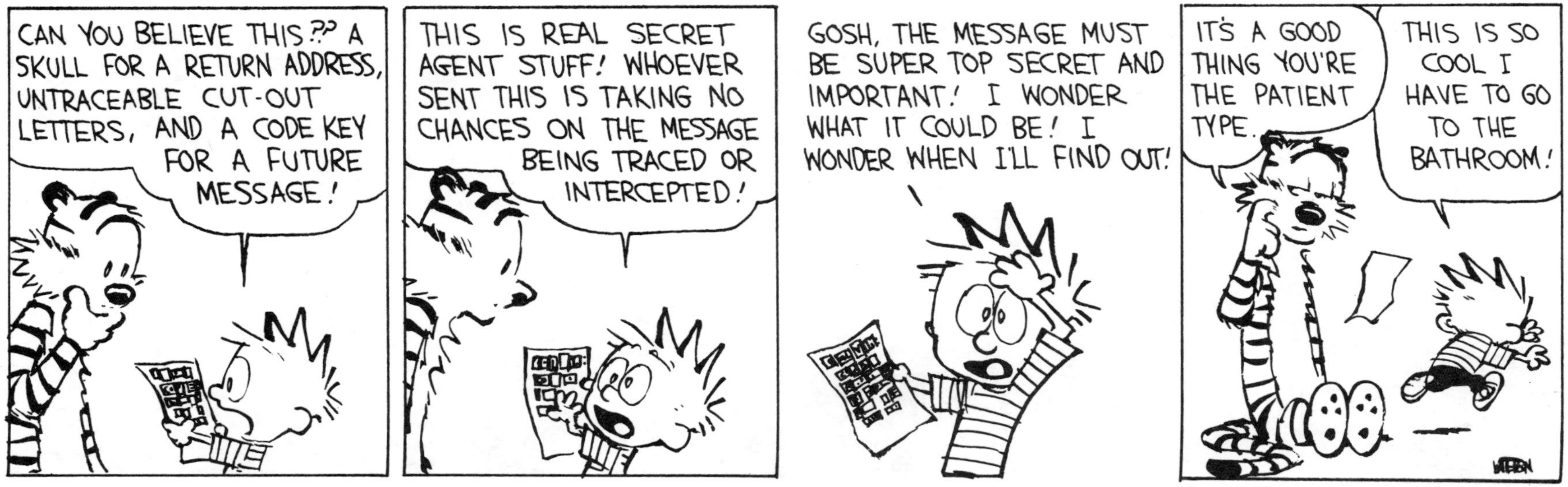
CAN YOU BELIEVE THIS?? A SKULL FOR A RETURN ADDRESS, UNTRACEABLE CUT-OUT LETTERS, AND A CODE KEY FOR A FUTURE MESSAGE!
THIS IS REAL SECRET AGENT STUFF! WHOEVER SENT THIS IS TAKING NO CHANCES ON THE MESSAGE BEING TRACED OR INTERCEPTED!
GOSH, THE MESSAGE MUST BE SUPER TOP SECRET AND IMPORTANT! I WONDER WHAT IT COULD BE! I WONDER WHEN I'LL FIND OUT!
IT'S A GOOD THING YOU'RE THE PATIENT TYPE.
THIS IS SO COOL I HAVE TO GO TO THE BATHROOM!

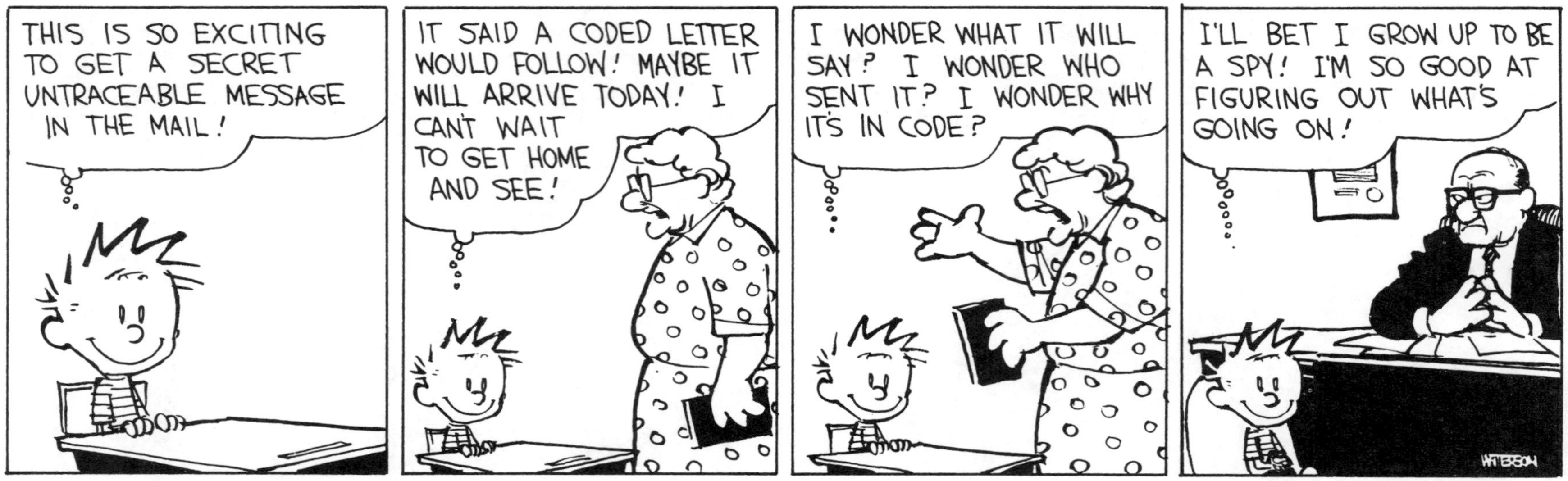
THIS IS SO EXCITING TO GET A SECRET UNTRACEABLE MESSAGE IN THE MAIL!
IT SAID A CODED LETTER WOULD FOLLOW! MAYBE IT WILL ARRIVE TODAY! I CAN'T WAIT TO GET HOME AND SEE!
I WONDER WHAT IT WILL SAY? I WONDER WHO SENT IT? I WONDER WHY IT'S IN CODE?
I'LL BET I GROW UP TO BE A SPY! I'M SO GOOD AT FIGURING OUT WHAT'S GOING ON!
WATTERSON

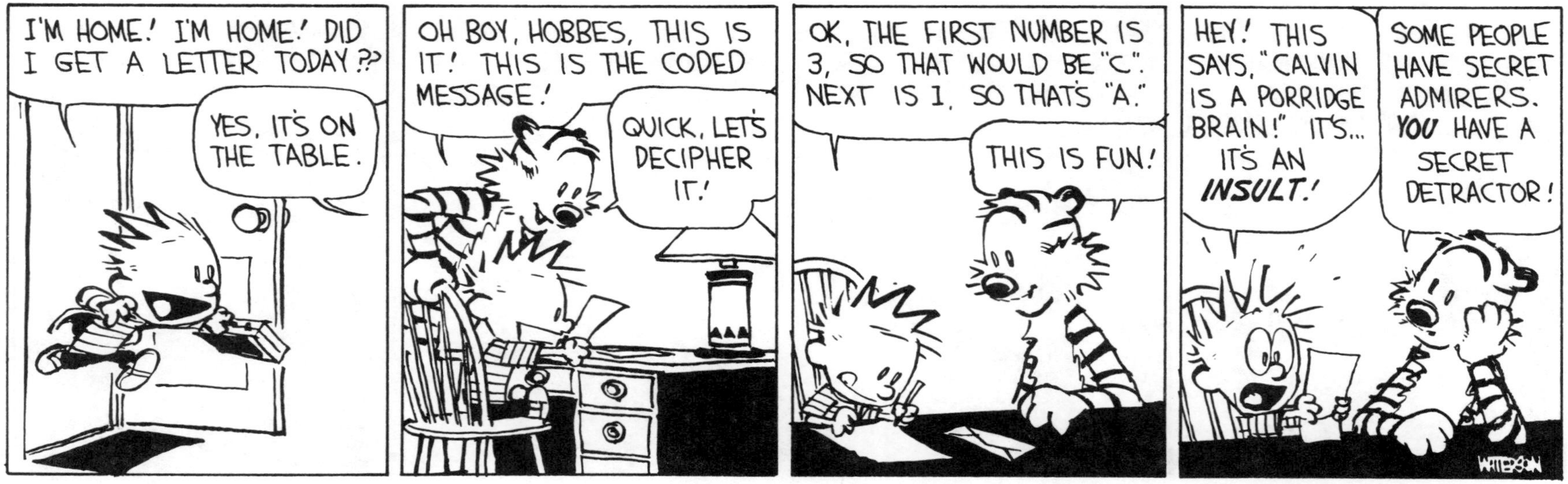
I'M HOME! I'M HOME! DID I GET A LETTER TODAY?!?
YES, IT'S ON THE TABLE.
OH BOY, HOBBES, THIS IS IT! THIS IS THE CODED MESSAGE!
QUICK, LET'S DECIPHER IT!
OK, THE FIRST NUMBER IS 3, SO THAT WOULD BE "C". NEXT IS 1, SO THAT'S "A."
THIS IS FUN!
HEY! THIS SAYS, "CALVIN IS A PORRIDGE BRAIN!" IT'S... IT'S AN **INSULT**!
SOME PEOPLE HAVE SECRET ADMIRERS. **YOU** HAVE A SECRET DETRACTOR!
WATTERSON

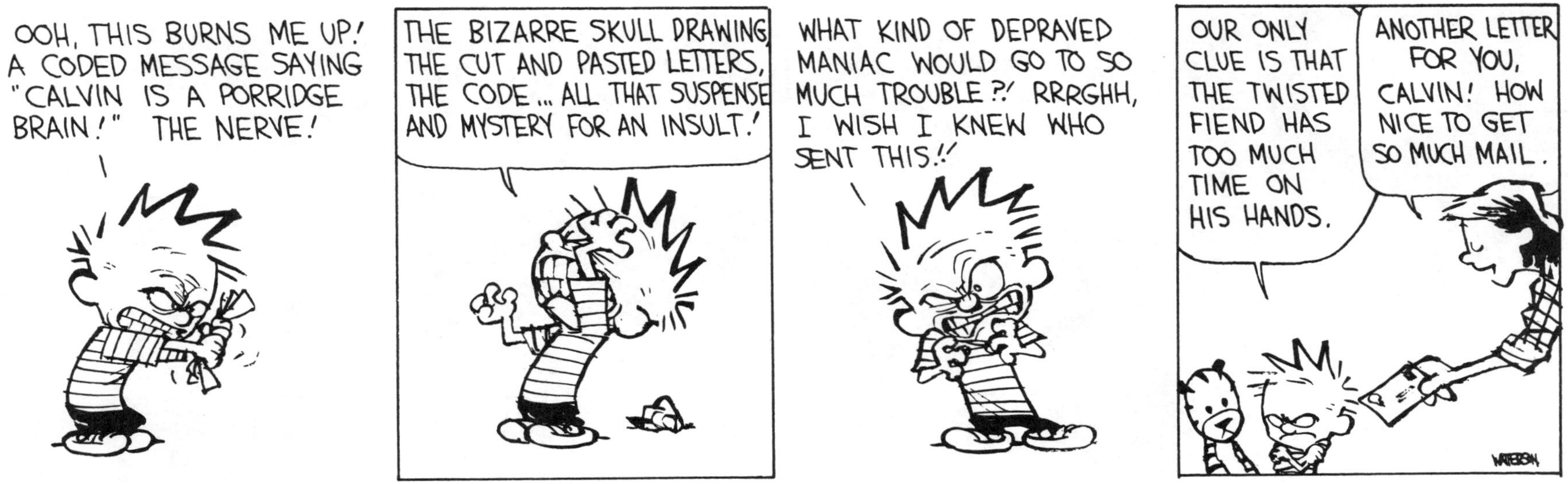
OOH, THIS BURNS ME UP! A CODED MESSAGE SAYING "CALVIN IS A PORRIDGE BRAIN!" THE NERVE!
THE BIZARRE SKULL DRAWING, THE CUT AND PASTED LETTERS, THE CODE... ALL THAT SUSPENSE AND MYSTERY FOR AN INSULT!
WHAT KIND OF DEPRAVED MANIAC WOULD GO TO SO MUCH TROUBLE?! RRRGHH, I WISH I KNEW WHO SENT THIS!!
OUR ONLY CLUE IS THAT THE TWISTED FIEND HAS TOO MUCH TIME ON HIS HANDS.
ANOTHER LETTER FOR YOU, CALVIN! HOW NICE TO GET SO MUCH MAIL.
WATTERSON

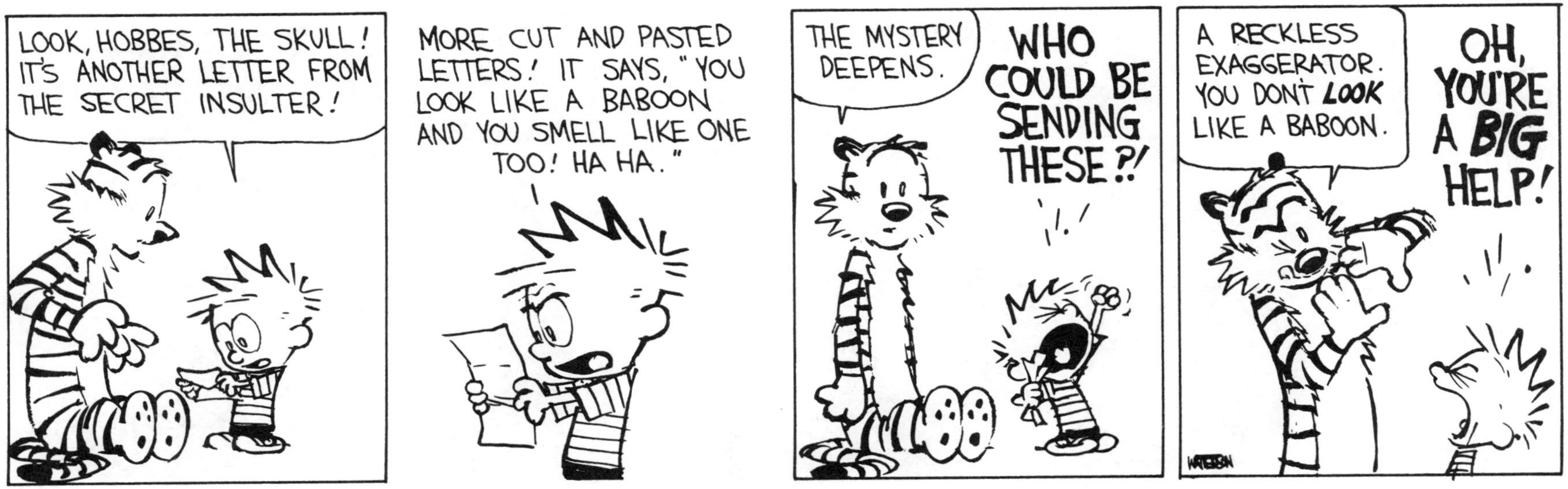
LOOK, HOBBES, THE SKULL! IT'S ANOTHER LETTER FROM THE SECRET INSULTER!
MORE CUT AND PASTED LETTERS! IT SAYS, "YOU LOOK LIKE A BABOON AND YOU SMELL LIKE ONE TOO! HA HA."
THE MYSTERY DEEPENS.
WHO COULD BE SENDING THESE?!
WATTERSON
A RECKLESS EXAGGERATOR. YOU DON'T LOOK LIKE A BABOON.
OH, YOU'RE A BIG HELP!

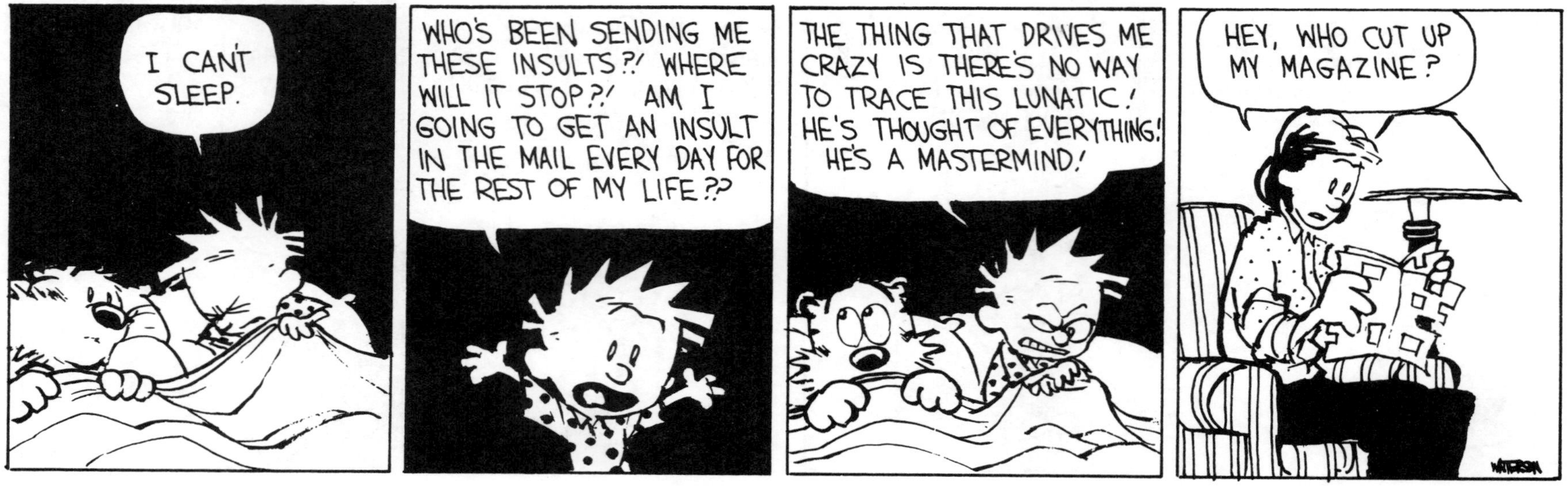
I CAN'T SLEEP.
WHO'S BEEN SENDING ME THESE INSULTS?! WHERE WILL IT STOP?! AM I GOING TO GET AN INSULT IN THE MAIL EVERY DAY FOR THE REST OF MY LIFE??
THE THING THAT DRIVES ME CRAZY IS THERE'S NO WAY TO TRACE THIS LUNATIC! HE'S THOUGHT OF EVERYTHING! HE'S A MASTERMIND!
HEY, WHO CUT UP MY MAGAZINE?

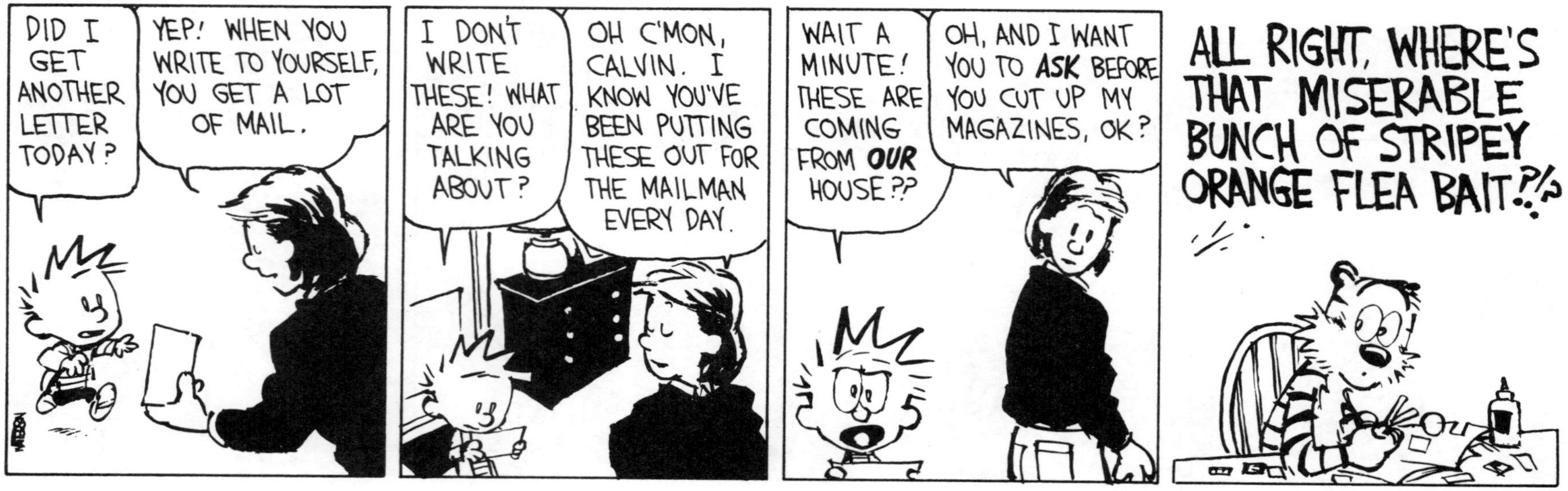
DID I GET ANOTHER LETTER TODAY?
YEP! WHEN YOU WRITE TO YOURSELF, YOU GET A LOT OF MAIL.
I DON'T WRITE THESE! WHAT ARE YOU TALKING ABOUT?
OH C'MON, CALVIN. I KNOW YOU'VE BEEN PUTTING THESE OUT FOR THE MAILMAN EVERY DAY.
WAIT A MINUTE! THESE ARE COMING FROM **OUR** HOUSE??
OH, AND I WANT YOU TO **ASK** BEFORE YOU CUT UP MY MAGAZINES, OK?
ALL RIGHT, WHERE'S THAT MISERABLE BUNCH OF STRIPEY ORANGE FLEA BAIT?!?

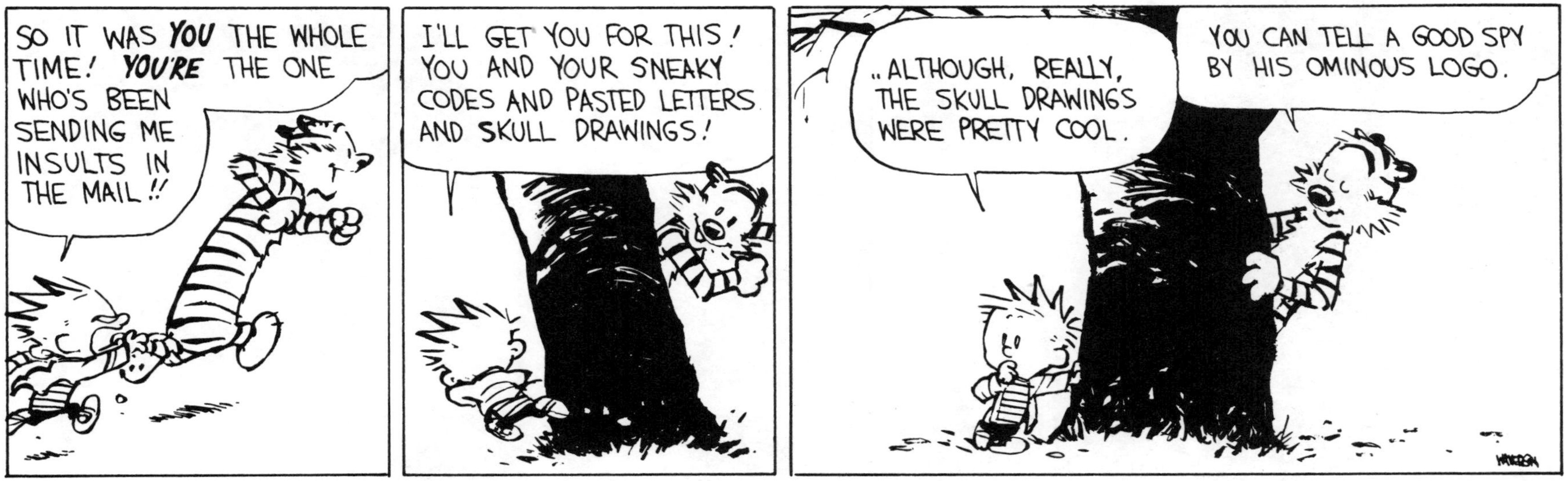
SO IT WAS **YOU** THE WHOLE TIME! **YOU'RE** THE ONE WHO'S BEEN SENDING ME INSULTS IN THE MAIL!!
I'LL GET YOU FOR THIS! YOU AND YOUR SNEAKY CODES AND PASTED LETTERS AND SKULL DRAWINGS!
..ALTHOUGH, REALLY, THE SKULL DRAWINGS WERE PRETTY COOL.
YOU CAN TELL A GOOD SPY BY HIS OMINOUS LOGO.

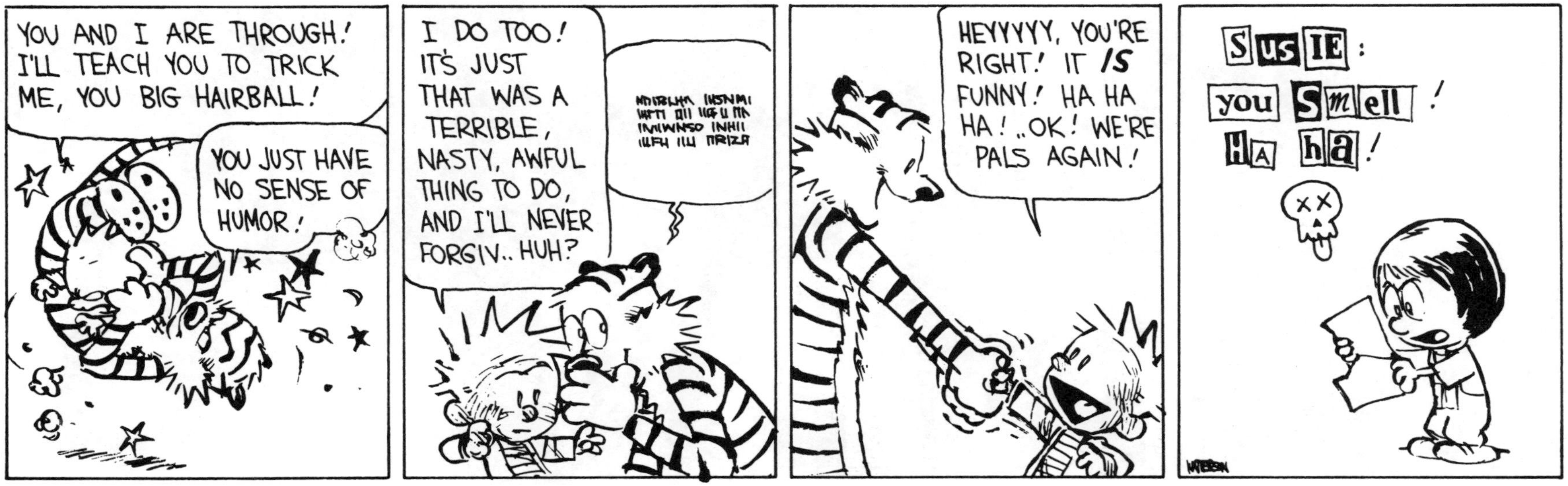
YOU AND I ARE THROUGH! I'LL TEACH YOU TO TRICK ME, YOU BIG HAIRBALL!
YOU JUST HAVE NO SENSE OF HUMOR!
I DO TOO! IT'S JUST THAT WAS A TERRIBLE, NASTY, AWFUL THING TO DO, AND I'LL NEVER FORGIV.. HUH?
HEYYYYY, YOU'RE RIGHT! IT ***IS*** FUNNY! HA HA HA! ..OK! WE'RE PALS AGAIN!
SusIE :
you Smell !
HA ha !

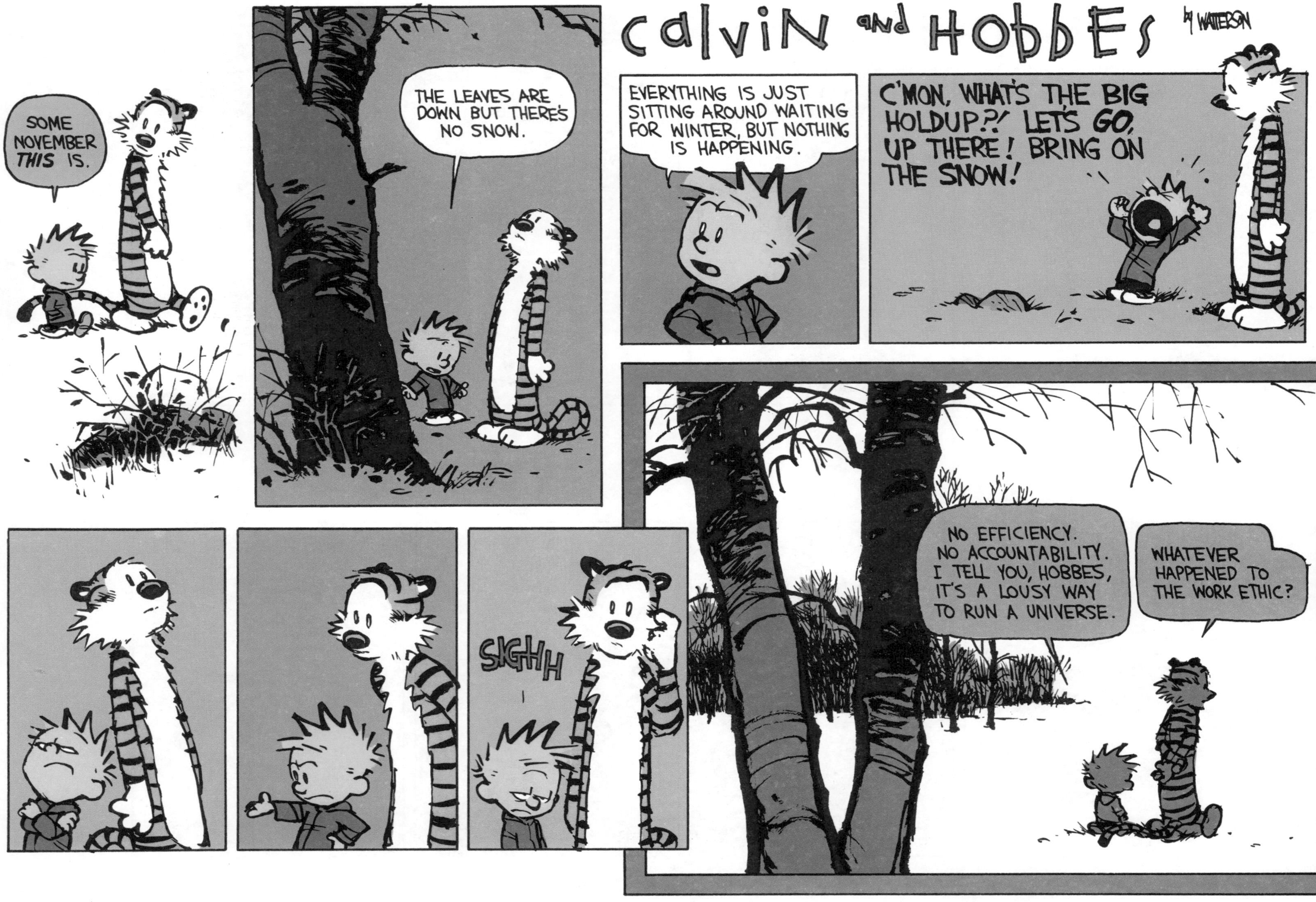
Calvin and Hobbes
by WATTERSON
SOME NOVEMBER THIS IS.
THE LEAVES ARE DOWN BUT THERE'S NO SNOW.
EVERYTHING IS JUST SITTING AROUND WAITING FOR WINTER, BUT NOTHING IS HAPPENING.
C'MON, WHAT'S THE BIG HOLDUP?! LET'S GO, UP THERE! BRING ON THE SNOW!
SIGHH
NO EFFICIENCY. NO ACCOUNTABILITY. I TELL YOU, HOBBES, IT'S A LOUSY WAY TO RUN A UNIVERSE.
WHATEVER HAPPENED TO THE WORK ETHIC?

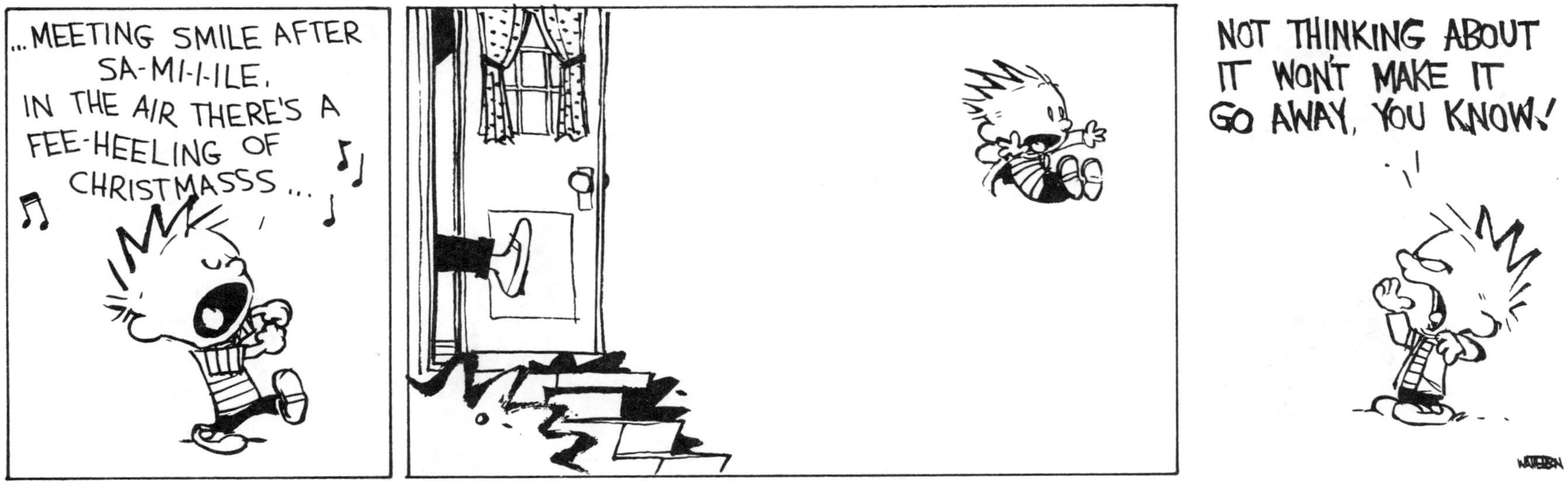
...MEETING SMILE AFTER SA-MI-I-ILE. IN THE AIR THERE'S A FEE-HEELING OF CHRISTMASSS...
NOT THINKING ABOUT IT WON'T MAKE IT GO AWAY, YOU KNOW!

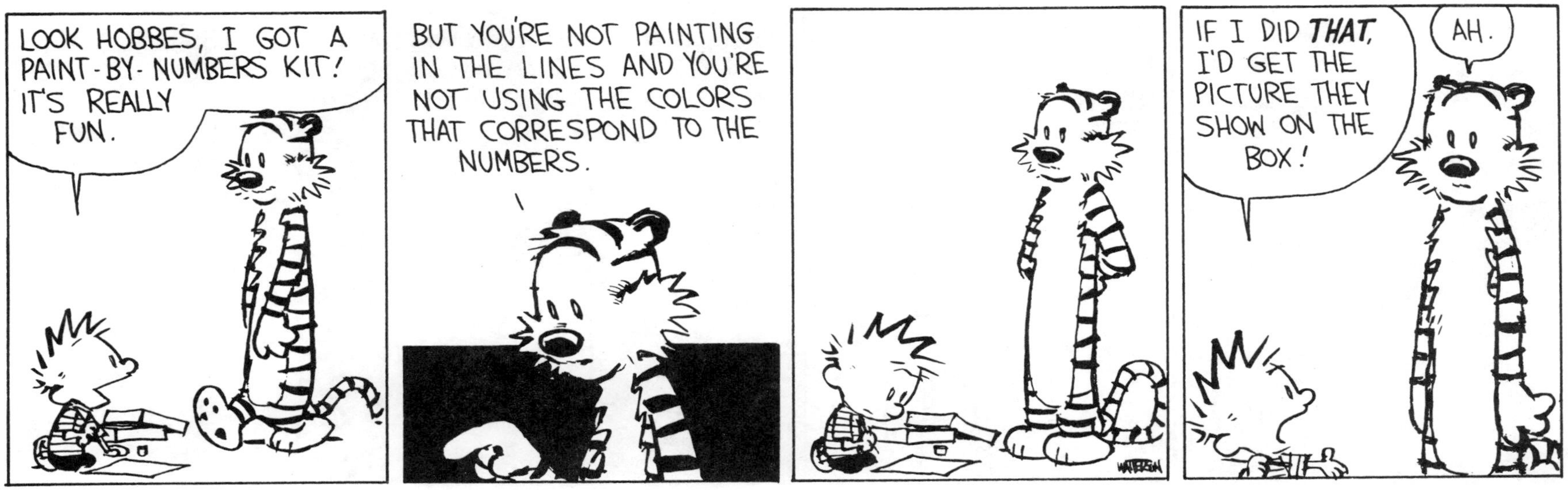
LOOK HOBBES, I GOT A PAINT-BY-NUMBERS KIT! IT'S REALLY FUN.
BUT YOU'RE NOT PAINTING IN THE LINES AND YOU'RE NOT USING THE COLORS THAT CORRESPOND TO THE NUMBERS.
IF I DID THAT, I'D GET THE PICTURE THEY SHOW ON THE BOX!
AH.

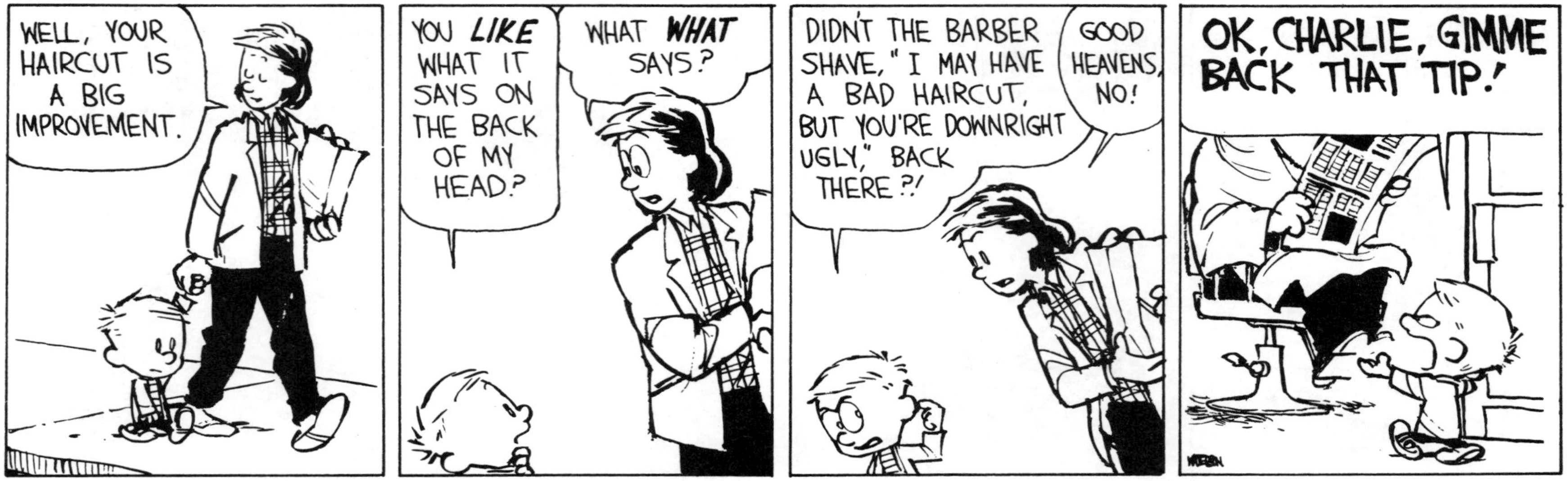
WELL, YOUR HAIRCUT IS A BIG IMPROVEMENT.
YOU *LIKE* WHAT IT SAYS ON THE BACK OF MY HEAD?
WHAT *WHAT* SAYS?
DIDN'T THE BARBER SHAVE, "I MAY HAVE A BAD HAIRCUT, BUT YOU'RE DOWNRIGHT UGLY," BACK THERE?!
GOOD HEAVENS, NO!
OK, CHARLIE, GIMME BACK THAT TIP!

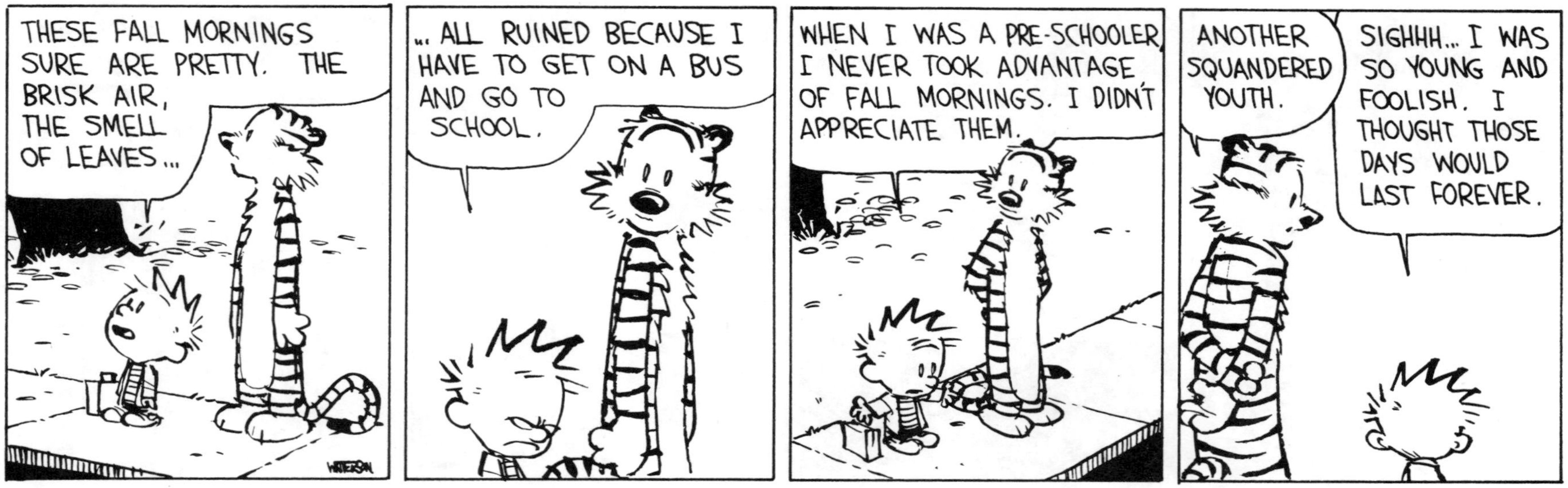
THESE FALL MORNINGS SURE ARE PRETTY. THE BRISK AIR, THE SMELL OF LEAVES...
... ALL RUINED BECAUSE I HAVE TO GET ON A BUS AND GO TO SCHOOL.
WHEN I WAS A PRE-SCHOOLER, I NEVER TOOK ADVANTAGE OF FALL MORNINGS. I DIDN'T APPRECIATE THEM.
ANOTHER SQUANDERED YOUTH.
SIGHHH... I WAS SO YOUNG AND FOOLISH. I THOUGHT THOSE DAYS WOULD LAST FOREVER.

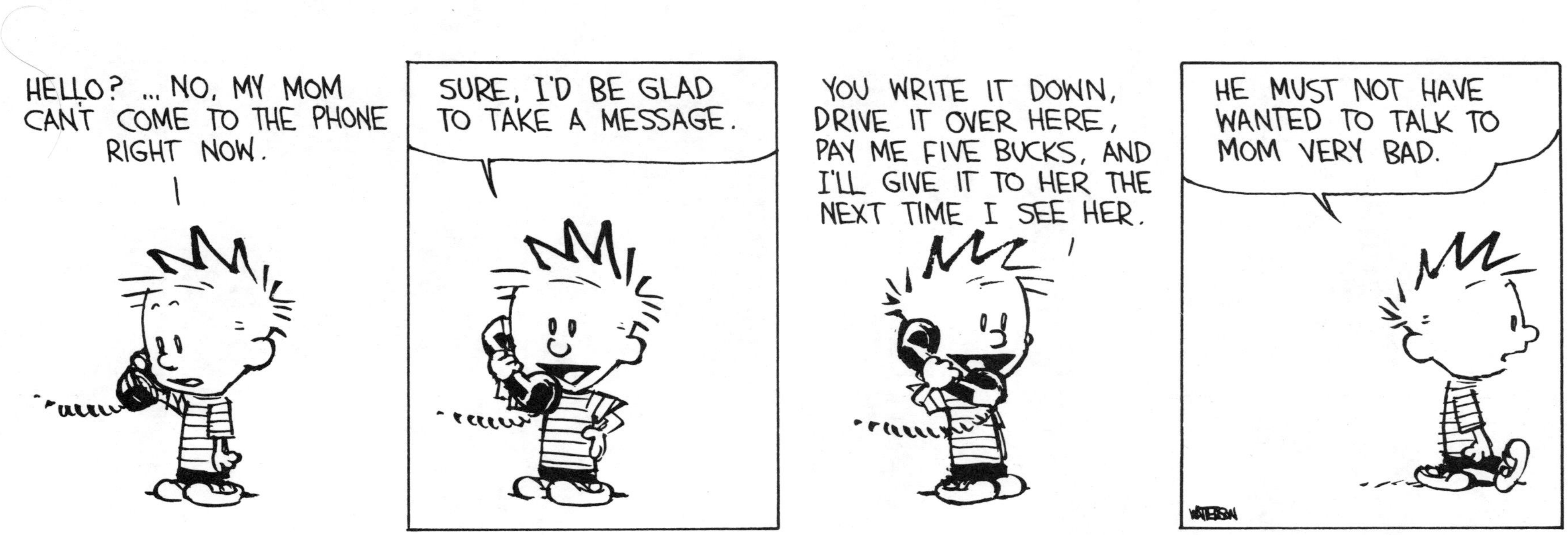
HELLO? ... NO, MY MOM CAN'T COME TO THE PHONE RIGHT NOW.
SURE, I'D BE GLAD TO TAKE A MESSAGE.
YOU WRITE IT DOWN, DRIVE IT OVER HERE, PAY ME FIVE BUCKS, AND I'LL GIVE IT TO HER THE NEXT TIME I SEE HER.
HE MUST NOT HAVE WANTED TO TALK TO MOM VERY BAD.

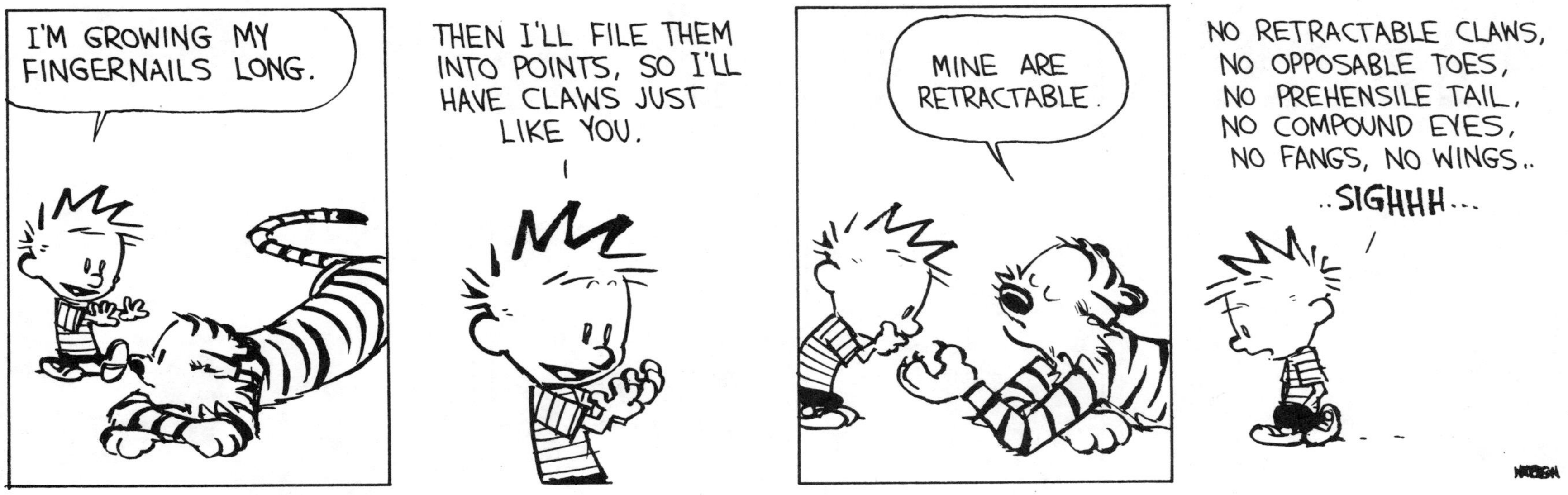
I'M GROWING MY FINGERNAILS LONG.
THEN I'LL FILE THEM INTO POINTS, SO I'LL HAVE CLAWS JUST LIKE YOU.
MINE ARE RETRACTABLE.
NO RETRACTABLE CLAWS, NO OPPOSABLE TOES, NO PREHENSILE TAIL, NO COMPOUND EYES, NO FANGS, NO WINGS..
..SIGHHH...

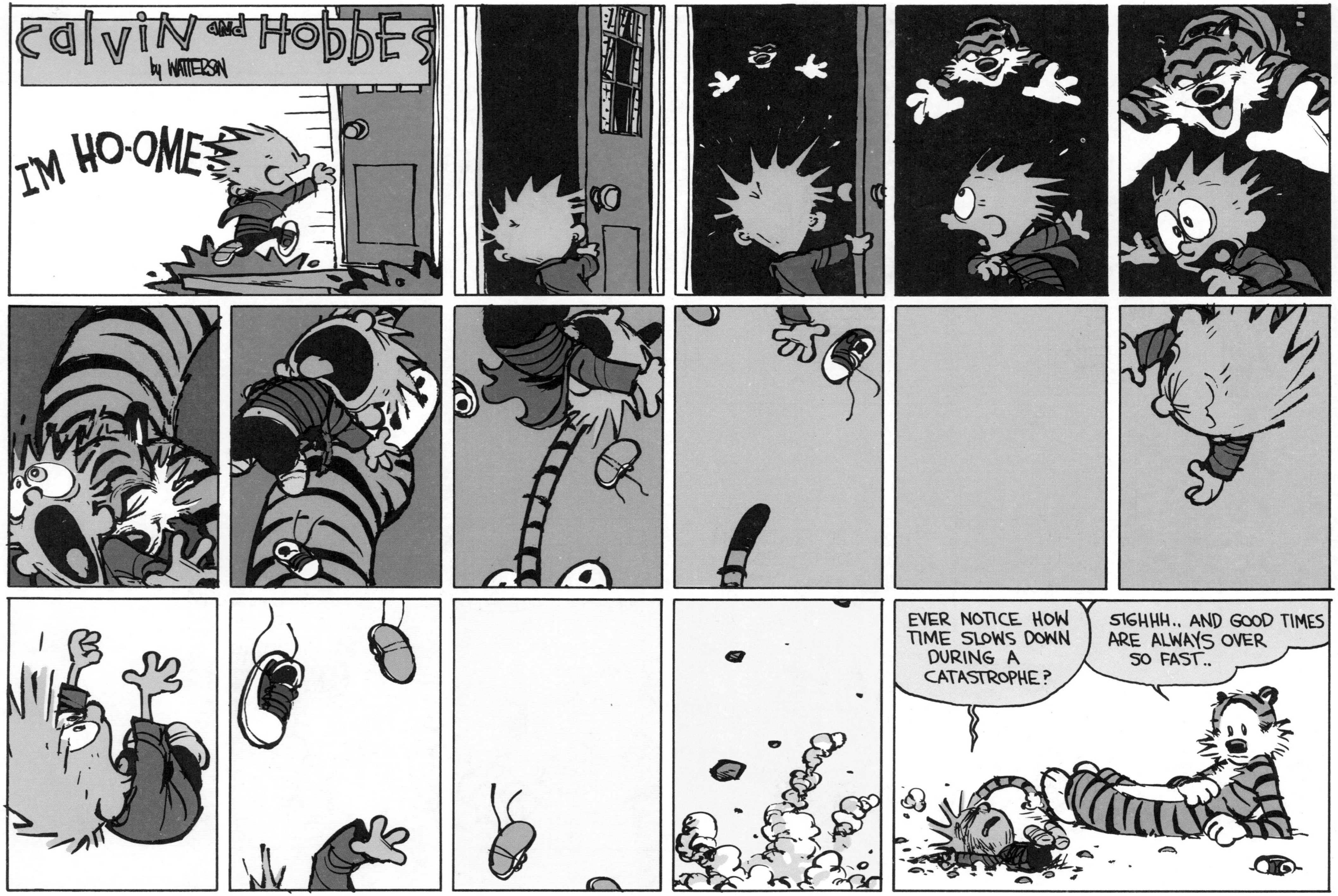

Calvin and Hobbes
by WATTERSON
I'M HO-OME
EVER NOTICE HOW TIME SLOWS DOWN DURING A CATASTROPHE?
SIGHHH.. AND GOOD TIMES ARE ALWAYS OVER SO FAST..

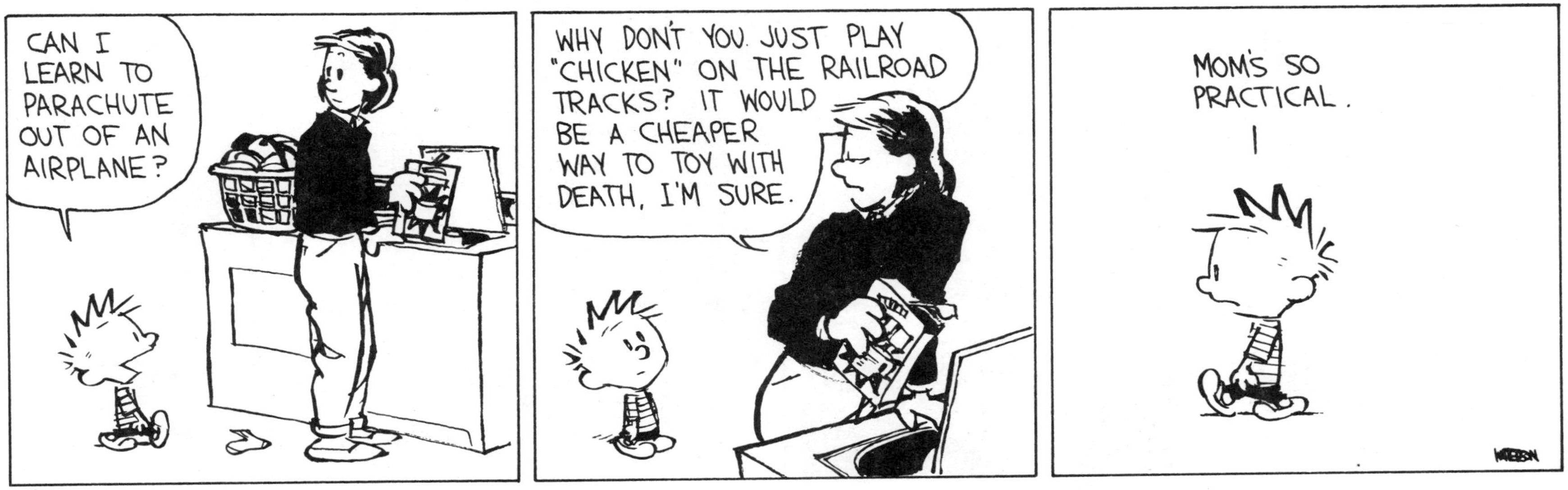
CAN I LEARN TO PARACHUTE OUT OF AN AIRPLANE?
WHY DON'T YOU JUST PLAY "CHICKEN" ON THE RAILROAD TRACKS? IT WOULD BE A CHEAPER WAY TO TOY WITH DEATH, I'M SURE.
MOM'S SO PRACTICAL.

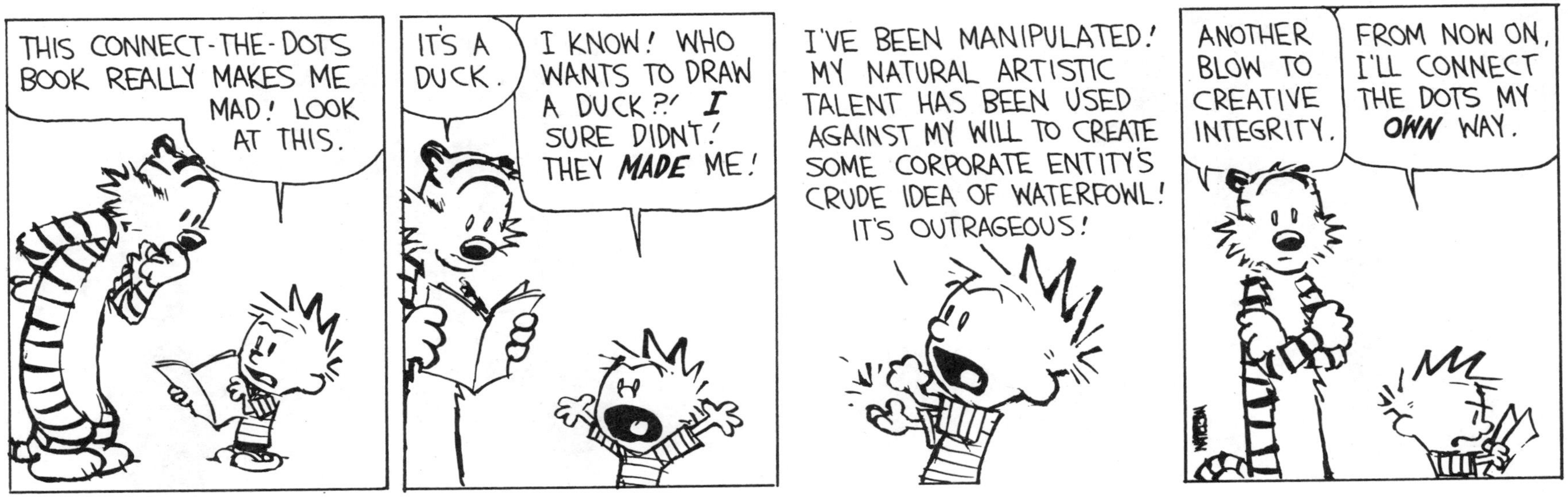
THIS CONNECT-THE-DOTS BOOK REALLY MAKES ME MAD! LOOK AT THIS.
IT'S A DUCK.
I KNOW! WHO WANTS TO DRAW A DUCK?! I SURE DIDN'T! THEY MADE ME!
I'VE BEEN MANIPULATED! MY NATURAL ARTISTIC TALENT HAS BEEN USED AGAINST MY WILL TO CREATE SOME CORPORATE ENTITY'S CRUDE IDEA OF WATERFOWL! IT'S OUTRAGEOUS!
ANOTHER BLOW TO CREATIVE INTEGRITY.
FROM NOW ON, I'LL CONNECT THE DOTS MY OWN WAY.

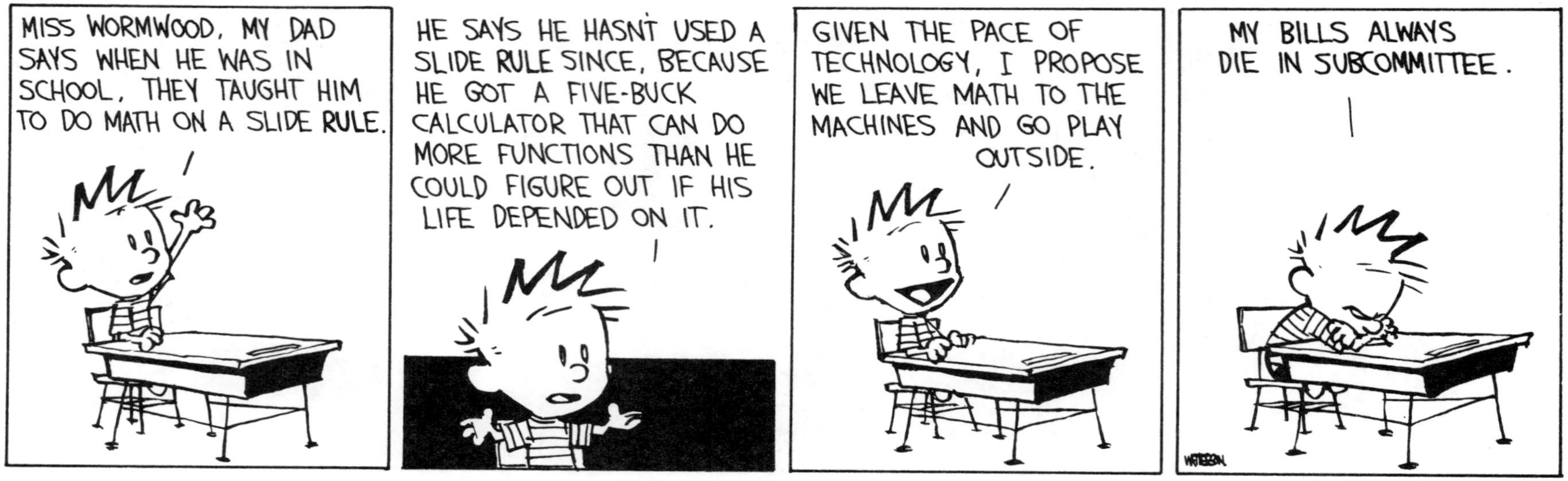
MISS WORMWOOD, MY DAD SAYS WHEN HE WAS IN SCHOOL, THEY TAUGHT HIM TO DO MATH ON A SLIDE RULE.
HE SAYS HE HASN'T USED A SLIDE RULE SINCE, BECAUSE HE GOT A FIVE-BUCK CALCULATOR THAT CAN DO MORE FUNCTIONS THAN HE COULD FIGURE OUT IF HIS LIFE DEPENDED ON IT.
GIVEN THE PACE OF TECHNOLOGY, I PROPOSE WE LEAVE MATH TO THE MACHINES AND GO PLAY OUTSIDE.
MY BILLS ALWAYS DIE IN SUBCOMMITTEE.

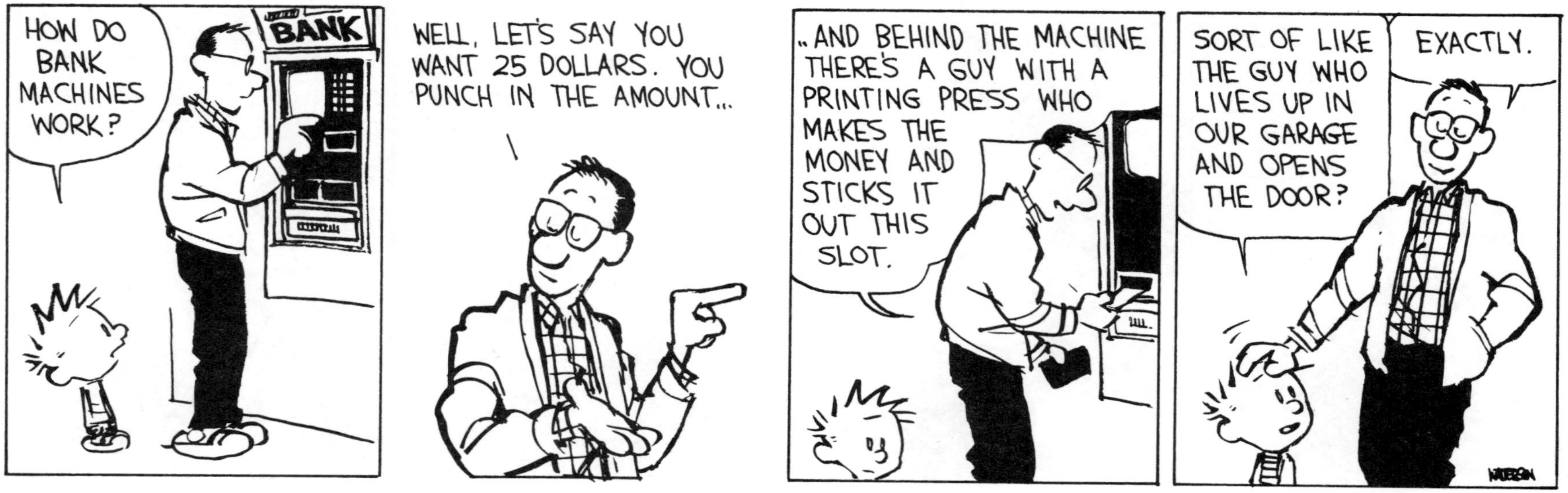
HOW DO BANK MACHINES WORK?
BANK
WELL, LET'S SAY YOU WANT 25 DOLLARS. YOU PUNCH IN THE AMOUNT...
..AND BEHIND THE MACHINE THERE'S A GUY WITH A PRINTING PRESS WHO MAKES THE MONEY AND STICKS IT OUT THIS SLOT.
SORT OF LIKE THE GUY WHO LIVES UP IN OUR GARAGE AND OPENS THE DOOR?
EXACTLY.

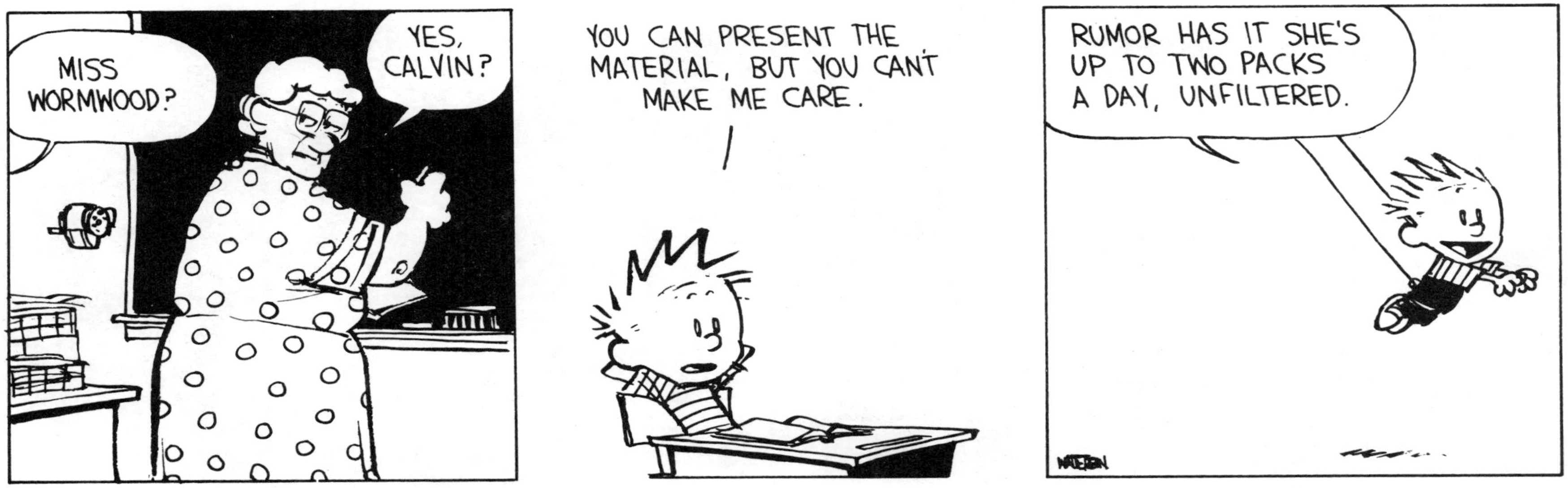
MISS WORMWOOD?
YES, CALVIN?
YOU CAN PRESENT THE MATERIAL, BUT YOU CAN'T MAKE ME CARE.
RUMOR HAS IT SHE'S UP TO TWO PACKS A DAY, UNFILTERED.

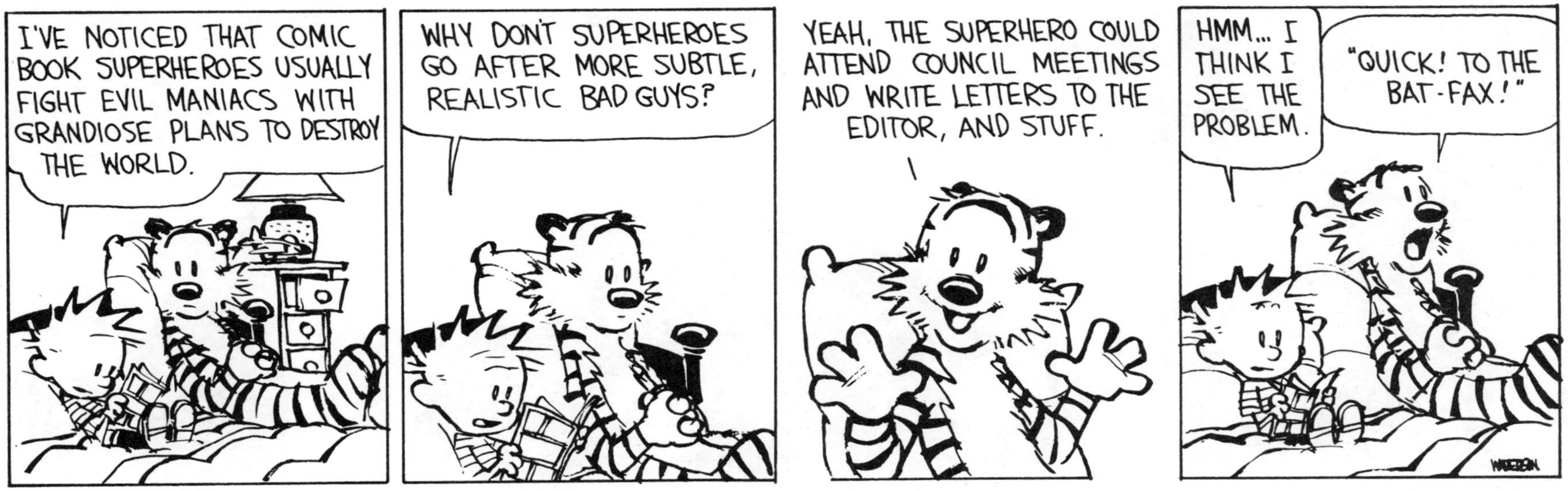
I'VE NOTICED THAT COMIC BOOK SUPERHEROES USUALLY FIGHT EVIL MANIACS WITH GRANDIOSE PLANS TO DESTROY THE WORLD.
WHY DON'T SUPERHEROES GO AFTER MORE SUBTLE, REALISTIC BAD GUYS?
YEAH, THE SUPERHERO COULD ATTEND COUNCIL MEETINGS AND WRITE LETTERS TO THE EDITOR, AND STUFF.
HMM... I THINK I SEE THE PROBLEM.
"QUICK! TO THE BAT-FAX!"

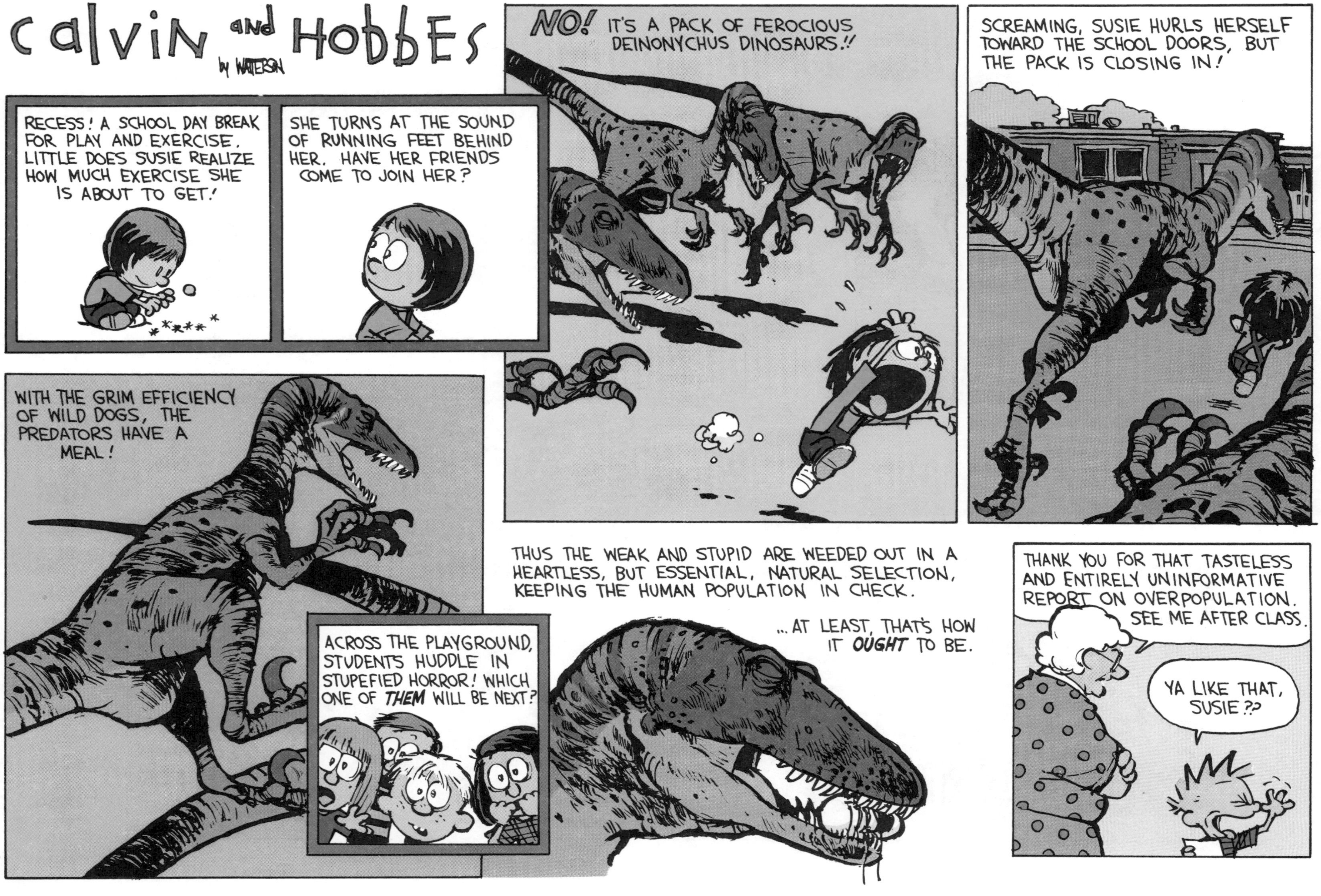
Calvin and Hobbes
by WATTERSON
RECESS! A SCHOOL DAY BREAK FOR PLAY AND EXERCISE. LITTLE DOES SUSIE REALIZE HOW MUCH EXERCISE SHE IS ABOUT TO GET!
SHE TURNS AT THE SOUND OF RUNNING FEET BEHIND HER. HAVE HER FRIENDS COME TO JOIN HER?
NO! IT'S A PACK OF FEROCIOUS DEINONYCHUS DINOSAURS!!
SCREAMING, SUSIE HURLS HERSELF TOWARD THE SCHOOL DOORS, BUT THE PACK IS CLOSING IN!
WITH THE GRIM EFFICIENCY OF WILD DOGS, THE PREDATORS HAVE A MEAL!
ACROSS THE PLAYGROUND, STUDENTS HUDDLE IN STUPEFIED HORROR! WHICH ONE OF THEM WILL BE NEXT?
THUS THE WEAK AND STUPID ARE WEEDED OUT IN A HEARTLESS, BUT ESSENTIAL, NATURAL SELECTION, KEEPING THE HUMAN POPULATION IN CHECK.
...AT LEAST, THAT'S HOW IT OUGHT TO BE.
THANK YOU FOR THAT TASTELESS AND ENTIRELY UNINFORMATIVE REPORT ON OVERPOPULATION. SEE ME AFTER CLASS.
YA LIKE THAT, SUSIE ?!?

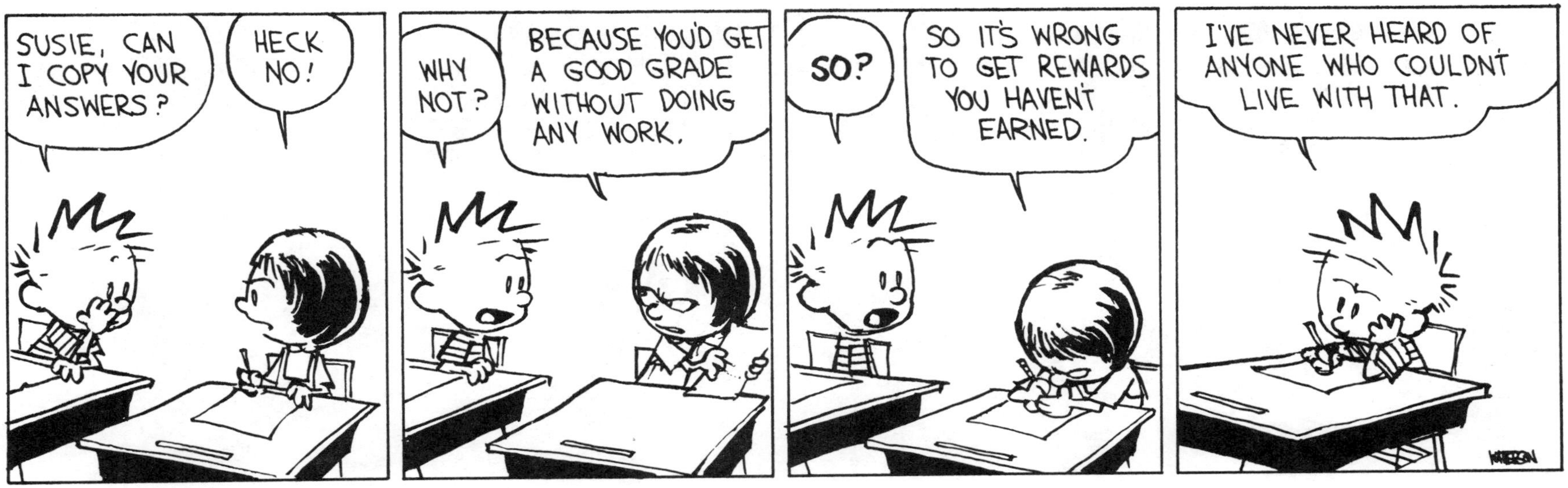
SUSIE, CAN I COPY YOUR ANSWERS?
HECK NO!
WHY NOT?
BECAUSE YOU'D GET A GOOD GRADE WITHOUT DOING ANY WORK.
SO?
SO IT'S WRONG TO GET REWARDS YOU HAVEN'T EARNED.
I'VE NEVER HEARD OF ANYONE WHO COULDN'T LIVE WITH THAT.

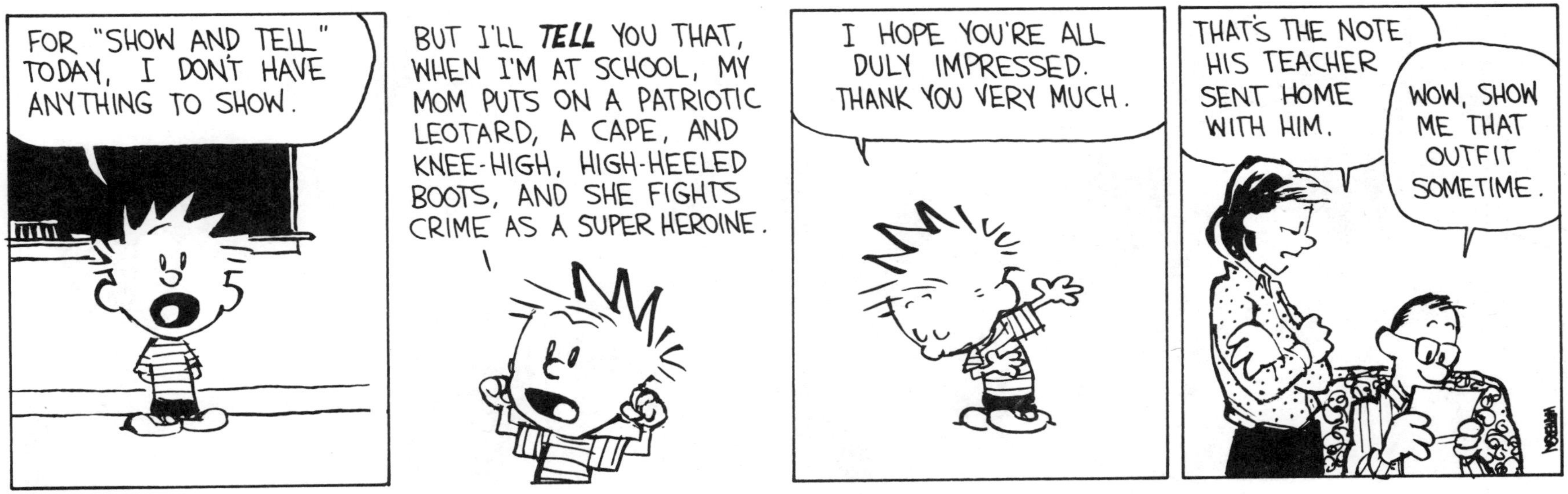
FOR "SHOW AND TELL" TODAY, I DON'T HAVE ANYTHING TO SHOW.
BUT I'LL TELL YOU THAT, WHEN I'M AT SCHOOL, MY MOM PUTS ON A PATRIOTIC LEOTARD, A CAPE, AND KNEE-HIGH, HIGH-HEELED BOOTS, AND SHE FIGHTS CRIME AS A SUPER HEROINE.
I HOPE YOU'RE ALL DULY IMPRESSED. THANK YOU VERY MUCH.
THAT'S THE NOTE HIS TEACHER SENT HOME WITH HIM.
WOW, SHOW ME THAT OUTFIT SOMETIME.

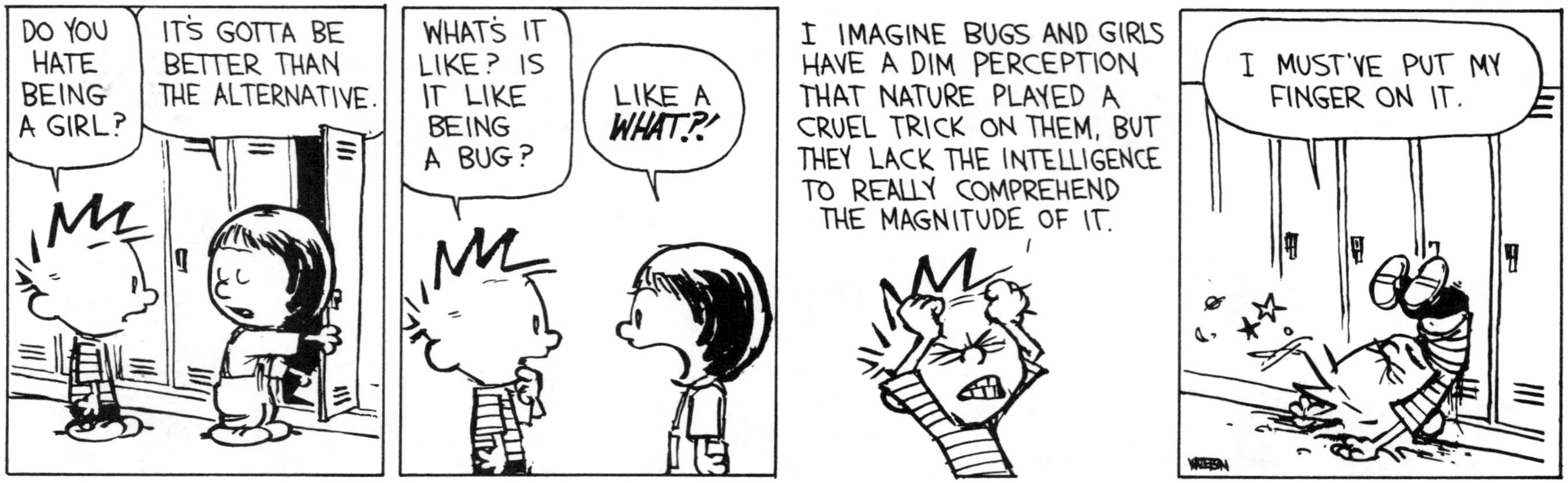
DO YOU HATE BEING A GIRL?
IT'S GOTTA BE BETTER THAN THE ALTERNATIVE.
WHAT'S IT LIKE? IS IT LIKE BEING A BUG?
LIKE A *WHAT?!*
I IMAGINE BUGS AND GIRLS HAVE A DIM PERCEPTION THAT NATURE PLAYED A CRUEL TRICK ON THEM, BUT THEY LACK THE INTELLIGENCE TO REALLY COMPREHEND THE MAGNITUDE OF IT.
I MUST'VE PUT MY FINGER ON IT.
WATTERSON

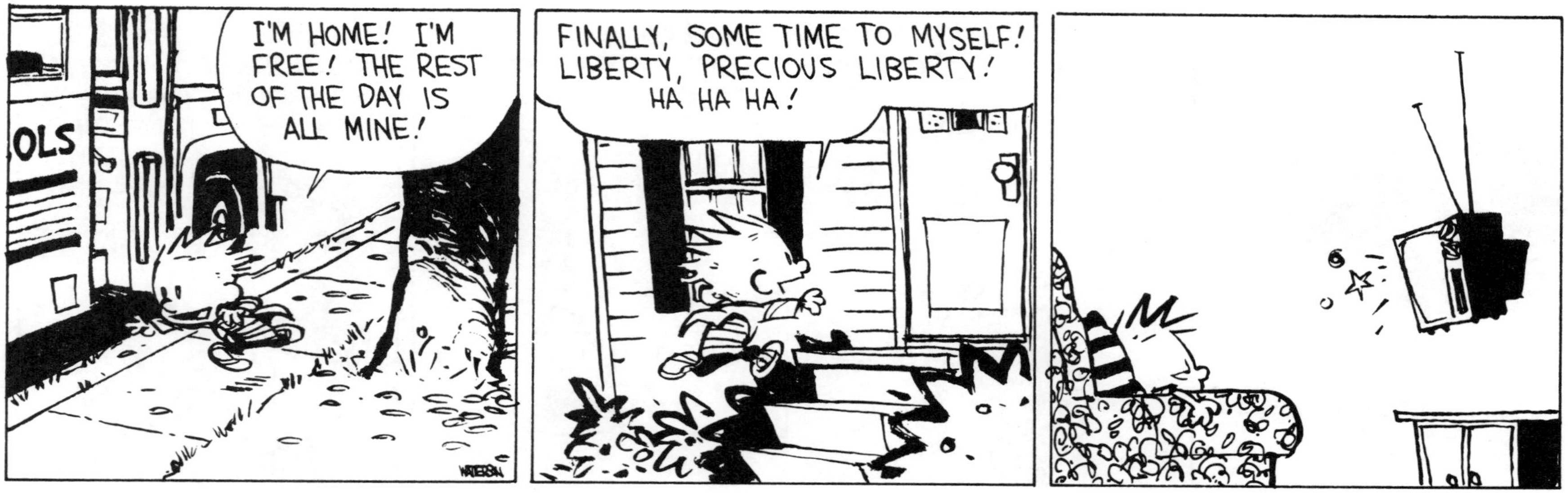
OLS
I'M HOME! I'M FREE! THE REST OF THE DAY IS ALL MINE!
WATTERSON
FINALLY, SOME TIME TO MYSELF! LIBERTY, PRECIOUS LIBERTY! HA HA HA!

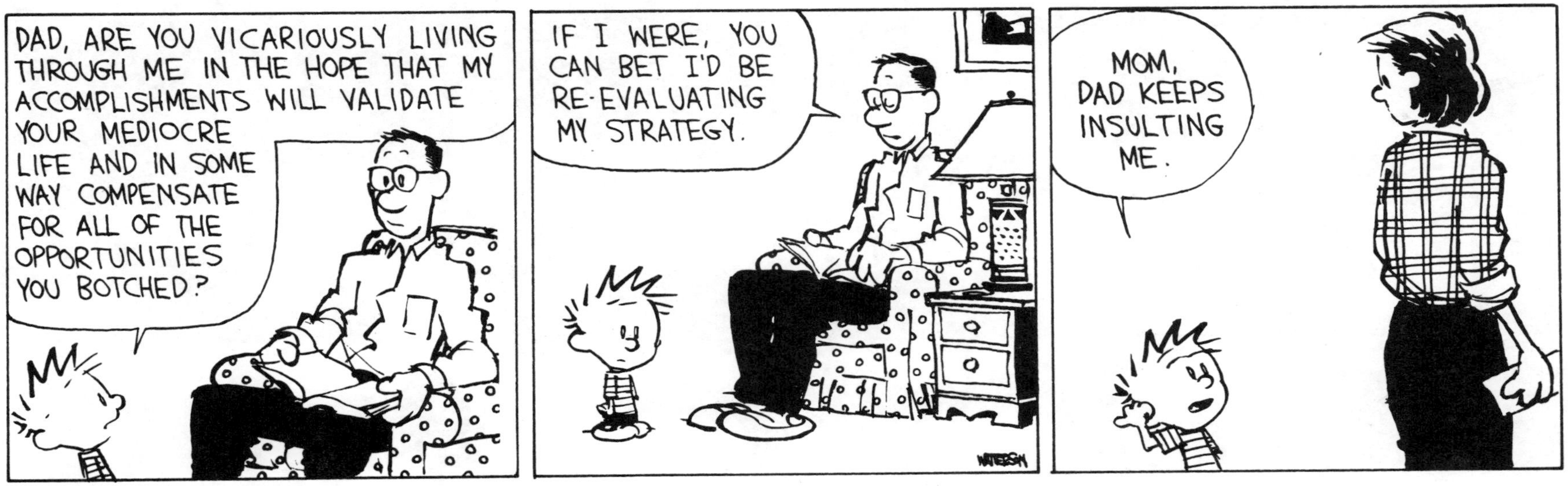
DAD, ARE YOU VICARIOUSLY LIVING THROUGH ME IN THE HOPE THAT MY ACCOMPLISHMENTS WILL VALIDATE YOUR MEDIOCRE LIFE AND IN SOME WAY COMPENSATE FOR ALL OF THE OPPORTUNITIES YOU BOTCHED?
IF I WERE, YOU CAN BET I'D BE RE-EVALUATING MY STRATEGY.
MOM, DAD KEEPS INSULTING ME.

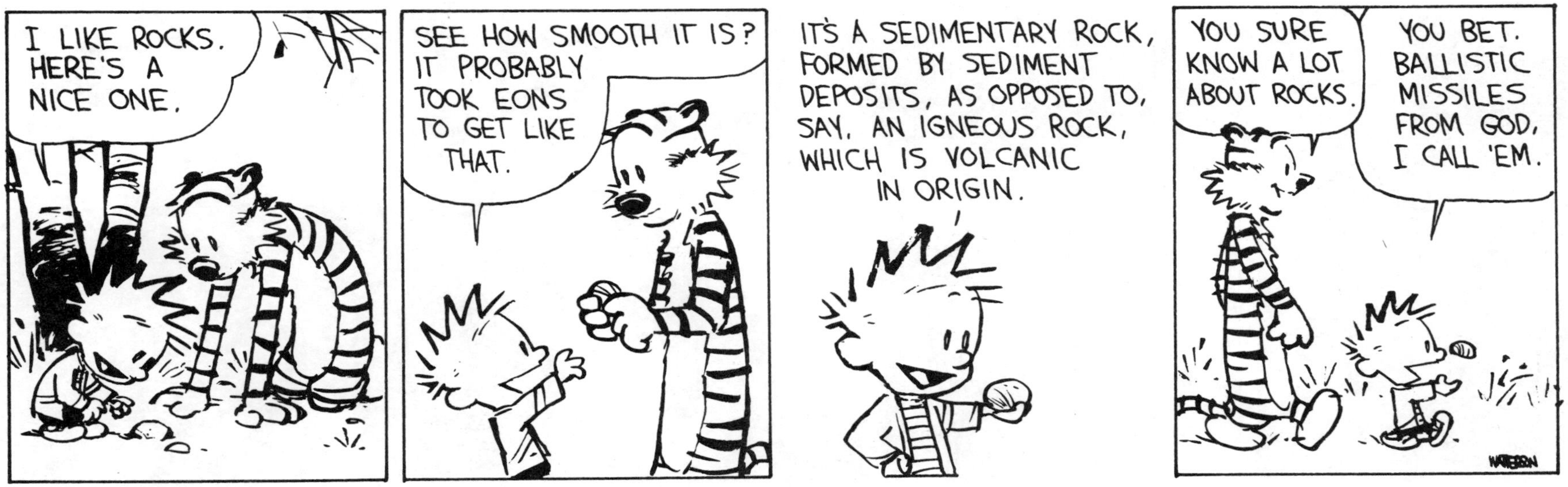
I LIKE ROCKS. HERE'S A NICE ONE.
SEE HOW SMOOTH IT IS? IT PROBABLY TOOK EONS TO GET LIKE THAT.
IT'S A SEDIMENTARY ROCK, FORMED BY SEDIMENT DEPOSITS, AS OPPOSED TO, SAY, AN IGNEOUS ROCK, WHICH IS VOLCANIC IN ORIGIN.
YOU SURE KNOW A LOT ABOUT ROCKS.
YOU BET. BALLISTIC MISSILES FROM GOD, I CALL 'EM.

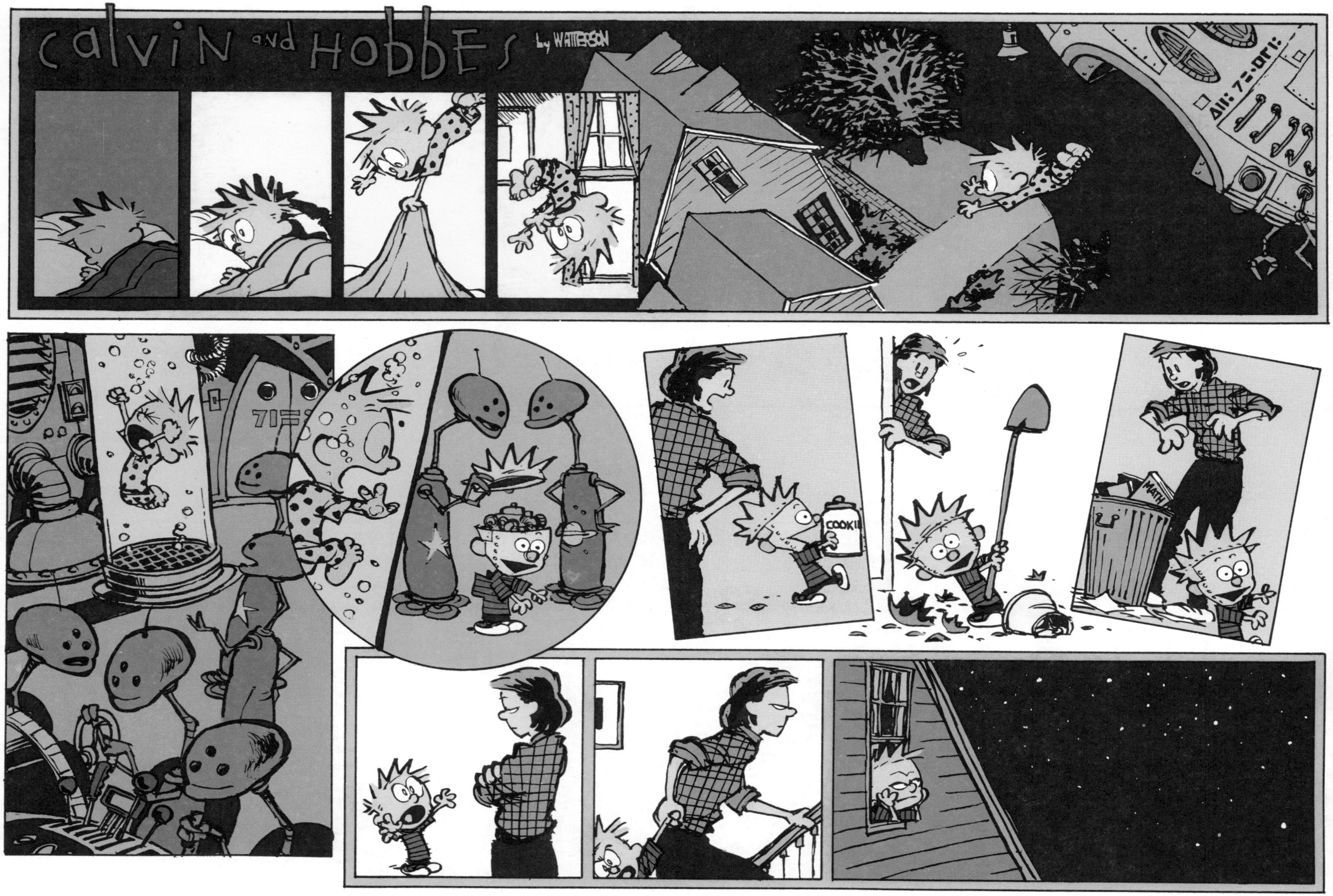
calvin and HOBBES
by WATTERSON
COOKI
MATH

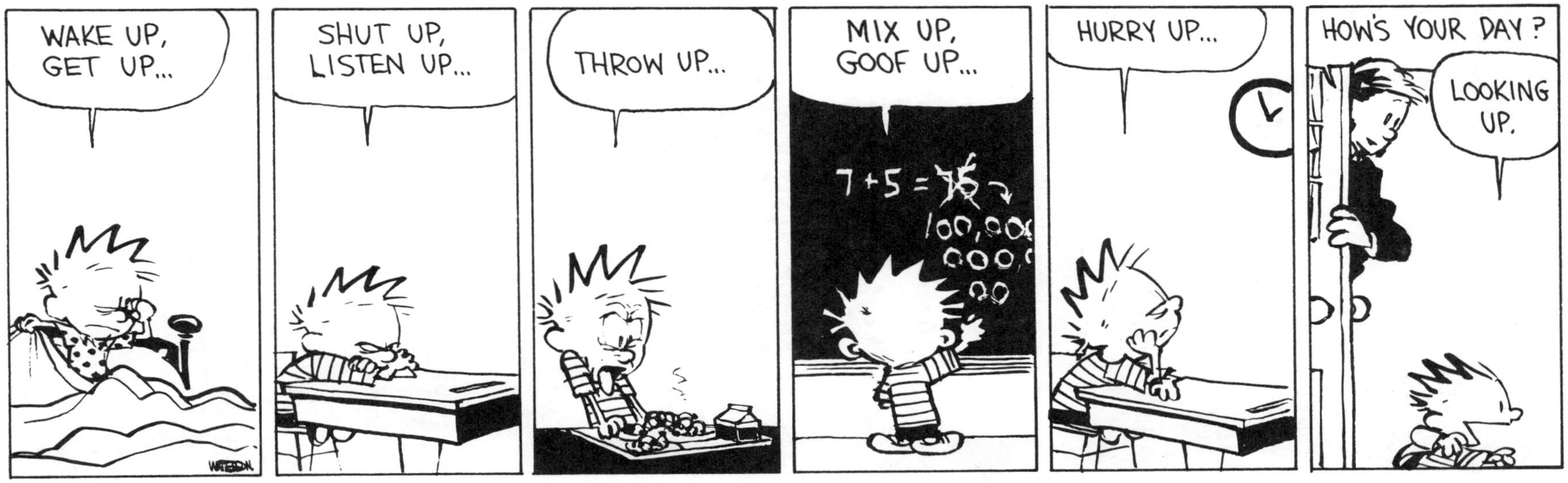
WAKE UP, GET UP...
SHUT UP, LISTEN UP...
THROW UP...
MIX UP, GOOF UP...
HURRY UP...
HOW'S YOUR DAY?
LOOKING UP.

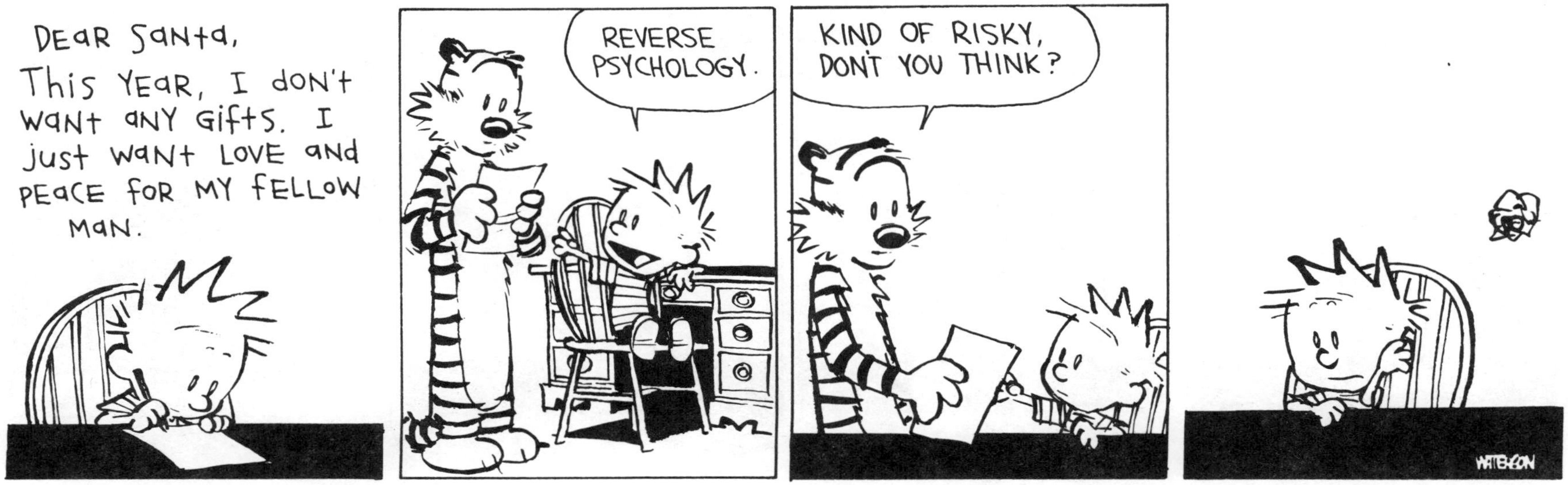
Dear Santa,
This Year, I don't want any Gifts. I just want Love and peace for my fellow man.
REVERSE PSYCHOLOGY.
KIND OF RISKY, DON'T YOU THINK?

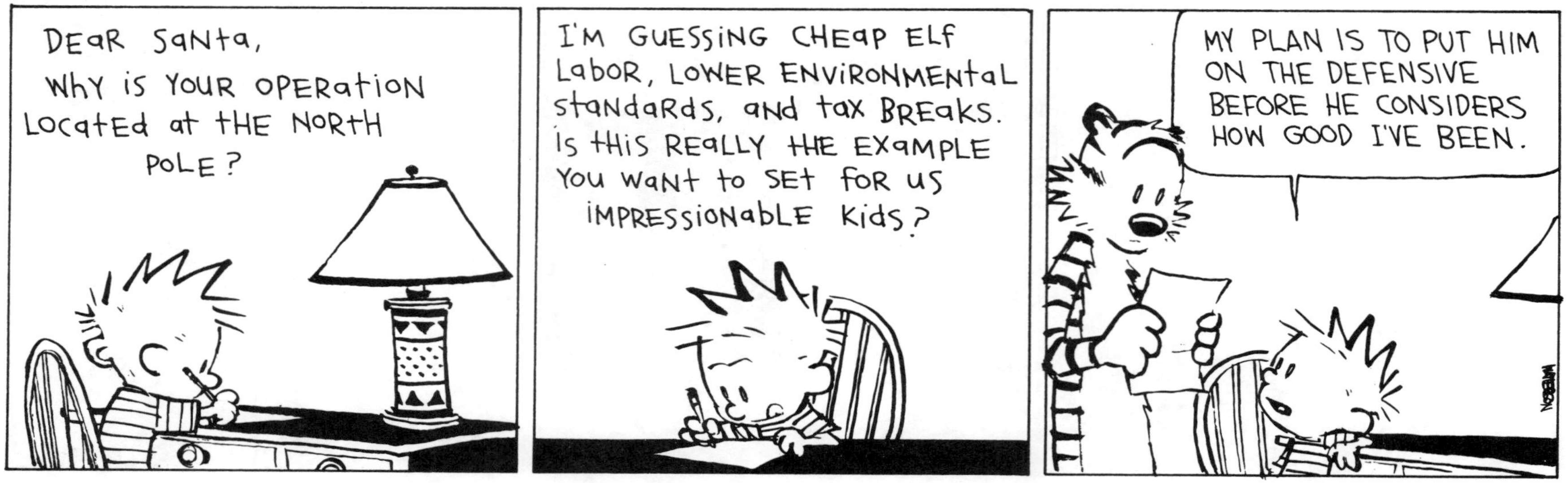
DEAR SANTA,
WHY IS YOUR OPERATION LOCATED AT THE NORTH POLE?
I'M GUESSING CHEAP ELF LABOR, LOWER ENVIRONMENTAL STANDARDS, AND TAX BREAKS. IS THIS REALLY THE EXAMPLE YOU WANT TO SET FOR US IMPRESSIONABLE KIDS?
MY PLAN IS TO PUT HIM ON THE DEFENSIVE BEFORE HE CONSIDERS HOW GOOD I'VE BEEN.

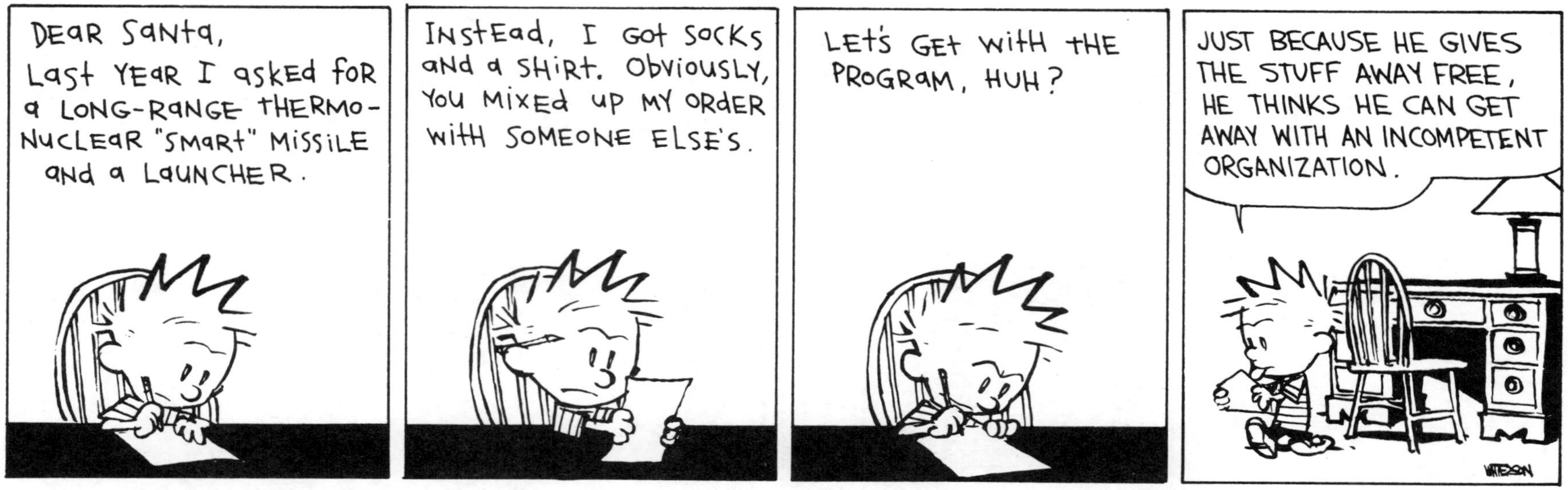
DEAR SANTA,
LAST YEAR I ASKED FOR A LONG-RANGE THERMO-NUCLEAR "SMART" MISSILE AND A LAUNCHER.
INSTEAD, I GOT SOCKS AND A SHIRT. OBVIOUSLY, YOU MIXED UP MY ORDER WITH SOMEONE ELSE'S.
LET'S GET WITH THE PROGRAM, HUH?
JUST BECAUSE HE GIVES THE STUFF AWAY FREE, HE THINKS HE CAN GET AWAY WITH AN INCOMPETENT ORGANIZATION.

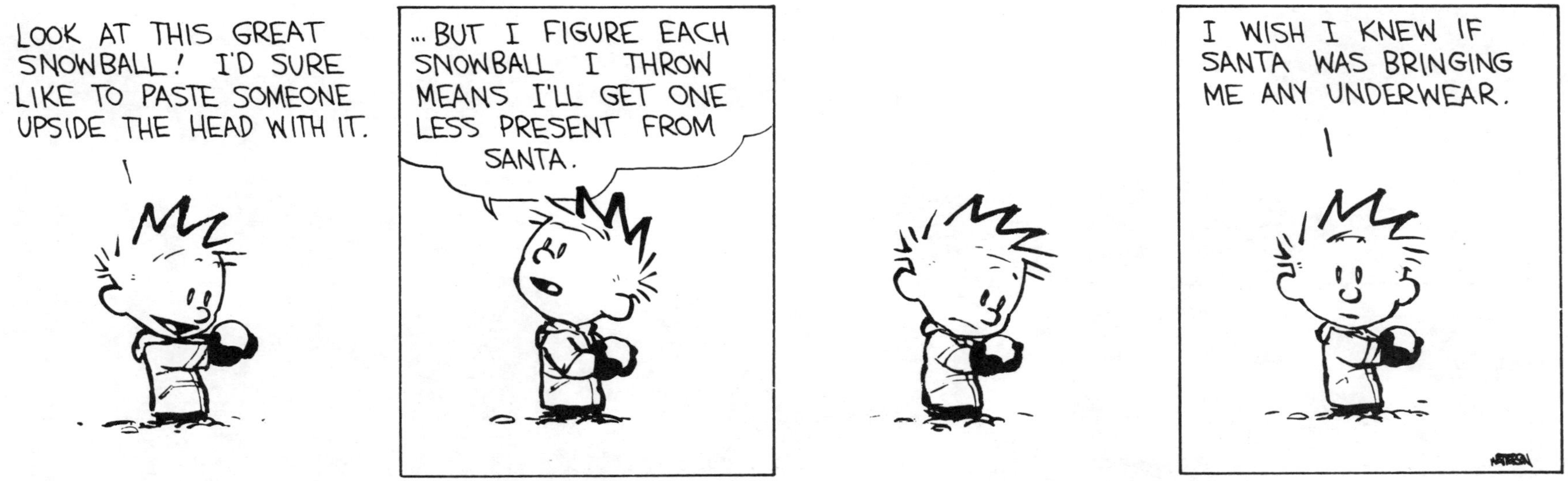
LOOK AT THIS GREAT SNOWBALL! I'D SURE LIKE TO PASTE SOMEONE UPSIDE THE HEAD WITH IT.
...BUT I FIGURE EACH SNOWBALL I THROW MEANS I'LL GET ONE LESS PRESENT FROM SANTA.
I WISH I KNEW IF SANTA WAS BRINGING ME ANY UNDERWEAR.

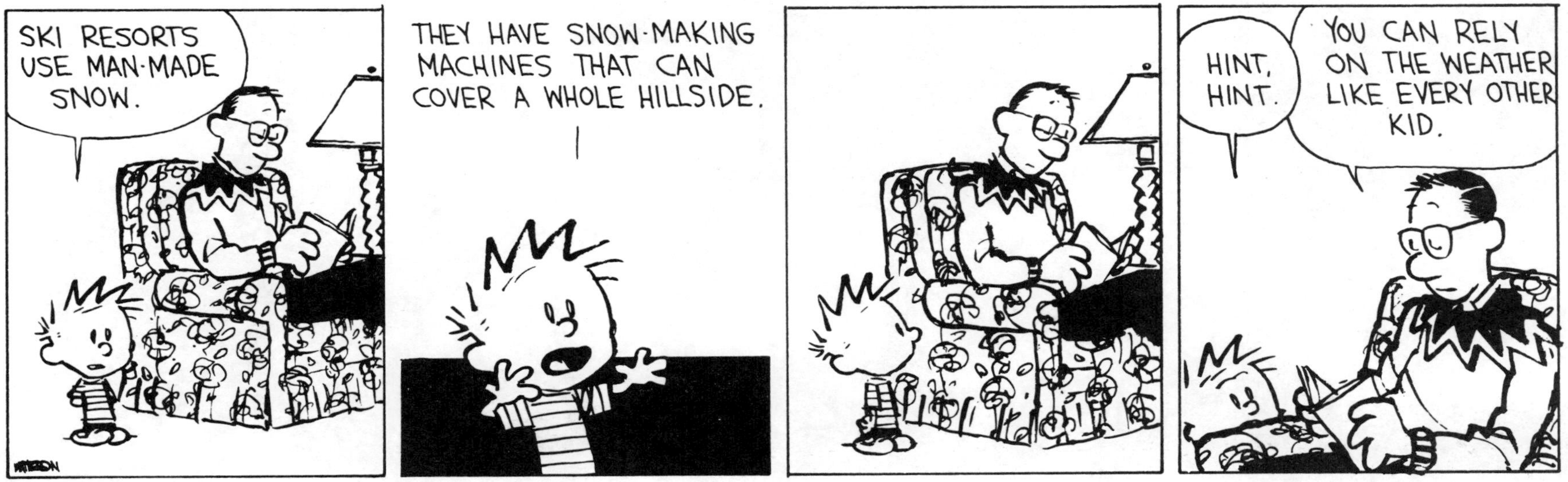
SKI RESORTS USE MAN-MADE SNOW.
THEY HAVE SNOW-MAKING MACHINES THAT CAN COVER A WHOLE HILLSIDE.
HINT, HINT.
YOU CAN RELY ON THE WEATHER LIKE EVERY OTHER KID.

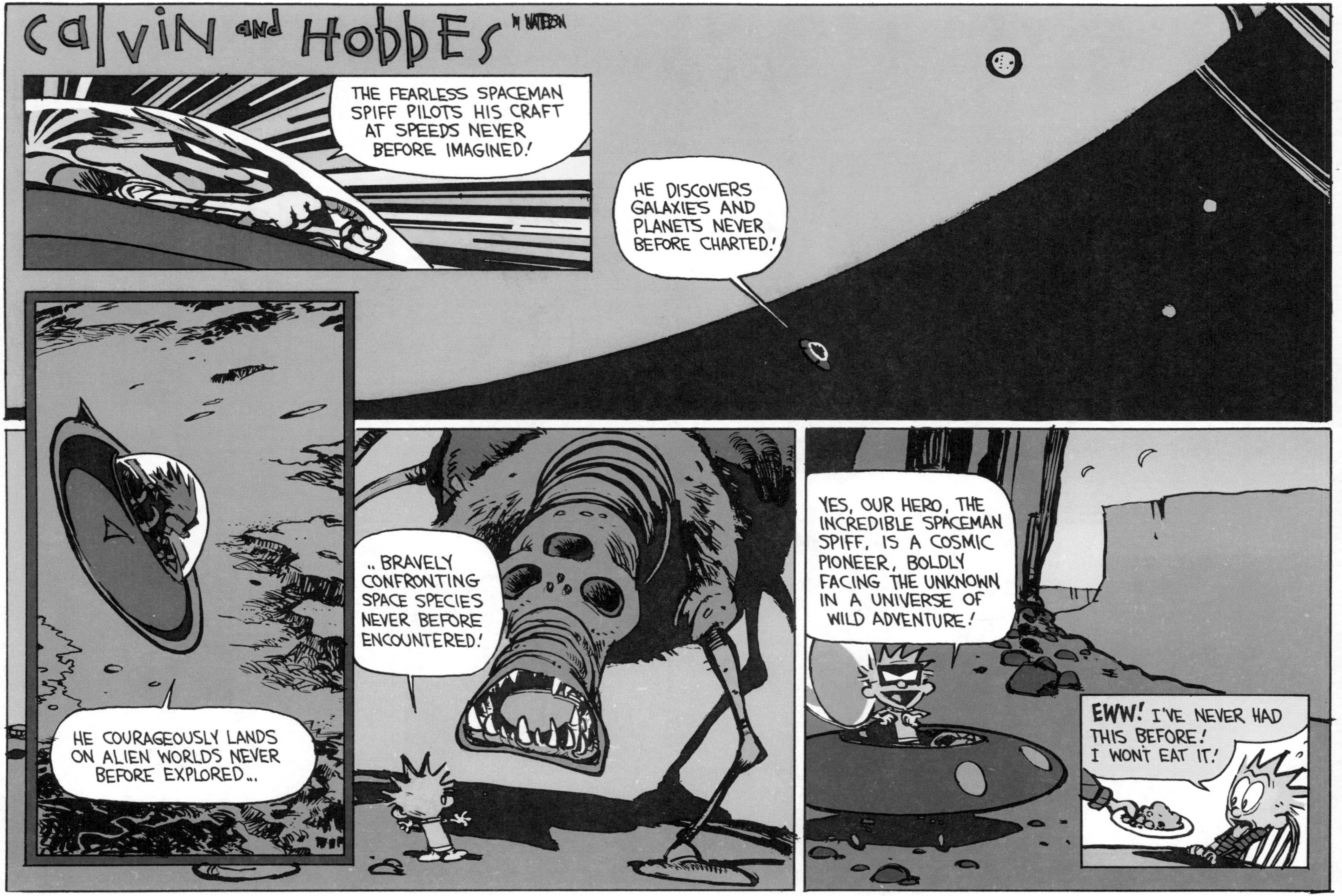
Calvin and HobbEs by WATTERSON
THE FEARLESS SPACEMAN SPIFF PILOTS HIS CRAFT AT SPEEDS NEVER BEFORE IMAGINED!
HE DISCOVERS GALAXIES AND PLANETS NEVER BEFORE CHARTED!
HE COURAGEOUSLY LANDS ON ALIEN WORLDS NEVER BEFORE EXPLORED..
.. BRAVELY CONFRONTING SPACE SPECIES NEVER BEFORE ENCOUNTERED!
YES, OUR HERO, THE INCREDIBLE SPACEMAN SPIFF, IS A COSMIC PIONEER, BOLDLY FACING THE UNKNOWN IN A UNIVERSE OF WILD ADVENTURE!
EWW! I'VE NEVER HAD THIS BEFORE! I WON'T EAT IT!

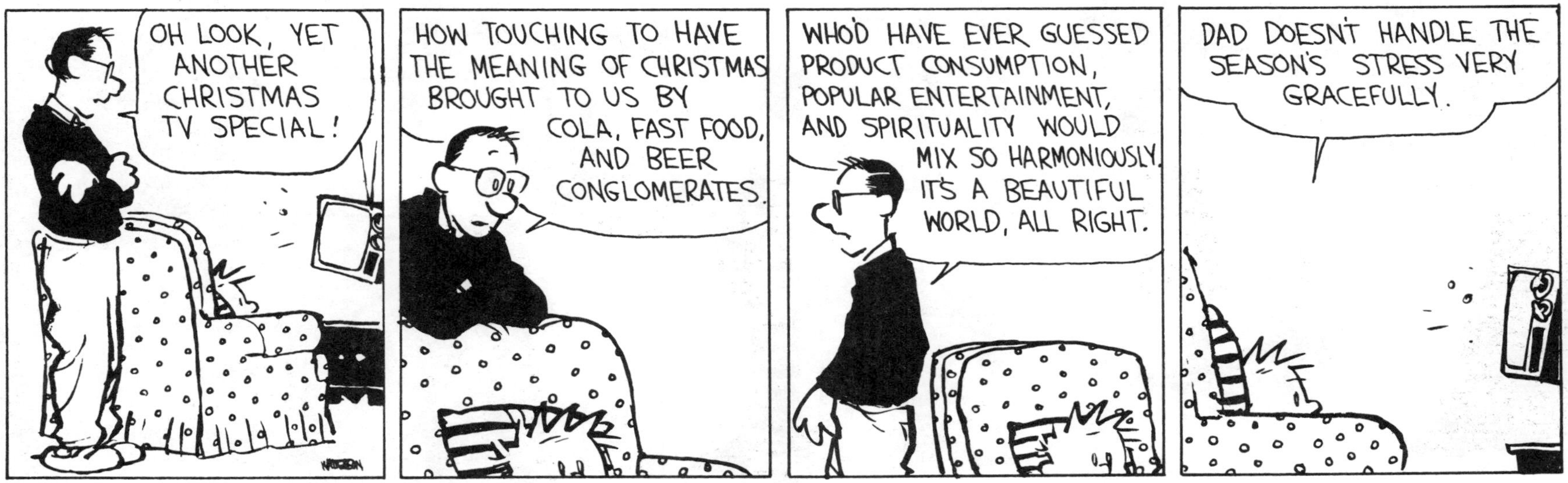
OH LOOK, YET ANOTHER CHRISTMAS TV SPECIAL!
HOW TOUCHING TO HAVE THE MEANING OF CHRISTMAS BROUGHT TO US BY COLA, FAST FOOD, AND BEER CONGLOMERATES.
WHO'D HAVE EVER GUESSED PRODUCT CONSUMPTION, POPULAR ENTERTAINMENT, AND SPIRITUALITY WOULD MIX SO HARMONIOUSLY. IT'S A BEAUTIFUL WORLD, ALL RIGHT.
DAD DOESN'T HANDLE THE SEASON'S STRESS VERY GRACEFULLY.

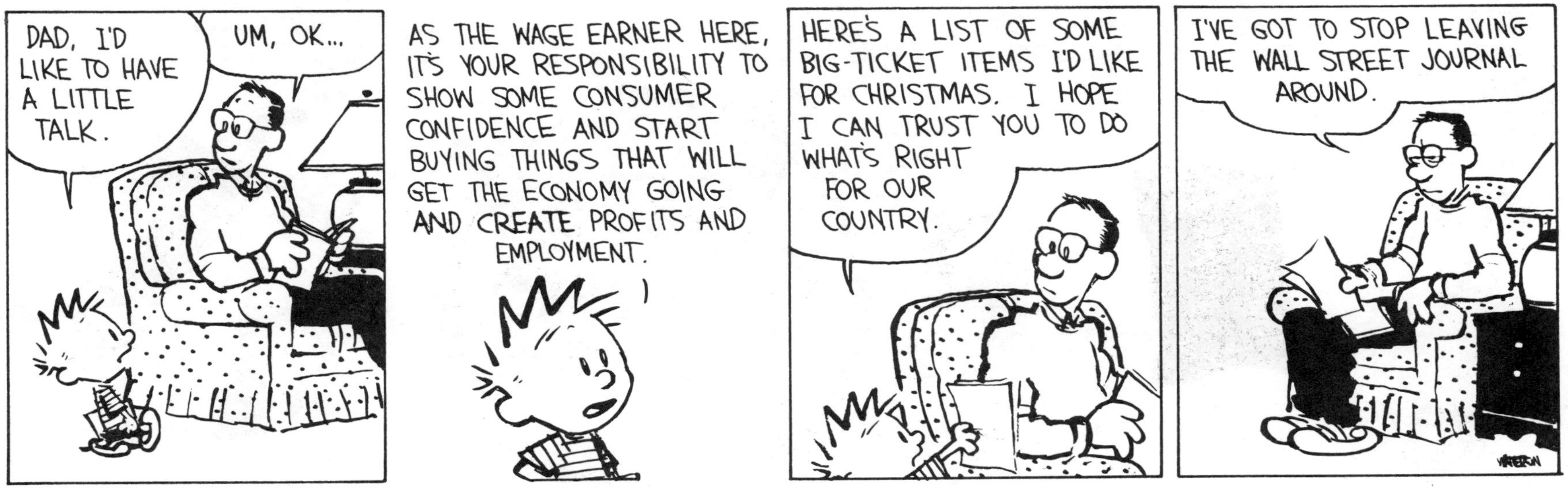
DAD, I'D LIKE TO HAVE A LITTLE TALK.
UM, OK...
AS THE WAGE EARNER HERE, IT'S YOUR RESPONSIBILITY TO SHOW SOME CONSUMER CONFIDENCE AND START BUYING THINGS THAT WILL GET THE ECONOMY GOING AND CREATE PROFITS AND EMPLOYMENT.
HERE'S A LIST OF SOME BIG-TICKET ITEMS I'D LIKE FOR CHRISTMAS. I HOPE I CAN TRUST YOU TO DO WHAT'S RIGHT FOR OUR COUNTRY.
I'VE GOT TO STOP LEAVING THE WALL STREET JOURNAL AROUND.

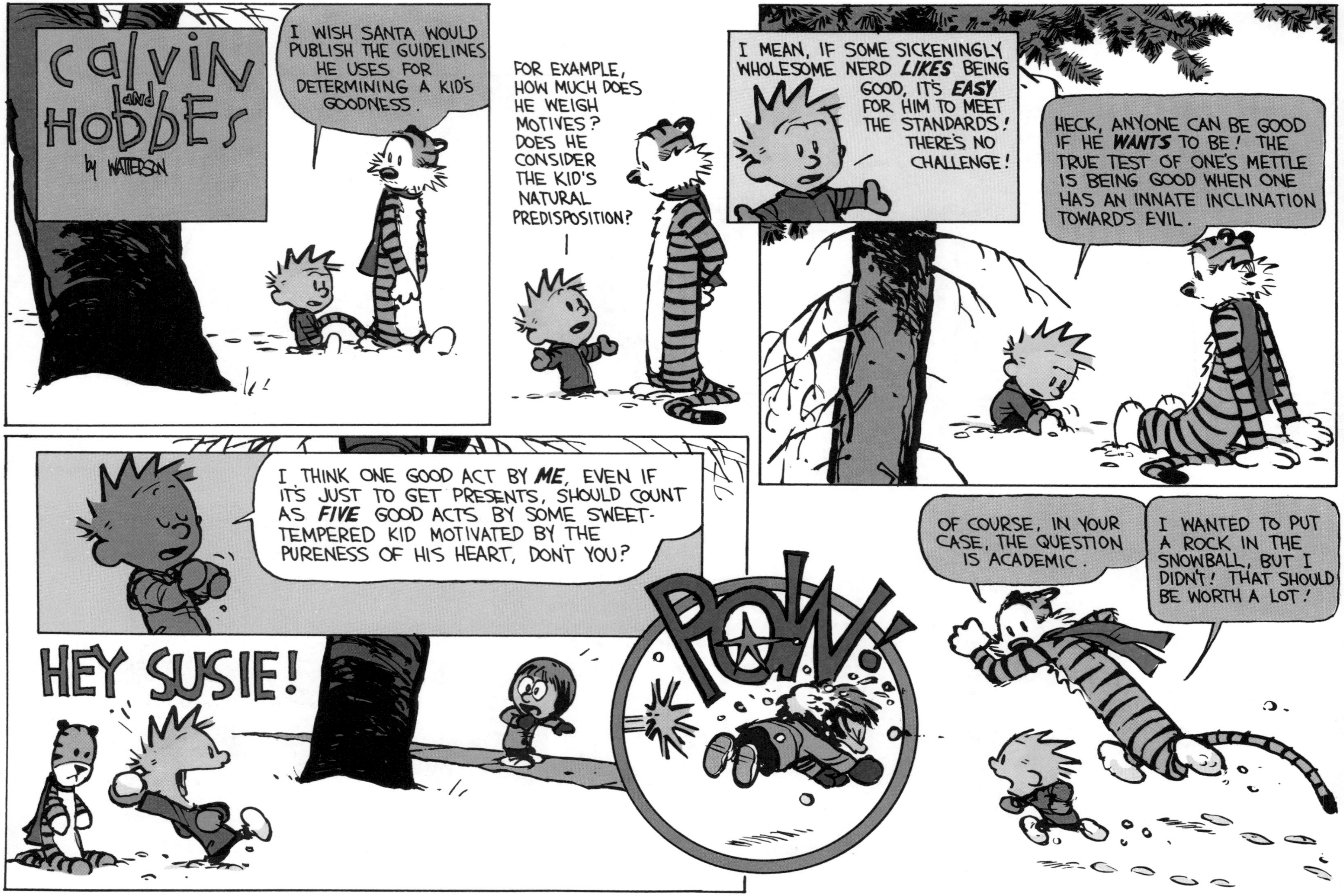
Calvin and Hobbes
by WATTERSON
I WISH SANTA WOULD PUBLISH THE GUIDELINES HE USES FOR DETERMINING A KID'S GOODNESS.
FOR EXAMPLE, HOW MUCH DOES HE WEIGH MOTIVES? DOES HE CONSIDER THE KID'S NATURAL PREDISPOSITION?
I MEAN, IF SOME SICKENINGLY WHOLESOME NERD LIKES BEING GOOD, IT'S EASY FOR HIM TO MEET THE STANDARDS! THERE'S NO CHALLENGE!
HECK, ANYONE CAN BE GOOD IF HE WANTS TO BE! THE TRUE TEST OF ONE'S METTLE IS BEING GOOD WHEN ONE HAS AN INNATE INCLINATION TOWARDS EVIL.
I THINK ONE GOOD ACT BY ME, EVEN IF IT'S JUST TO GET PRESENTS, SHOULD COUNT AS FIVE GOOD ACTS BY SOME SWEET-TEMPERED KID MOTIVATED BY THE PURENESS OF HIS HEART, DON'T YOU?
HEY SUSIE!
POW!
OF COURSE, IN YOUR CASE, THE QUESTION IS ACADEMIC.
I WANTED TO PUT A ROCK IN THE SNOWBALL, BUT I DIDN'T! THAT SHOULD BE WORTH A LOT!

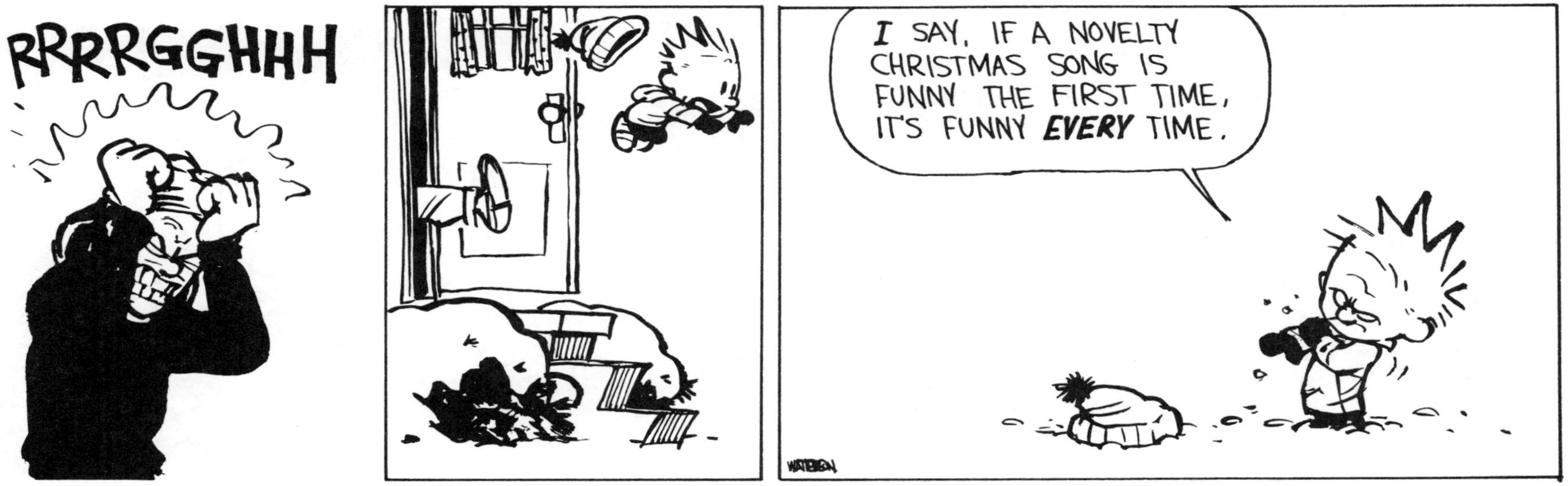
RRRRGGHHH
I SAY, IF A NOVELTY CHRISTMAS SONG IS FUNNY THE FIRST TIME, IT'S FUNNY **EVERY** TIME.

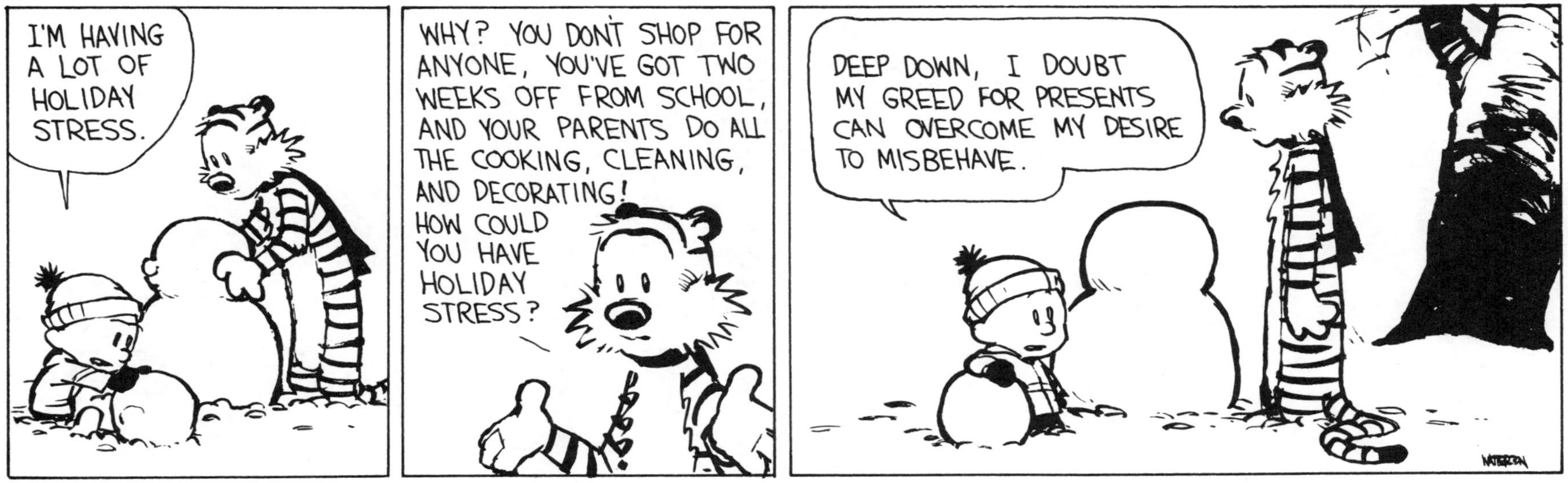
I'M HAVING A LOT OF HOLIDAY STRESS.
WHY? YOU DON'T SHOP FOR ANYONE, YOU'VE GOT TWO WEEKS OFF FROM SCHOOL, AND YOUR PARENTS DO ALL THE COOKING, CLEANING, AND DECORATING! HOW COULD YOU HAVE HOLIDAY STRESS?
DEEP DOWN, I DOUBT MY GREED FOR PRESENTS CAN OVERCOME MY DESIRE TO MISBEHAVE.

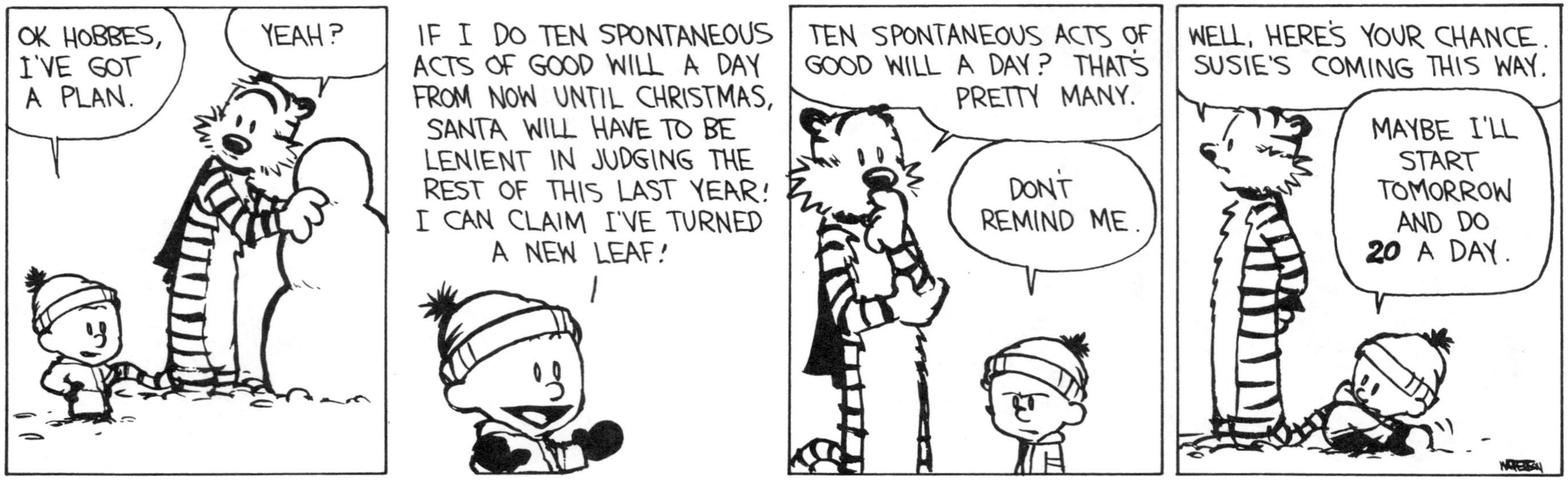
OK HOBBES, I'VE GOT A PLAN.
YEAH?
IF I DO TEN SPONTANEOUS ACTS OF GOOD WILL A DAY FROM NOW UNTIL CHRISTMAS, SANTA WILL HAVE TO BE LENIENT IN JUDGING THE REST OF THIS LAST YEAR! I CAN CLAIM I'VE TURNED A NEW LEAF!
TEN SPONTANEOUS ACTS OF GOOD WILL A DAY? THAT'S PRETTY MANY.
DON'T REMIND ME.
WELL, HERE'S YOUR CHANCE. SUSIE'S COMING THIS WAY.
MAYBE I'LL START TOMORROW AND DO **20** A DAY.

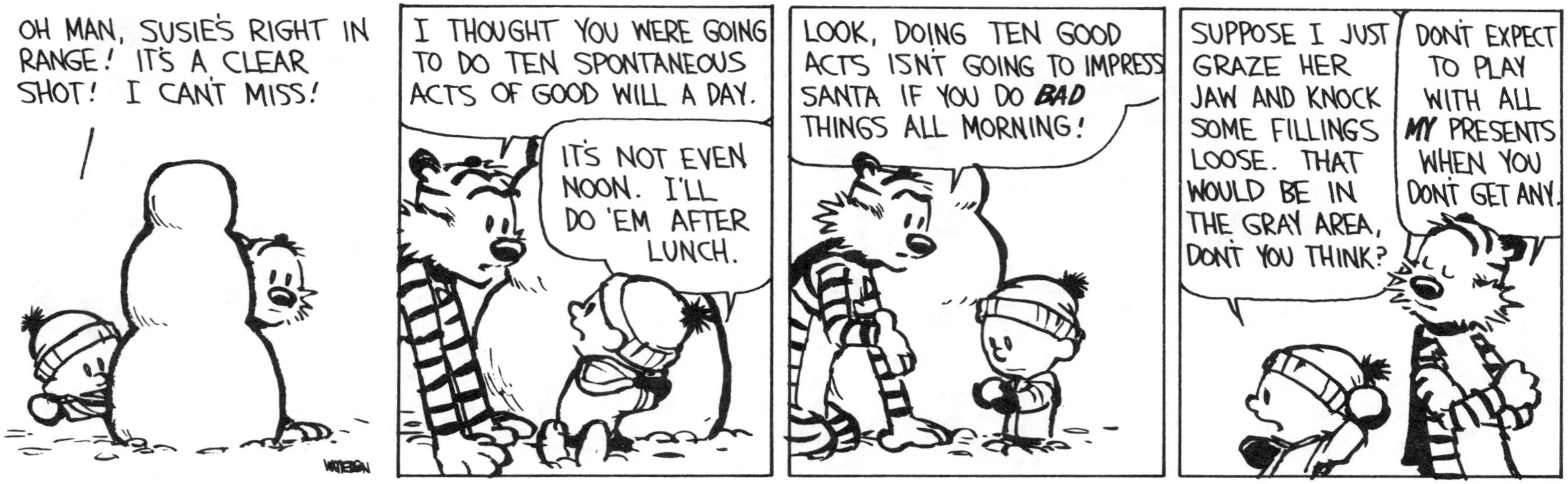
OH MAN, SUSIE'S RIGHT IN RANGE! IT'S A CLEAR SHOT! I CAN'T MISS!
I THOUGHT YOU WERE GOING TO DO TEN SPONTANEOUS ACTS OF GOOD WILL A DAY.
IT'S NOT EVEN NOON. I'LL DO 'EM AFTER LUNCH.
LOOK, DOING TEN GOOD ACTS ISN'T GOING TO IMPRESS SANTA IF YOU DO ***BAD*** THINGS ALL MORNING!
SUPPOSE I JUST GRAZE HER JAW AND KNOCK SOME FILLINGS LOOSE. THAT WOULD BE IN THE GRAY AREA, DON'T YOU THINK?
DON'T EXPECT TO PLAY WITH ALL ***MY*** PRESENTS WHEN YOU DON'T GET ANY.

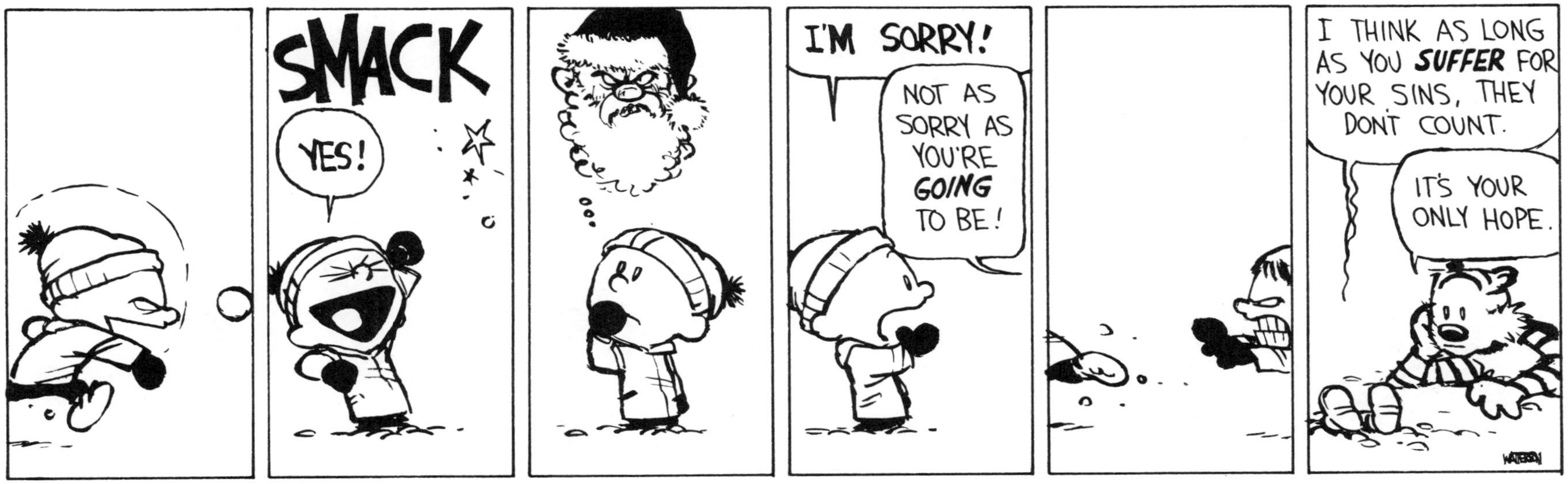
SMACK
YES!
I'M SORRY!
NOT AS SORRY AS YOU'RE GOING TO BE!
I THINK AS LONG AS YOU SUFFER FOR YOUR SINS, THEY DON'T COUNT.
IT'S YOUR ONLY HOPE.

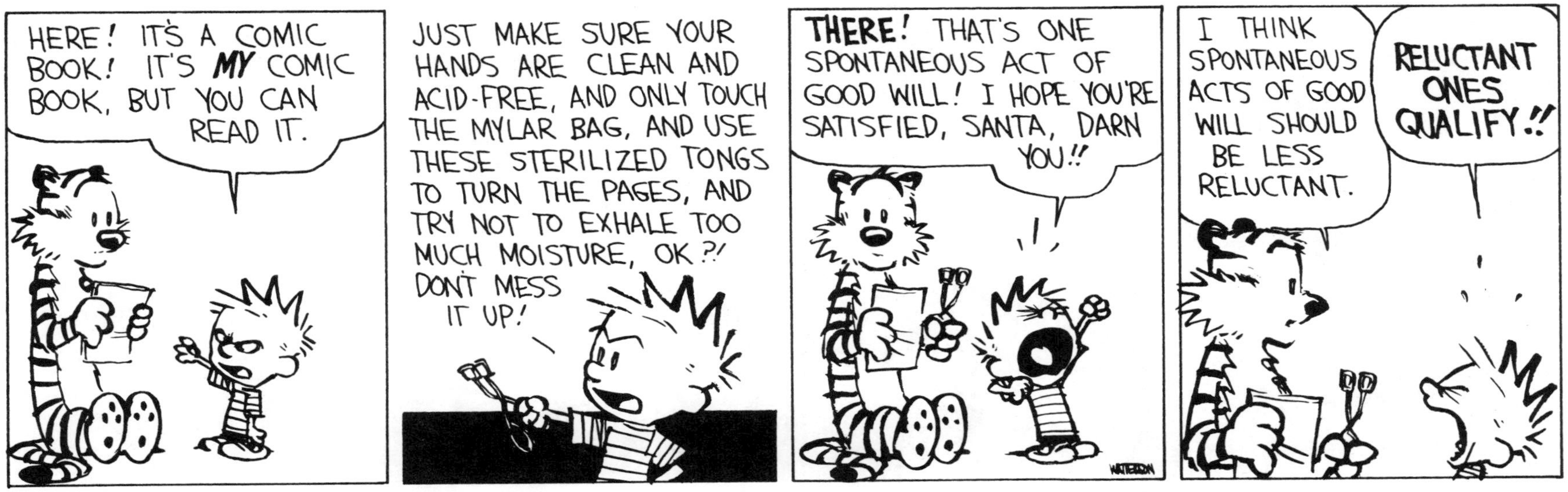
HERE! IT'S A COMIC BOOK! IT'S MY COMIC BOOK, BUT YOU CAN READ IT.
JUST MAKE SURE YOUR HANDS ARE CLEAN AND ACID-FREE, AND ONLY TOUCH THE MYLAR BAG, AND USE THESE STERILIZED TONGS TO TURN THE PAGES, AND TRY NOT TO EXHALE TOO MUCH MOISTURE, OK?! DON'T MESS IT UP!
THERE! THAT'S ONE SPONTANEOUS ACT OF GOOD WILL! I HOPE YOU'RE SATISFIED, SANTA, DARN YOU!!
I THINK SPONTANEOUS ACTS OF GOOD WILL SHOULD BE LESS RELUCTANT.
RELUCTANT ONES QUALIFY!!

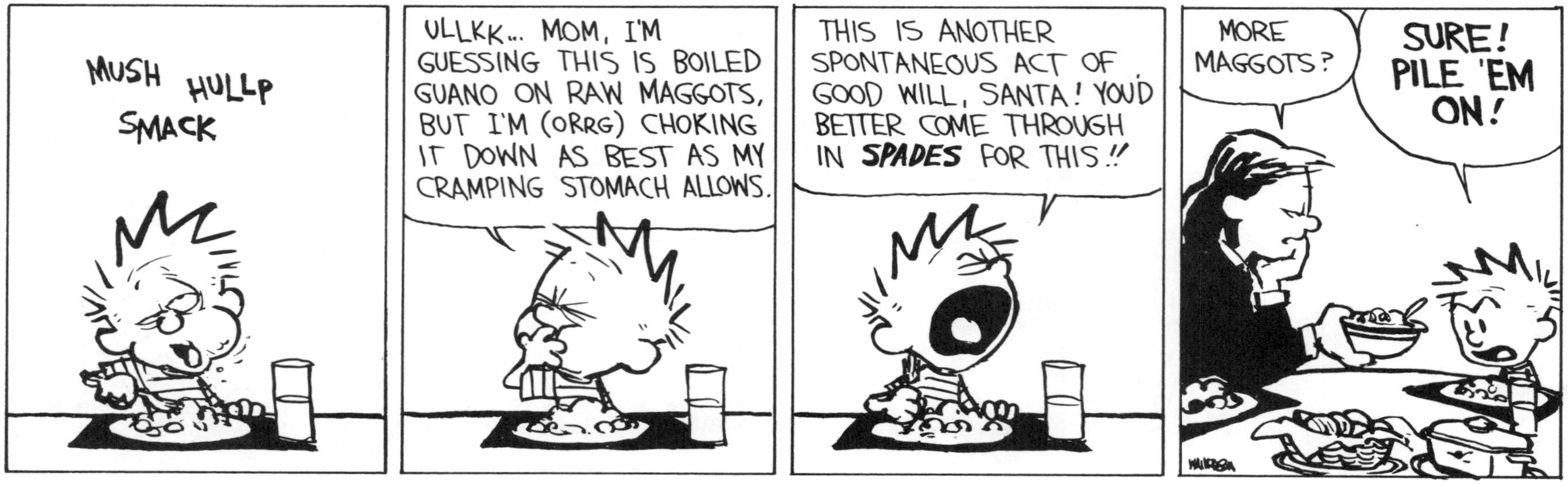
MUSH
HULLP
SMACK
ULLKK... MOM, I'M GUESSING THIS IS BOILED GUANO ON RAW MAGGOTS, BUT I'M (ORRG) CHOKING IT DOWN AS BEST AS MY CRAMPING STOMACH ALLOWS.
THIS IS ANOTHER SPONTANEOUS ACT OF GOOD WILL, SANTA! YOU'D BETTER COME THROUGH IN SPADES FOR THIS!!
MORE MAGGOTS?
SURE! PILE 'EM ON!

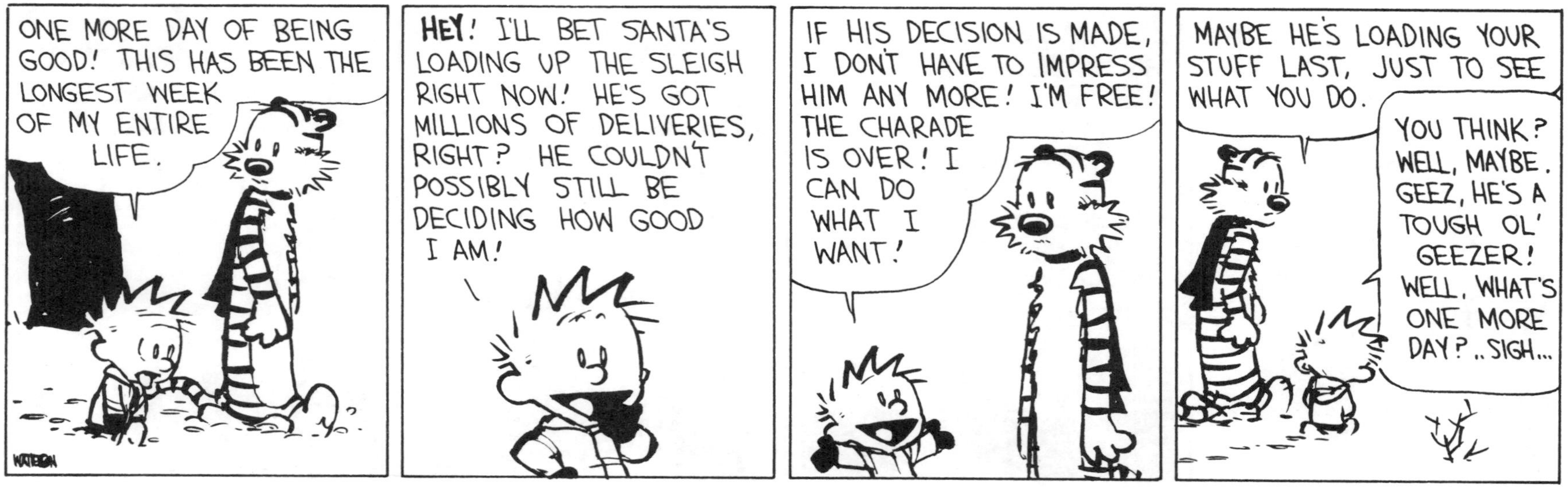
ONE MORE DAY OF BEING GOOD! THIS HAS BEEN THE LONGEST WEEK OF MY ENTIRE LIFE.
HEY! I'LL BET SANTA'S LOADING UP THE SLEIGH RIGHT NOW! HE'S GOT MILLIONS OF DELIVERIES, RIGHT? HE COULDN'T POSSIBLY STILL BE DECIDING HOW GOOD I AM!
IF HIS DECISION IS MADE, I DON'T HAVE TO IMPRESS HIM ANY MORE! I'M FREE! THE CHARADE IS OVER! I CAN DO WHAT I WANT!
MAYBE HE'S LOADING YOUR STUFF LAST, JUST TO SEE WHAT YOU DO.
YOU THINK? WELL, MAYBE. GEEZ, HE'S A TOUGH OL' GEEZER! WELL, WHAT'S ONE MORE DAY? .. SIGH...

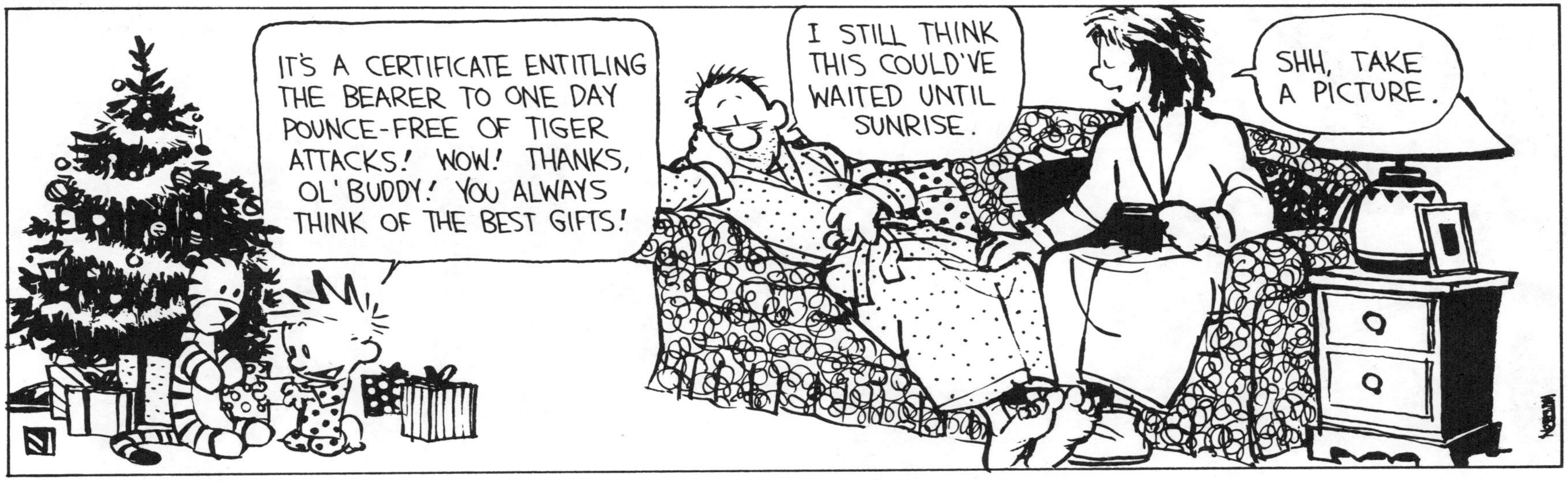
IT'S A CERTIFICATE ENTITLING THE BEARER TO ONE DAY POUNCE-FREE OF TIGER ATTACKS! WOW! THANKS, OL' BUDDY! YOU ALWAYS THINK OF THE BEST GIFTS!
I STILL THINK THIS COULD'VE WAITED UNTIL SUNRISE.
SHH, TAKE A PICTURE.

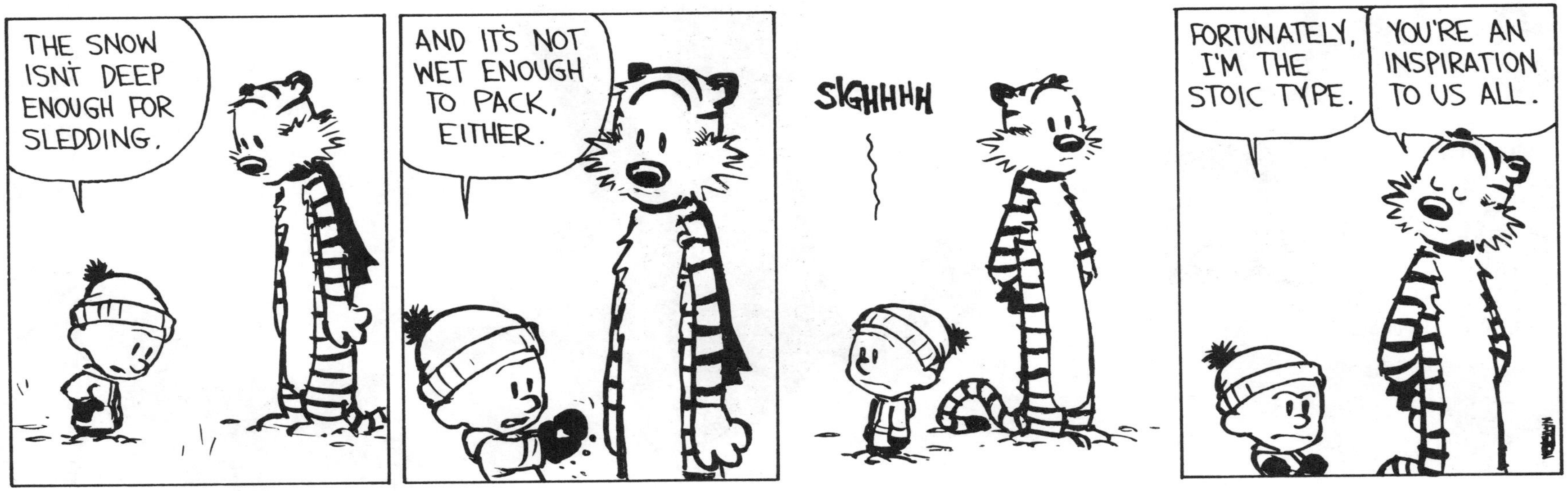
THE SNOW ISN'T DEEP ENOUGH FOR SLEDDING.
AND IT'S NOT WET ENOUGH TO PACK, EITHER.
SIGHHHH
FORTUNATELY, I'M THE STOIC TYPE.
YOU'RE AN INSPIRATION TO US ALL.

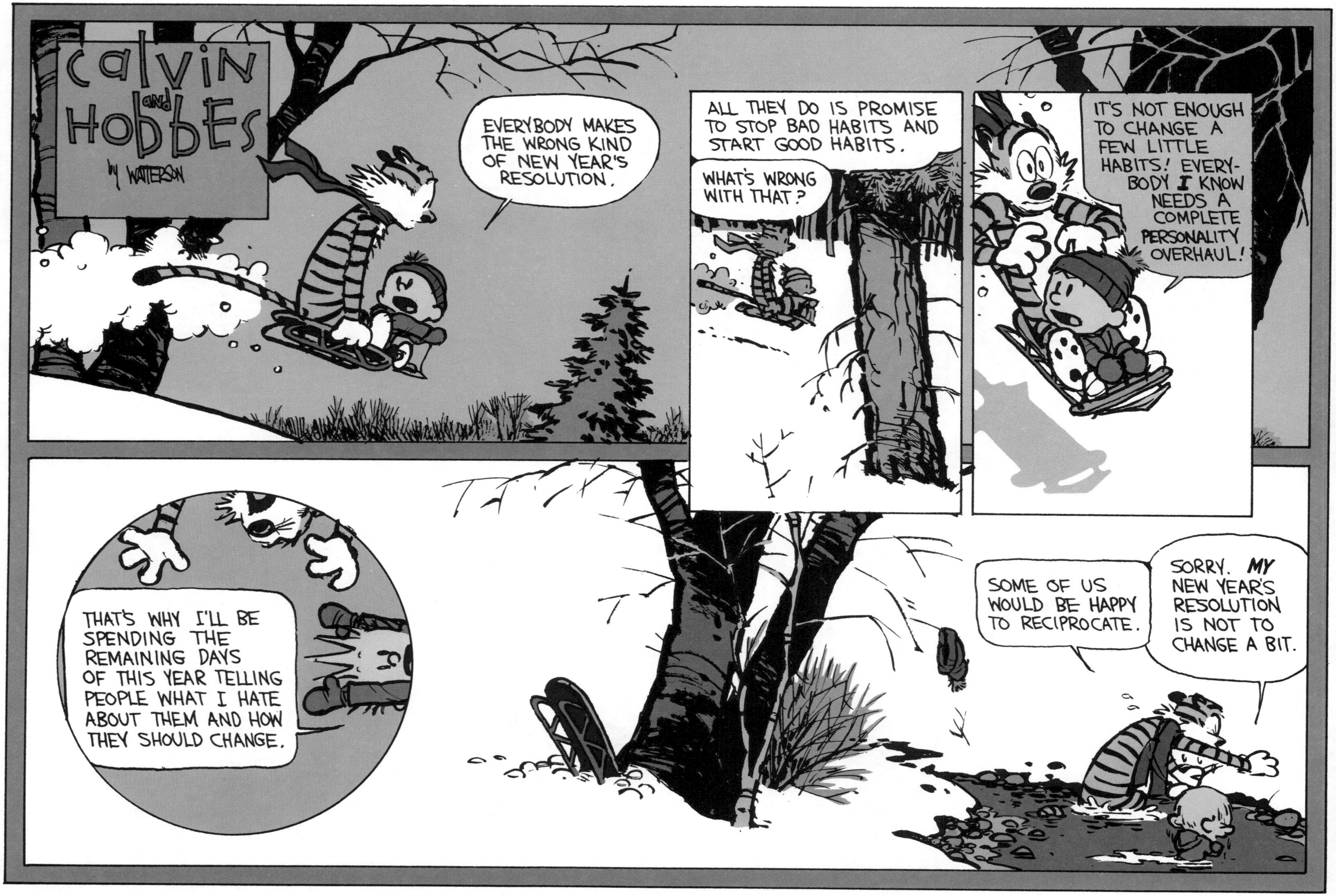
Calvin and Hobbes
by WATTERSON
EVERYBODY MAKES THE WRONG KIND OF NEW YEAR'S RESOLUTION.
ALL THEY DO IS PROMISE TO STOP BAD HABITS AND START GOOD HABITS.
WHAT'S WRONG WITH THAT?
IT'S NOT ENOUGH TO CHANGE A FEW LITTLE HABITS! EVERYBODY I KNOW NEEDS A COMPLETE PERSONALITY OVERHAUL!
THAT'S WHY I'LL BE SPENDING THE REMAINING DAYS OF THIS YEAR TELLING PEOPLE WHAT I HATE ABOUT THEM AND HOW THEY SHOULD CHANGE.
SOME OF US WOULD BE HAPPY TO RECIPROCATE.
SORRY. MY NEW YEAR'S RESOLUTION IS NOT TO CHANGE A BIT.

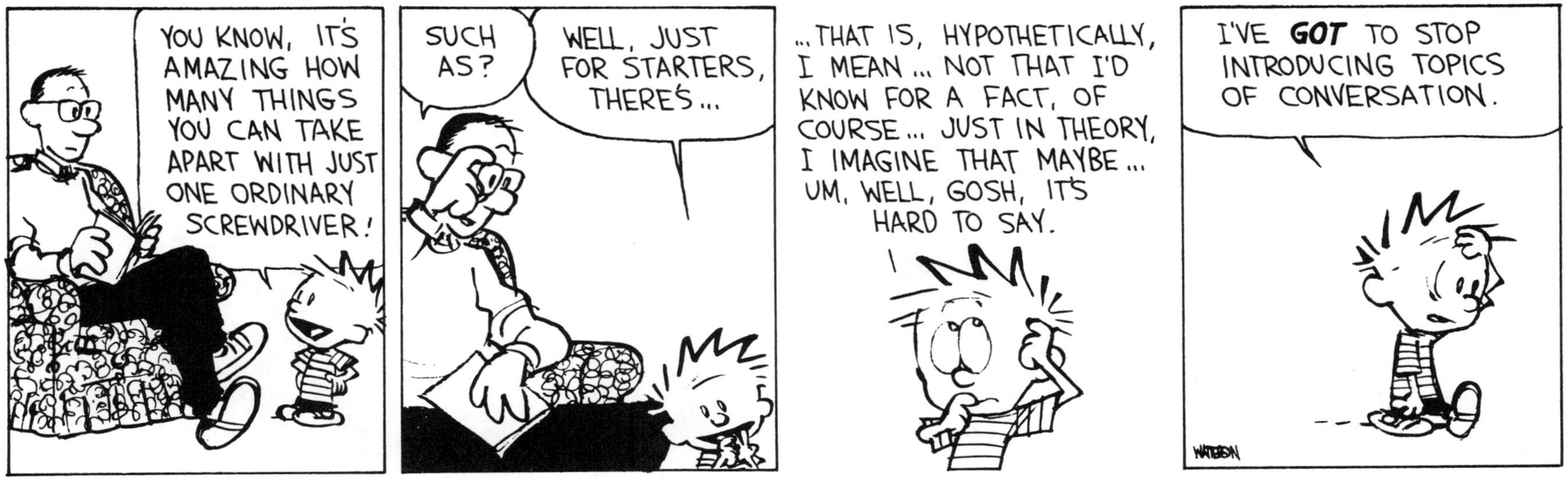
YOU KNOW, IT'S AMAZING HOW MANY THINGS YOU CAN TAKE APART WITH JUST ONE ORDINARY SCREWDRIVER!
SUCH AS?
WELL, JUST FOR STARTERS, THERE'S...
...THAT IS, HYPOTHETICALLY, I MEAN... NOT THAT I'D KNOW FOR A FACT, OF COURSE... JUST IN THEORY, I IMAGINE THAT MAYBE... UM, WELL, GOSH, IT'S HARD TO SAY.
I'VE **GOT** TO STOP INTRODUCING TOPICS OF CONVERSATION.

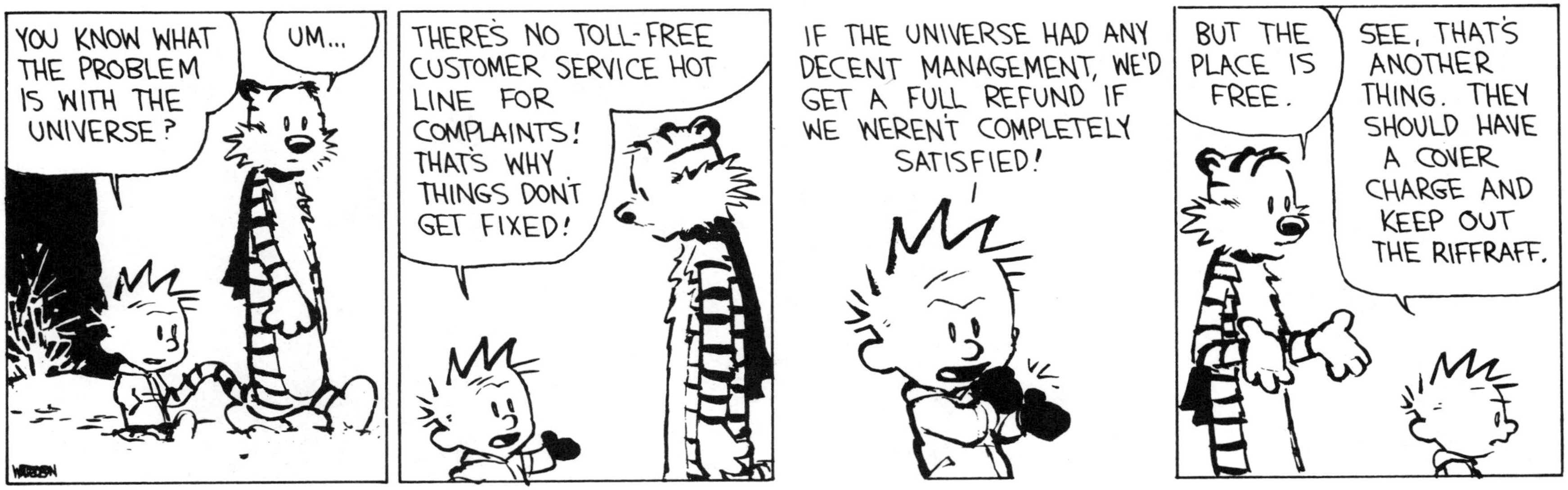
YOU KNOW WHAT THE PROBLEM IS WITH THE UNIVERSE?
UM...
THERE'S NO TOLL-FREE CUSTOMER SERVICE HOT LINE FOR COMPLAINTS! THAT'S WHY THINGS DON'T GET FIXED!
IF THE UNIVERSE HAD ANY DECENT MANAGEMENT, WE'D GET A FULL REFUND IF WE WEREN'T COMPLETELY SATISFIED!
BUT THE PLACE IS FREE.
SEE, THAT'S ANOTHER THING. THEY SHOULD HAVE A COVER CHARGE AND KEEP OUT THE RIFFRAFF.

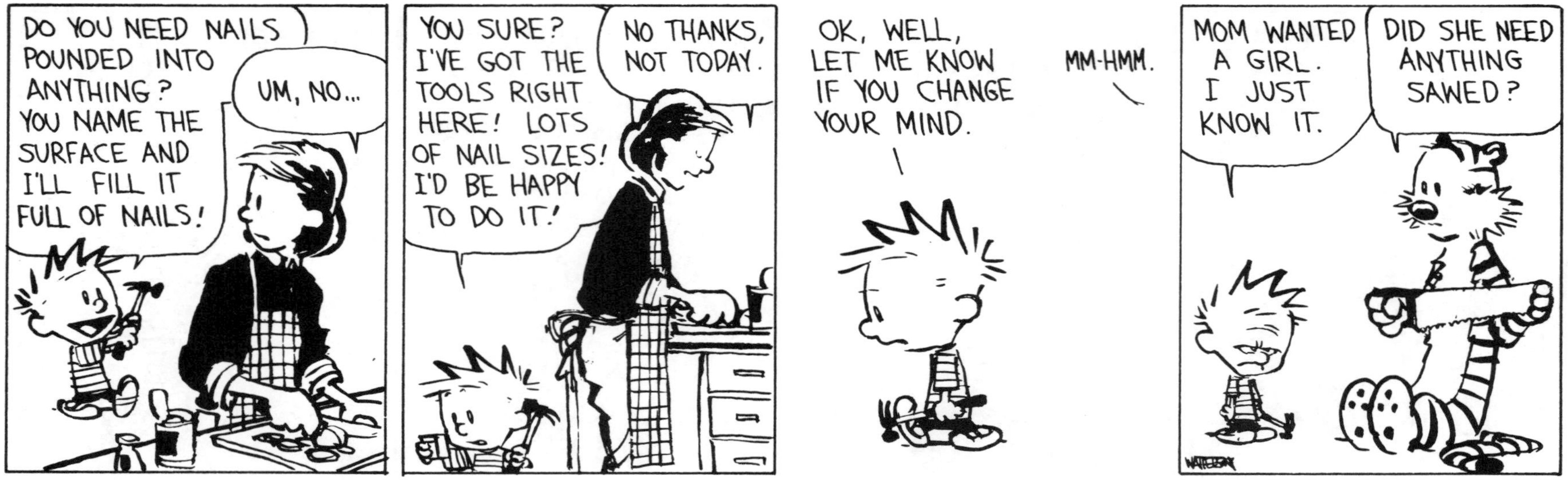
DO YOU NEED NAILS POUNDED INTO ANYTHING? YOU NAME THE SURFACE AND I'LL FILL IT FULL OF NAILS!
UM, NO...
YOU SURE? I'VE GOT THE TOOLS RIGHT HERE! LOTS OF NAIL SIZES! I'D BE HAPPY TO DO IT!
NO THANKS, NOT TODAY.
OK, WELL, LET ME KNOW IF YOU CHANGE YOUR MIND.
MM-HMM.
MOM WANTED A GIRL. I JUST KNOW IT.
DID SHE NEED ANYTHING SAWED?

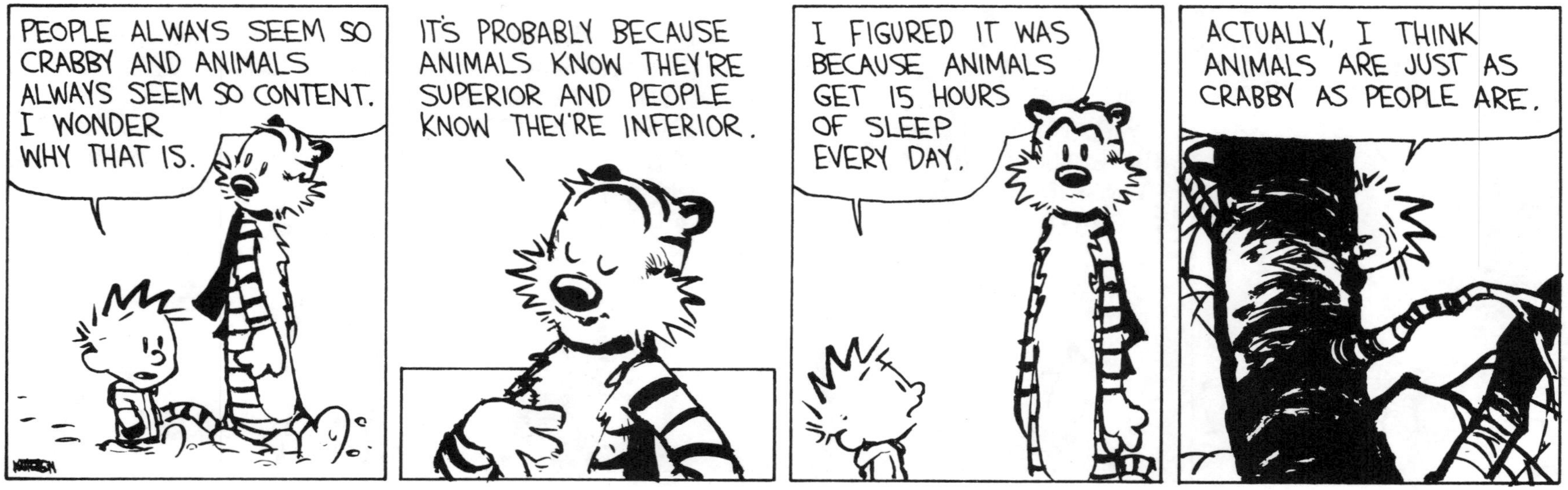
PEOPLE ALWAYS SEEM SO CRABBY AND ANIMALS ALWAYS SEEM SO CONTENT. I WONDER WHY THAT IS.
IT'S PROBABLY BECAUSE ANIMALS KNOW THEY'RE SUPERIOR AND PEOPLE KNOW THEY'RE INFERIOR.
I FIGURED IT WAS BECAUSE ANIMALS GET 15 HOURS OF SLEEP EVERY DAY.
ACTUALLY, I THINK ANIMALS ARE JUST AS CRABBY AS PEOPLE ARE.

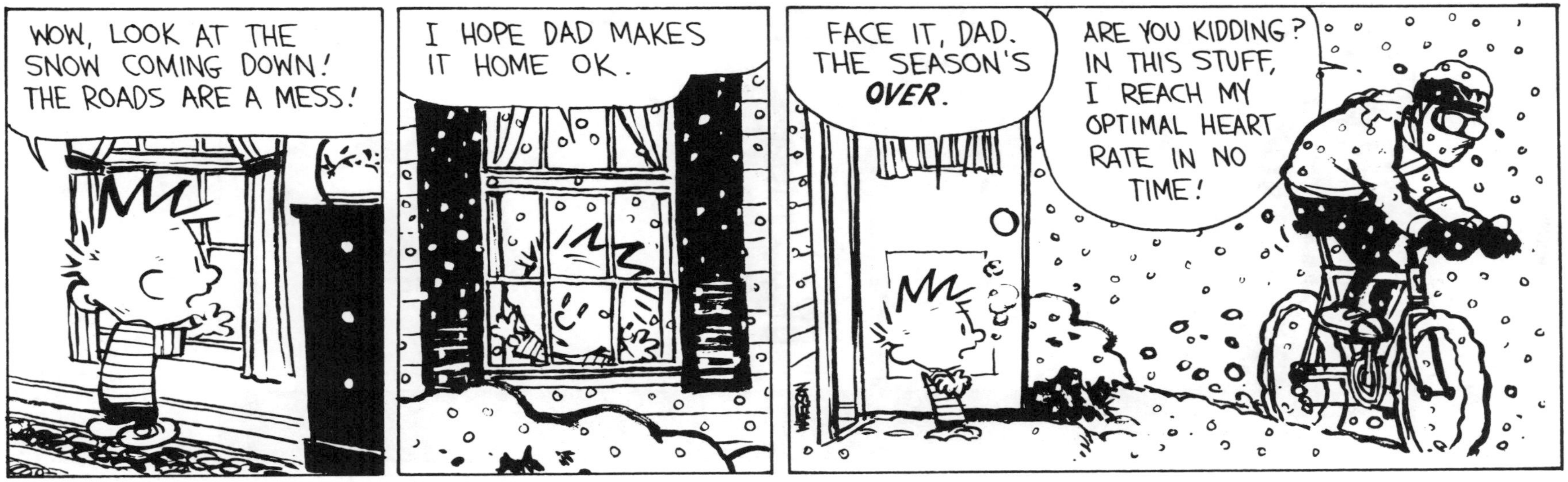
WOW, LOOK AT THE SNOW COMING DOWN! THE ROADS ARE A MESS!
I HOPE DAD MAKES IT HOME OK.
FACE IT, DAD. THE SEASON'S **OVER**.
ARE YOU KIDDING? IN THIS STUFF, I REACH MY OPTIMAL HEART RATE IN NO TIME!

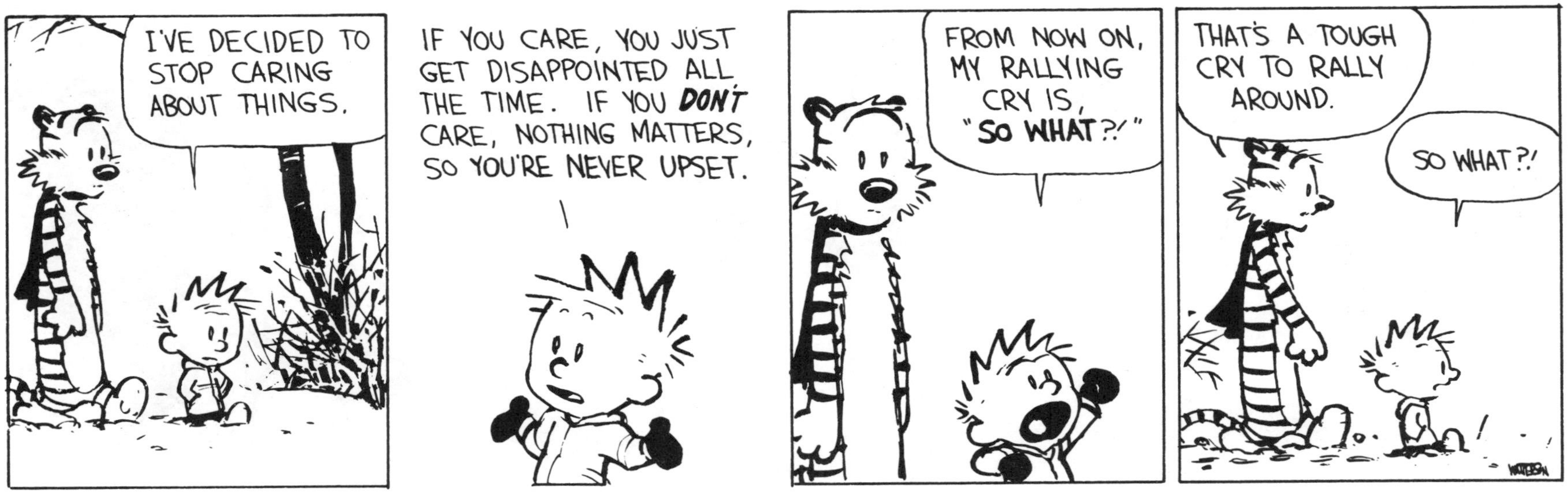
I'VE DECIDED TO STOP CARING ABOUT THINGS.
IF YOU CARE, YOU JUST GET DISAPPOINTED ALL THE TIME. IF YOU **DON'T** CARE, NOTHING MATTERS, SO YOU'RE NEVER UPSET.
FROM NOW ON, MY RALLYING CRY IS, "**SO WHAT**?!"
THAT'S A TOUGH CRY TO RALLY AROUND.
SO WHAT?!

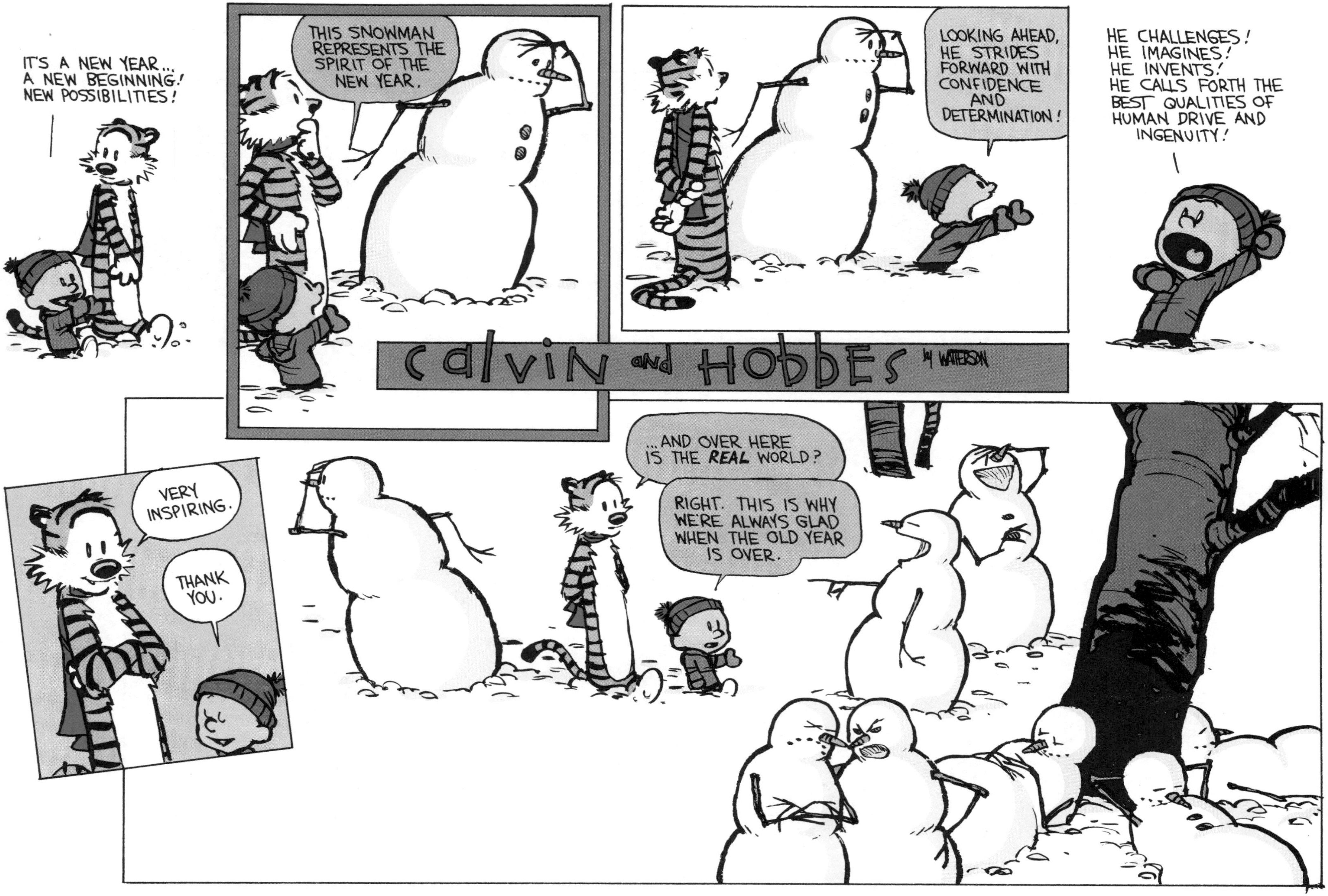
IT'S A NEW YEAR... A NEW BEGINNING! NEW POSSIBILITIES!
THIS SNOWMAN REPRESENTS THE SPIRIT OF THE NEW YEAR.
LOOKING AHEAD, HE STRIDES FORWARD WITH CONFIDENCE AND DETERMINATION!
HE CHALLENGES! HE IMAGINES! HE INVENTS! HE CALLS FORTH THE BEST QUALITIES OF HUMAN DRIVE AND INGENUITY!
Calvin and HOBBES by WATTERSON
VERY INSPIRING.
THANK YOU.
...AND OVER HERE IS THE REAL WORLD?
RIGHT. THIS IS WHY WE'RE ALWAYS GLAD WHEN THE OLD YEAR IS OVER.

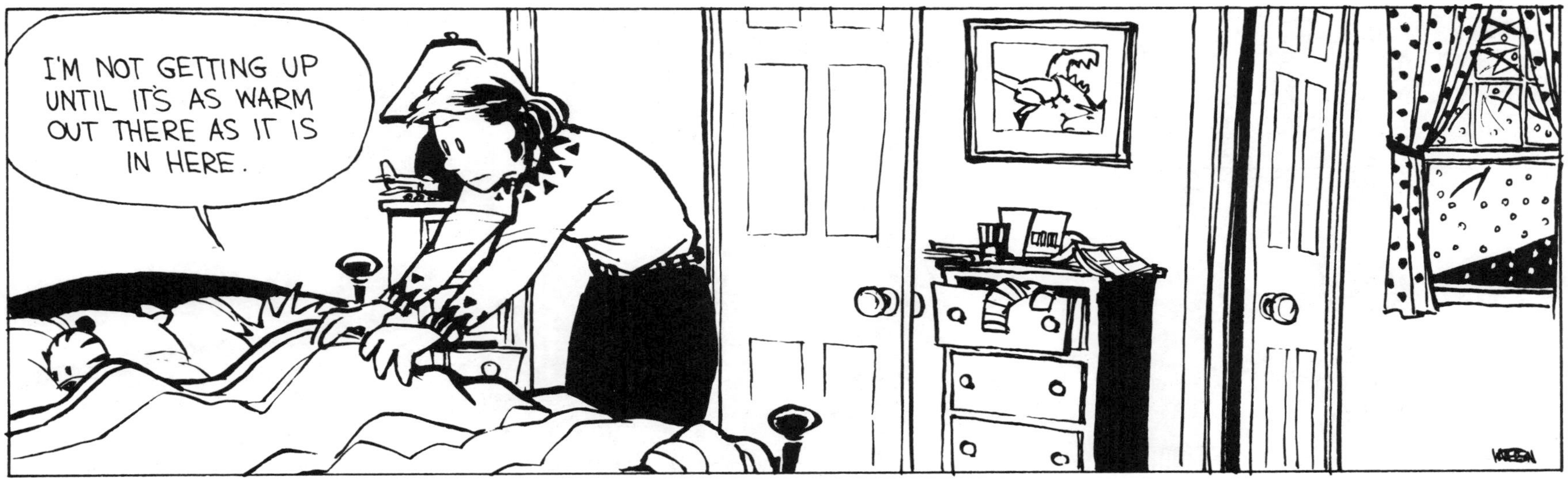
I'M NOT GETTING UP UNTIL IT'S AS WARM OUT THERE AS IT IS IN HERE.

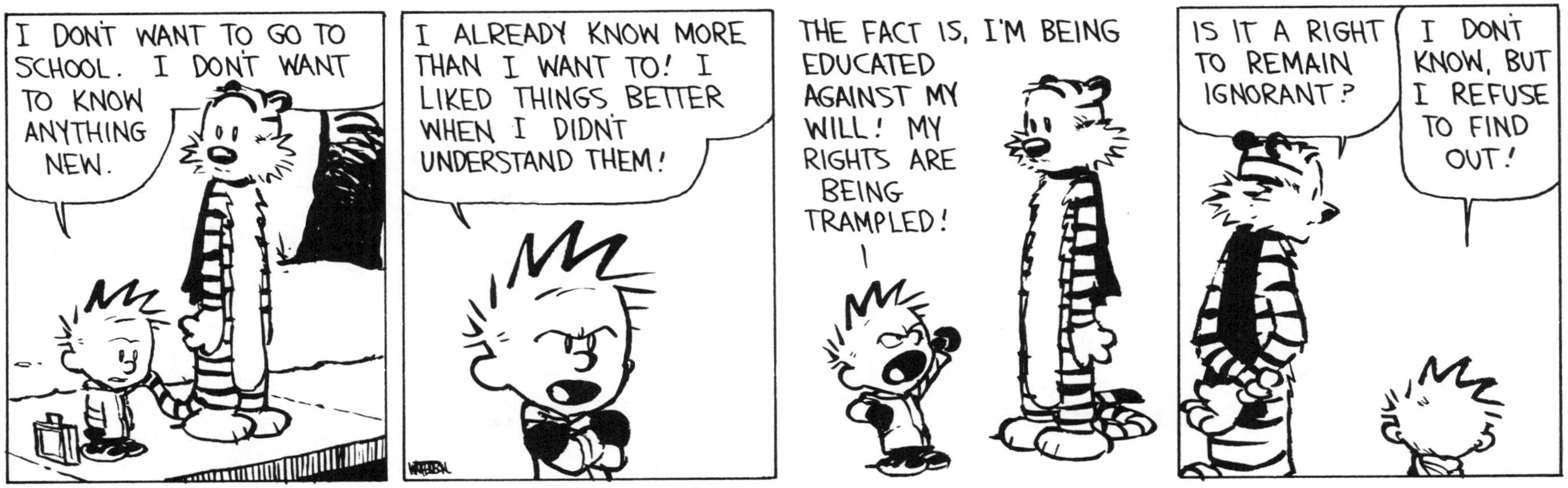
I DON'T WANT TO GO TO SCHOOL. I DON'T WANT TO KNOW ANYTHING NEW.
I ALREADY KNOW MORE THAN I WANT TO! I LIKED THINGS BETTER WHEN I DIDN'T UNDERSTAND THEM!
THE FACT IS, I'M BEING EDUCATED AGAINST MY WILL! MY RIGHTS ARE BEING TRAMPLED!
IS IT A RIGHT TO REMAIN IGNORANT?
I DON'T KNOW, BUT I REFUSE TO FIND OUT!

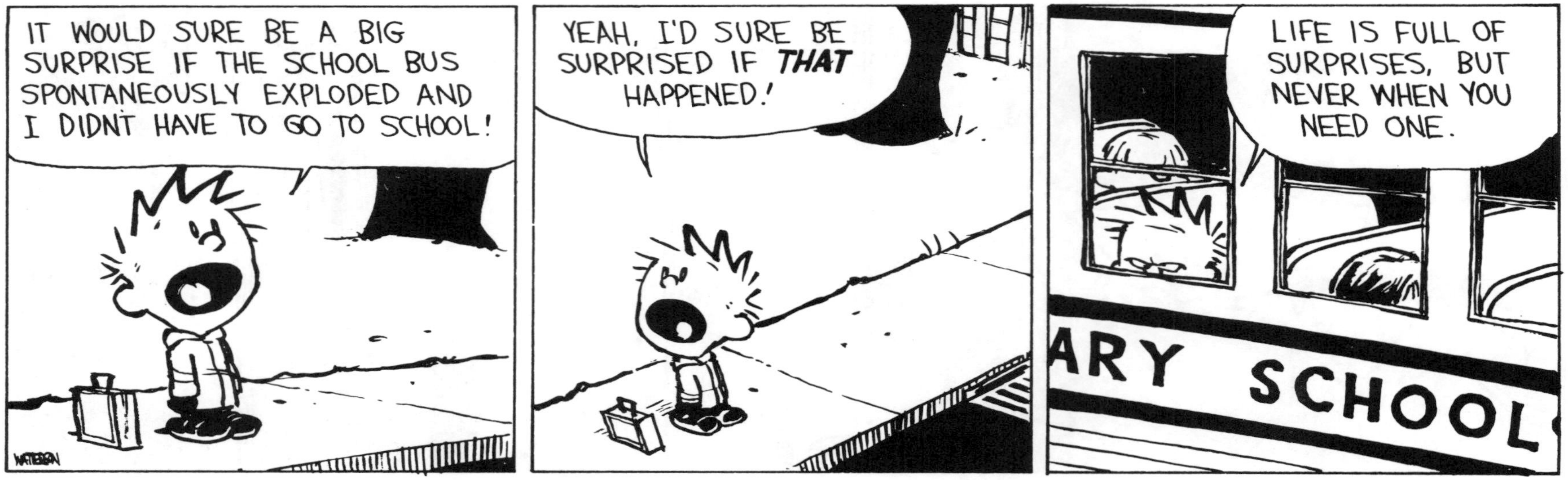
IT WOULD SURE BE A BIG SURPRISE IF THE SCHOOL BUS SPONTANEOUSLY EXPLODED AND I DIDN'T HAVE TO GO TO SCHOOL!
YEAH, I'D SURE BE SURPRISED IF *THAT* HAPPENED!
LIFE IS FULL OF SURPRISES, BUT NEVER WHEN YOU NEED ONE.
ARY SCHOOL

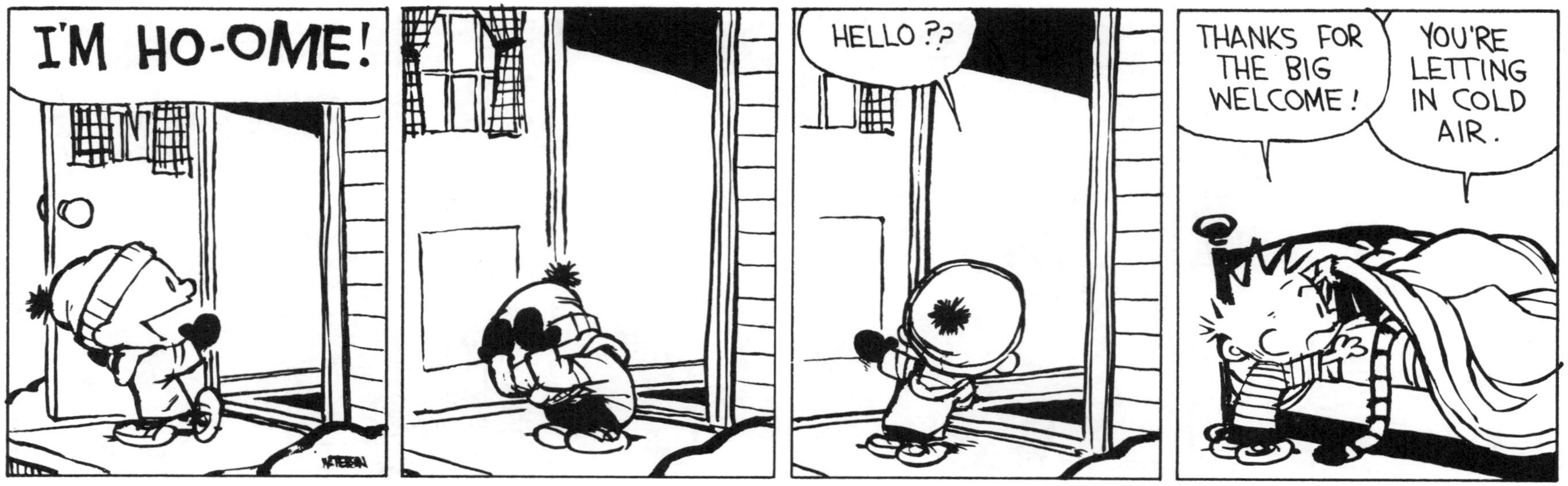
I'M HO-OME!
HELLO ??
THANKS FOR THE BIG WELCOME!
YOU'RE LETTING IN COLD AIR.

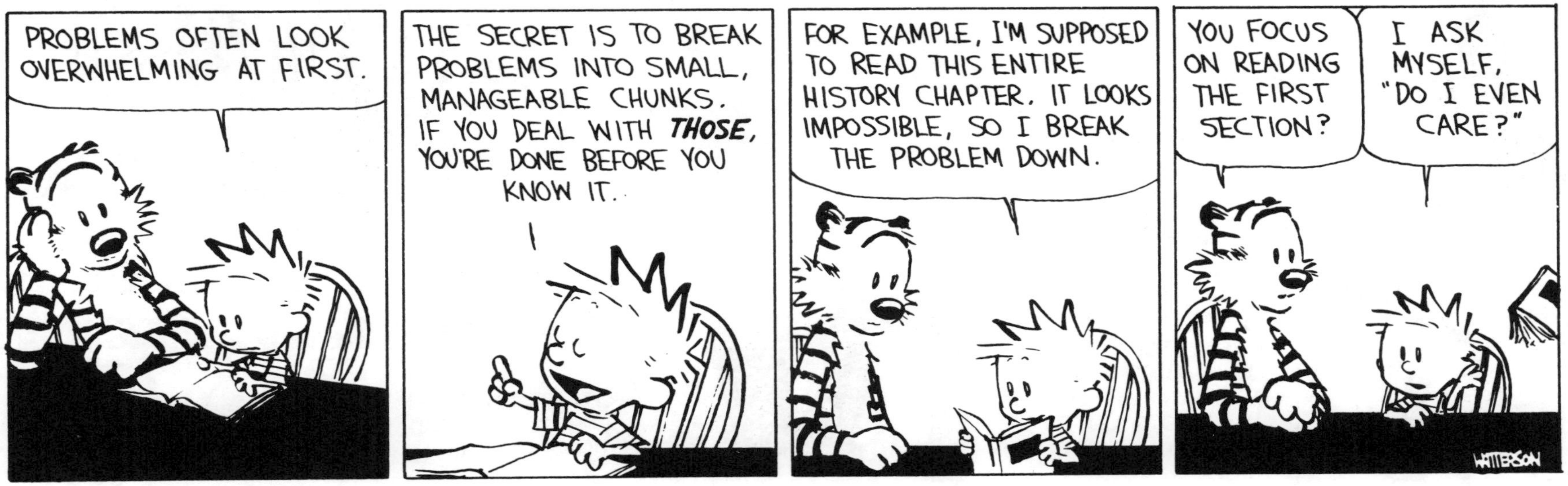
PROBLEMS OFTEN LOOK OVERWHELMING AT FIRST.
THE SECRET IS TO BREAK PROBLEMS INTO SMALL, MANAGEABLE CHUNKS. IF YOU DEAL WITH THOSE, YOU'RE DONE BEFORE YOU KNOW IT.
FOR EXAMPLE, I'M SUPPOSED TO READ THIS ENTIRE HISTORY CHAPTER. IT LOOKS IMPOSSIBLE, SO I BREAK THE PROBLEM DOWN.
YOU FOCUS ON READING THE FIRST SECTION?
I ASK MYSELF, "DO I EVEN CARE?"
WATTERSON

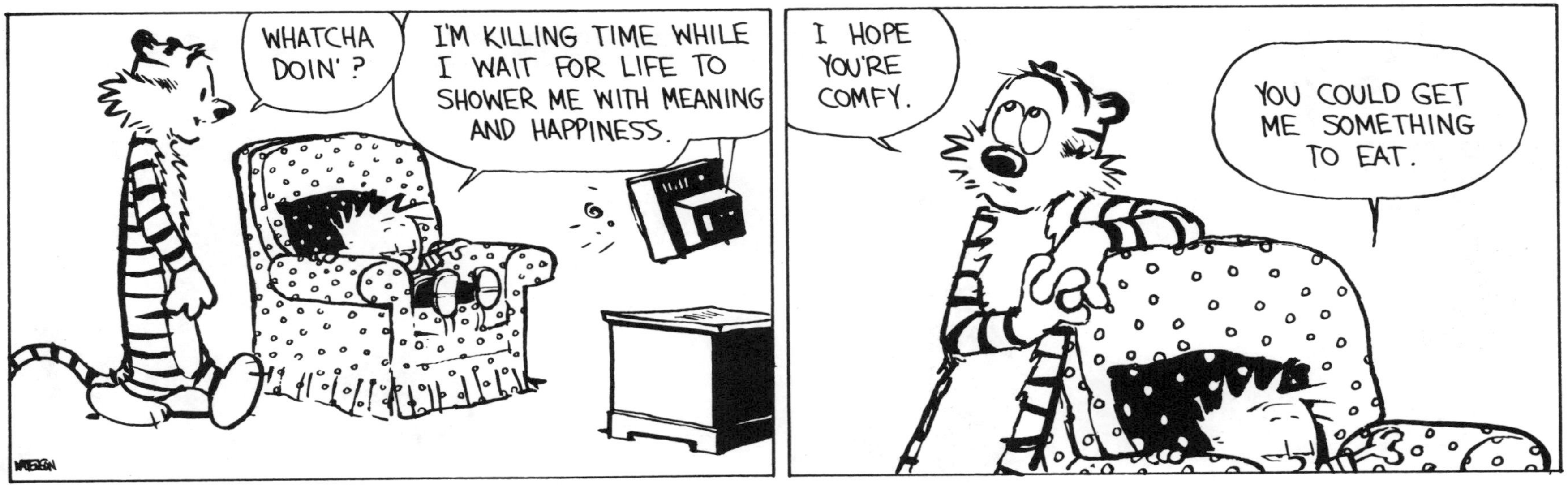
WHATCHA DOIN'?
I'M KILLING TIME WHILE I WAIT FOR LIFE TO SHOWER ME WITH MEANING AND HAPPINESS.
I HOPE YOU'RE COMFY.
YOU COULD GET ME SOMETHING TO EAT.

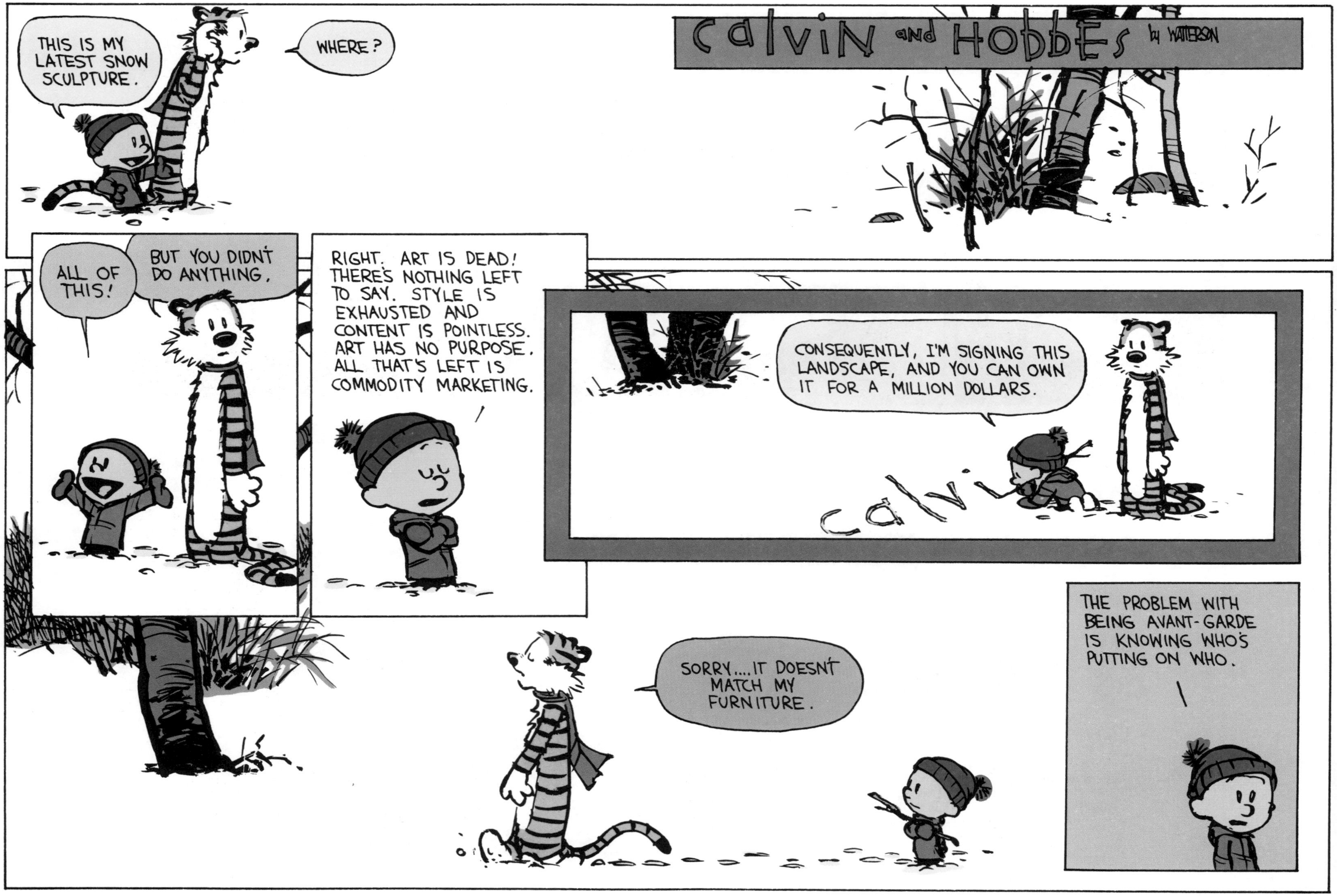
Calvin and HOBBES by WATTERSON
THIS IS MY LATEST SNOW SCULPTURE.
WHERE?
ALL OF THIS!
BUT YOU DIDN'T DO ANYTHING.
RIGHT. ART IS DEAD! THERE'S NOTHING LEFT TO SAY. STYLE IS EXHAUSTED AND CONTENT IS POINTLESS. ART HAS NO PURPOSE. ALL THAT'S LEFT IS COMMODITY MARKETING.
CONSEQUENTLY, I'M SIGNING THIS LANDSCAPE, AND YOU CAN OWN IT FOR A MILLION DOLLARS.
SORRY.... IT DOESN'T MATCH MY FURNITURE.
THE PROBLEM WITH BEING AVANT-GARDE IS KNOWING WHO'S PUTTING ON WHO.

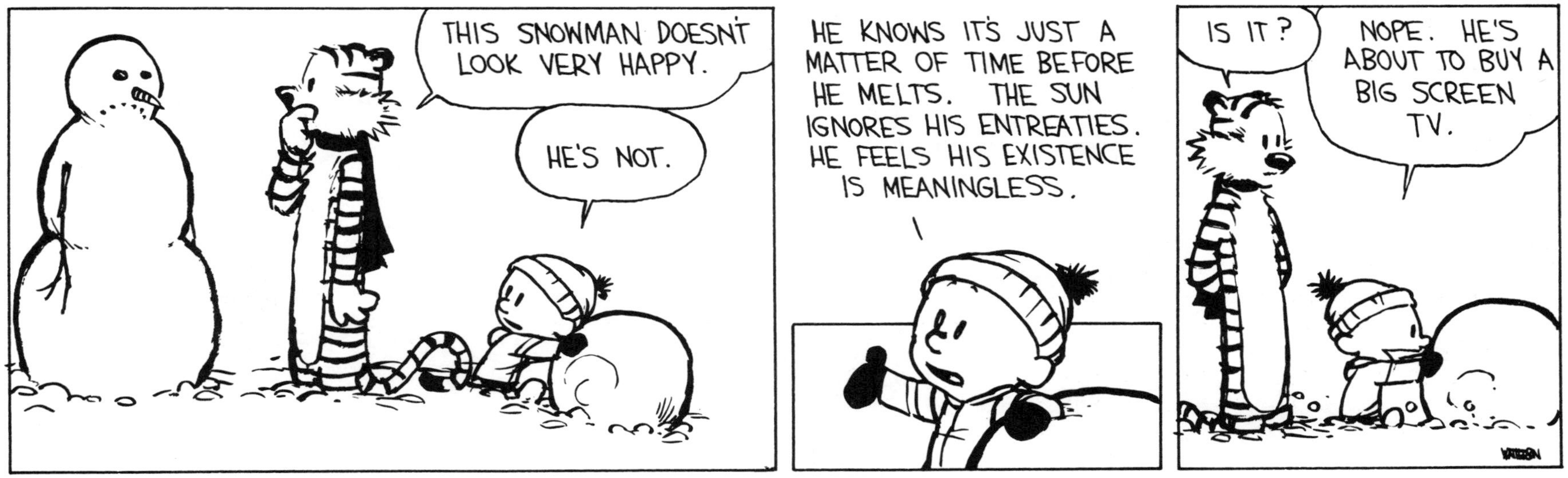
THIS SNOWMAN DOESN'T LOOK VERY HAPPY.
HE'S NOT.
HE KNOWS IT'S JUST A MATTER OF TIME BEFORE HE MELTS. THE SUN IGNORES HIS ENTREATIES. HE FEELS HIS EXISTENCE IS MEANINGLESS.
IS IT?
NOPE. HE'S ABOUT TO BUY A BIG SCREEN TV.

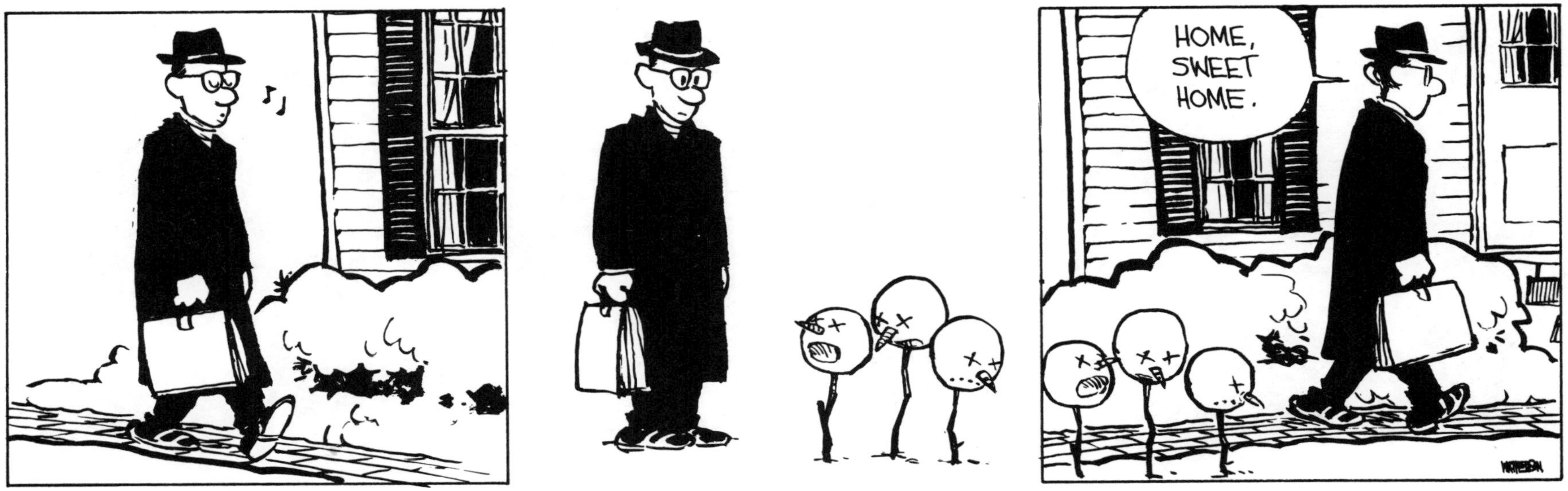
HOME, SWEET HOME.

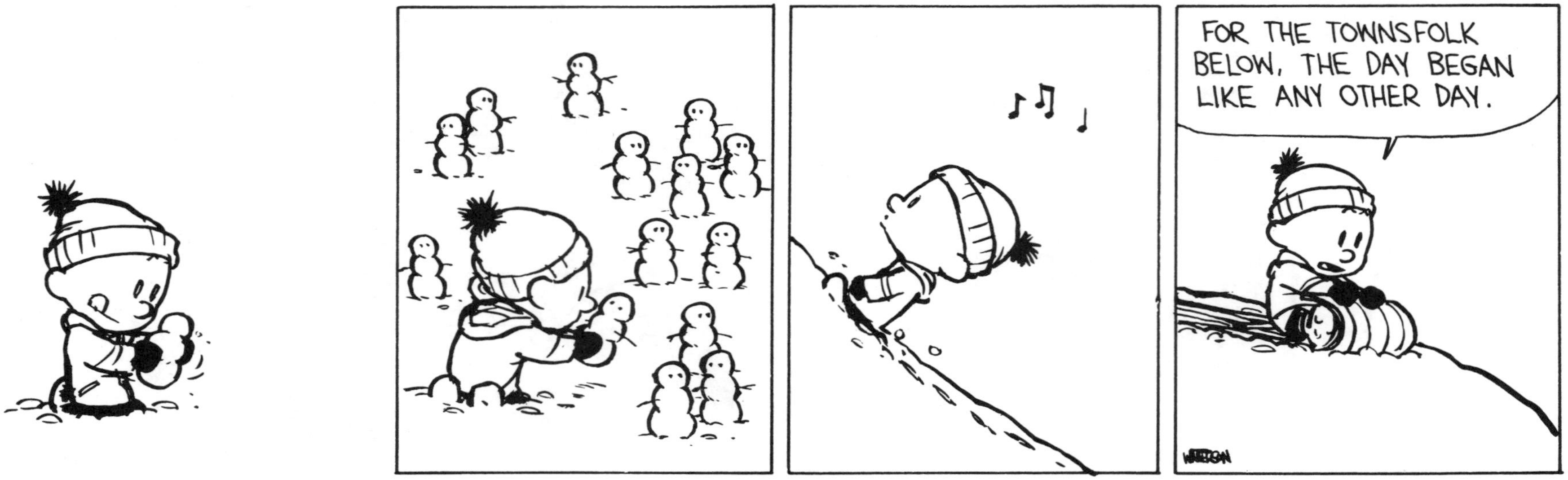
FOR THE TOWNSFOLK BELOW, THE DAY BEGAN LIKE ANY OTHER DAY.

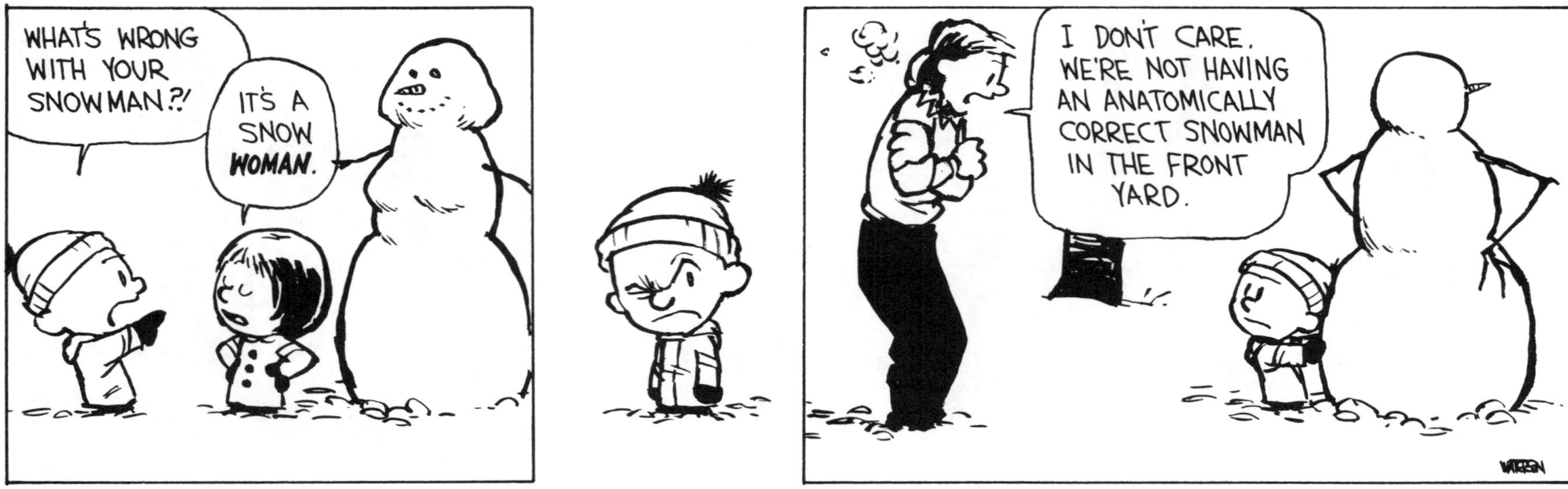
WHAT'S WRONG WITH YOUR SNOWMAN?!
IT'S A SNOW **WOMAN**.
I DON'T CARE. WE'RE NOT HAVING AN ANATOMICALLY CORRECT SNOWMAN IN THE FRONT YARD.

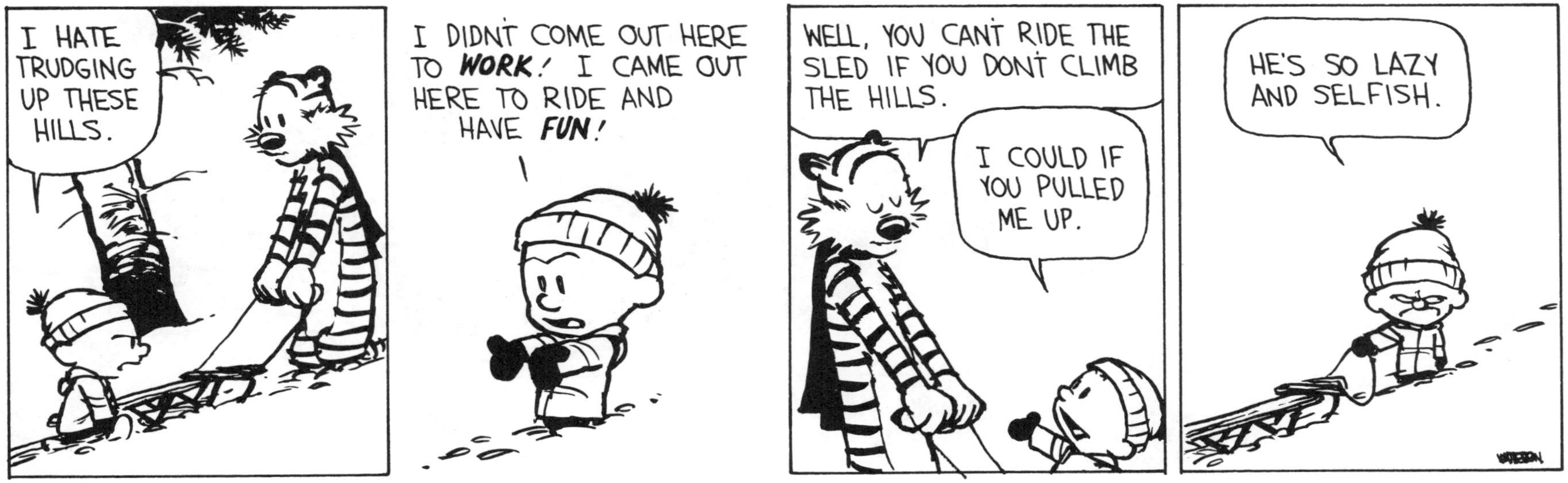
I HATE TRUDGING UP THESE HILLS.
I DIDN'T COME OUT HERE TO **WORK**! I CAME OUT HERE TO RIDE AND HAVE **FUN**!
WELL, YOU CAN'T RIDE THE SLED IF YOU DON'T CLIMB THE HILLS.
I COULD IF YOU PULLED ME UP.
HE'S SO LAZY AND SELFISH.
WATTERSON

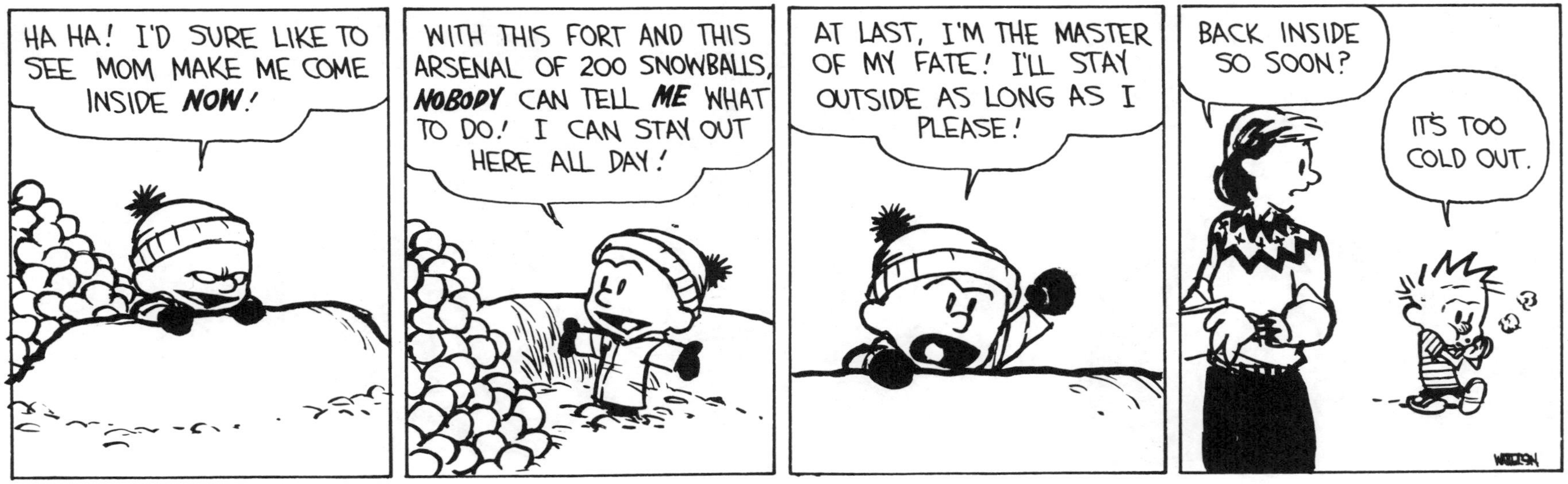
HA HA! I'D SURE LIKE TO SEE MOM MAKE ME COME INSIDE **NOW**!
WITH THIS FORT AND THIS ARSENAL OF 200 SNOWBALLS, **NOBODY** CAN TELL **ME** WHAT TO DO! I CAN STAY OUT HERE ALL DAY!
AT LAST, I'M THE MASTER OF MY FATE! I'LL STAY OUTSIDE AS LONG AS I PLEASE!
BACK INSIDE SO SOON?
IT'S TOO COLD OUT.
WATTERSON

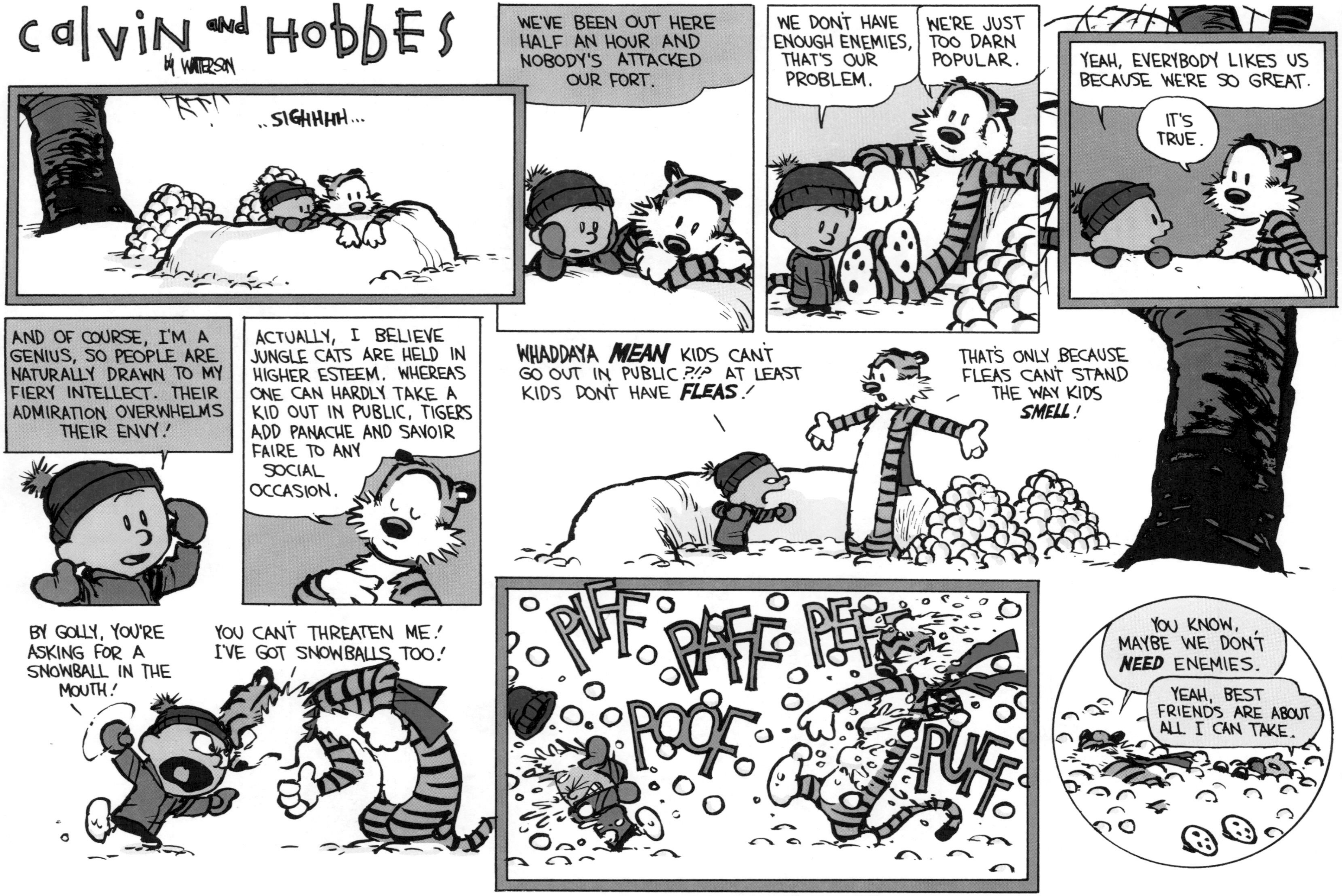
calvin and HOBBES
by WATTERSON
..SIGHHHH...
WE'VE BEEN OUT HERE HALF AN HOUR AND NOBODY'S ATTACKED OUR FORT.
WE DON'T HAVE ENOUGH ENEMIES, THAT'S OUR PROBLEM.
WE'RE JUST TOO DARN POPULAR.
YEAH, EVERYBODY LIKES US BECAUSE WE'RE SO GREAT.
IT'S TRUE.
AND OF COURSE, I'M A GENIUS, SO PEOPLE ARE NATURALLY DRAWN TO MY FIERY INTELLECT. THEIR ADMIRATION OVERWHELMS THEIR ENVY!
ACTUALLY, I BELIEVE JUNGLE CATS ARE HELD IN HIGHER ESTEEM. WHEREAS ONE CAN HARDLY TAKE A KID OUT IN PUBLIC, TIGERS ADD PANACHE AND SAVOIR FAIRE TO ANY SOCIAL OCCASION.
WHADDAYA MEAN KIDS CAN'T GO OUT IN PUBLIC?!? AT LEAST KIDS DON'T HAVE FLEAS!
THAT'S ONLY BECAUSE FLEAS CAN'T STAND THE WAY KIDS SMELL!
BY GOLLY, YOU'RE ASKING FOR A SNOWBALL IN THE MOUTH!
YOU CAN'T THREATEN ME! I'VE GOT SNOWBALLS TOO!
PIFF
PAFF
PEFF
POOF
PUFF
YOU KNOW, MAYBE WE DON'T NEED ENEMIES.
YEAH, BEST FRIENDS ARE ABOUT ALL I CAN TAKE.

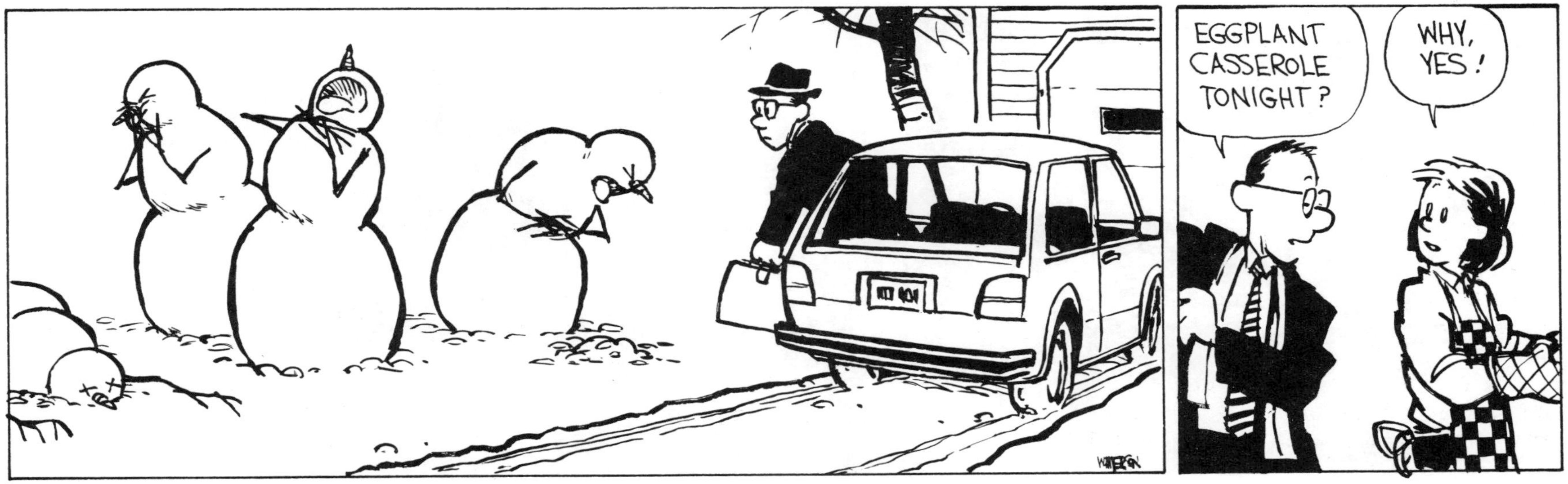
EGGPLANT CASSEROLE TONIGHT?
WHY, YES!

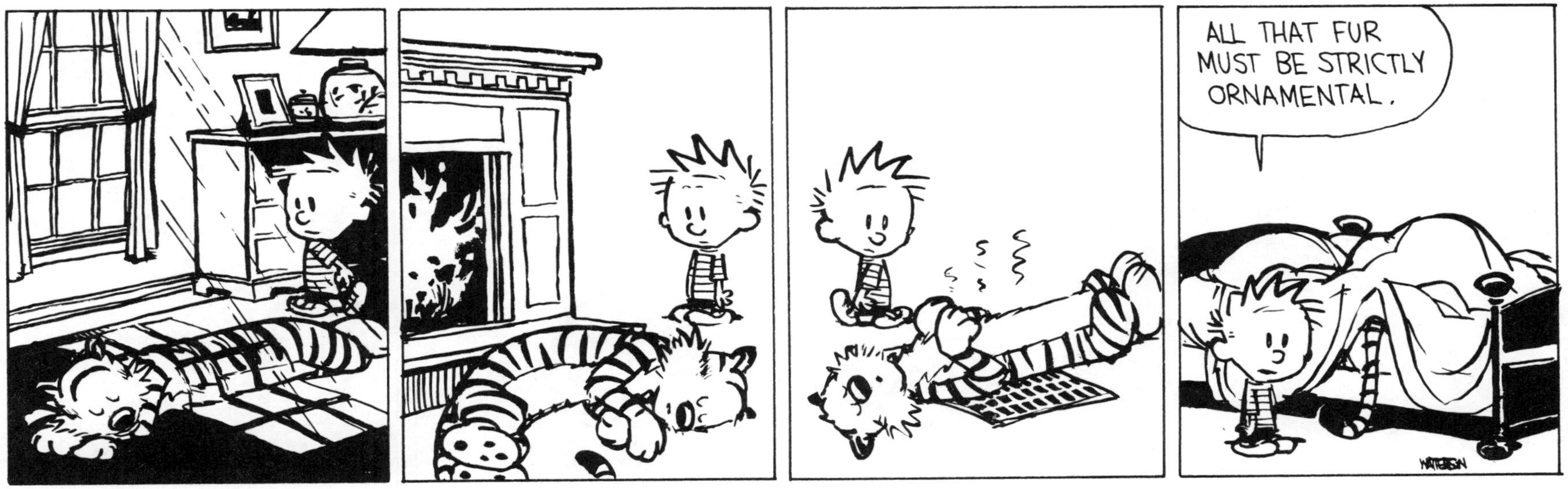
ALL THAT FUR MUST BE STRICTLY ORNAMENTAL.

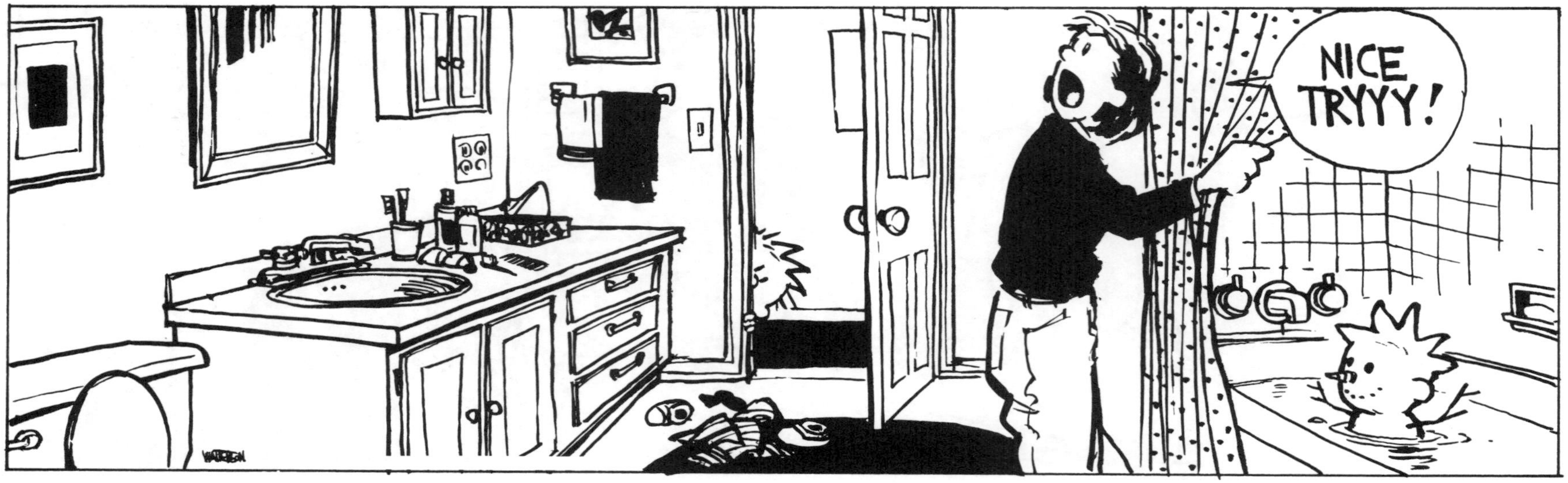
NICE TRYYY!

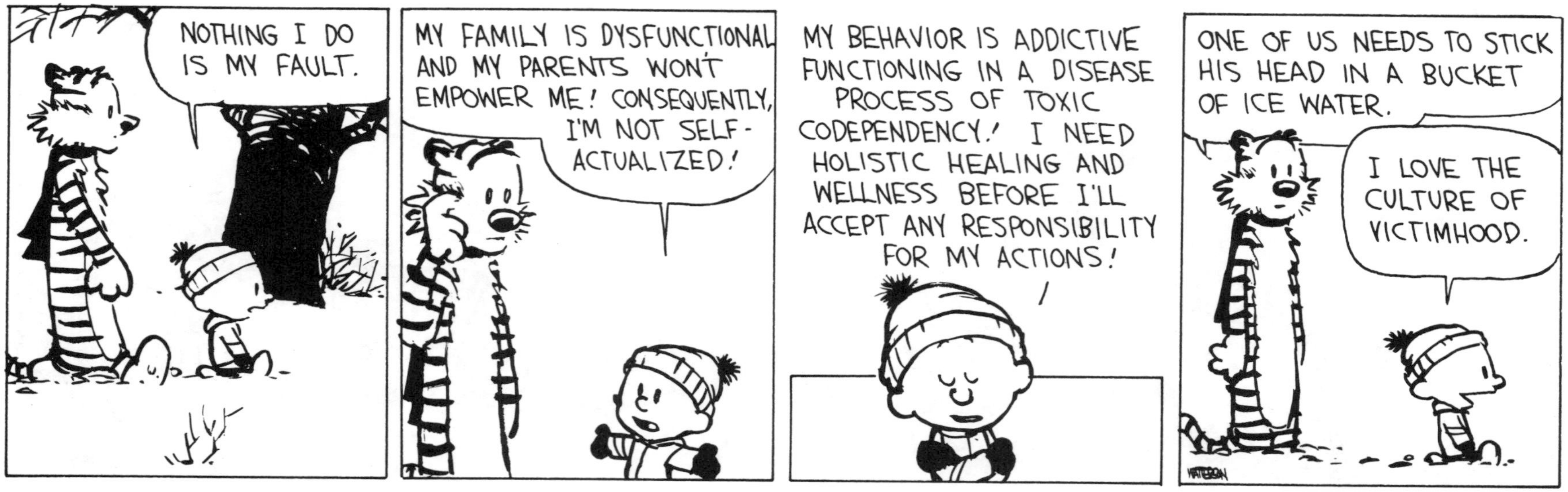
NOTHING I DO IS MY FAULT.
MY FAMILY IS DYSFUNCTIONAL AND MY PARENTS WON'T EMPOWER ME! CONSEQUENTLY, I'M NOT SELF-ACTUALIZED!
MY BEHAVIOR IS ADDICTIVE FUNCTIONING IN A DISEASE PROCESS OF TOXIC CODEPENDENCY! I NEED HOLISTIC HEALING AND WELLNESS BEFORE I'LL ACCEPT ANY RESPONSIBILITY FOR MY ACTIONS!
ONE OF US NEEDS TO STICK HIS HEAD IN A BUCKET OF ICE WATER.
I LOVE THE CULTURE OF VICTIMHOOD.

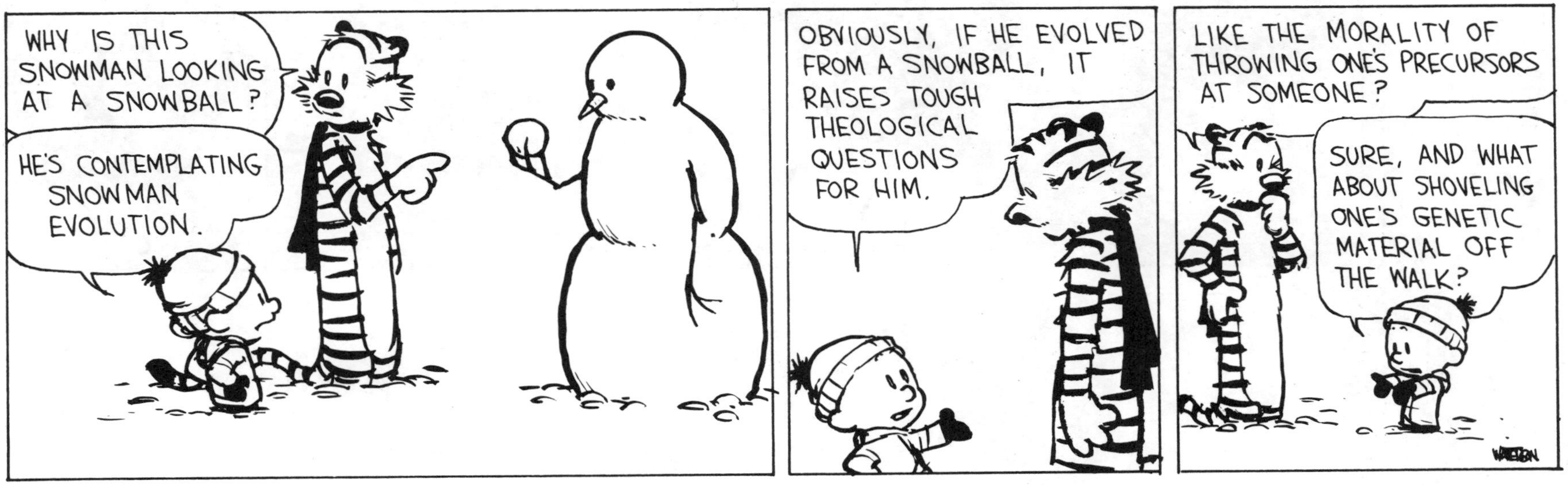
WHY IS THIS SNOWMAN LOOKING AT A SNOWBALL?
HE'S CONTEMPLATING SNOWMAN EVOLUTION.
OBVIOUSLY, IF HE EVOLVED FROM A SNOWBALL, IT RAISES TOUGH THEOLOGICAL QUESTIONS FOR HIM.
LIKE THE MORALITY OF THROWING ONE'S PRECURSORS AT SOMEONE?
SURE, AND WHAT ABOUT SHOVELING ONE'S GENETIC MATERIAL OFF THE WALK?

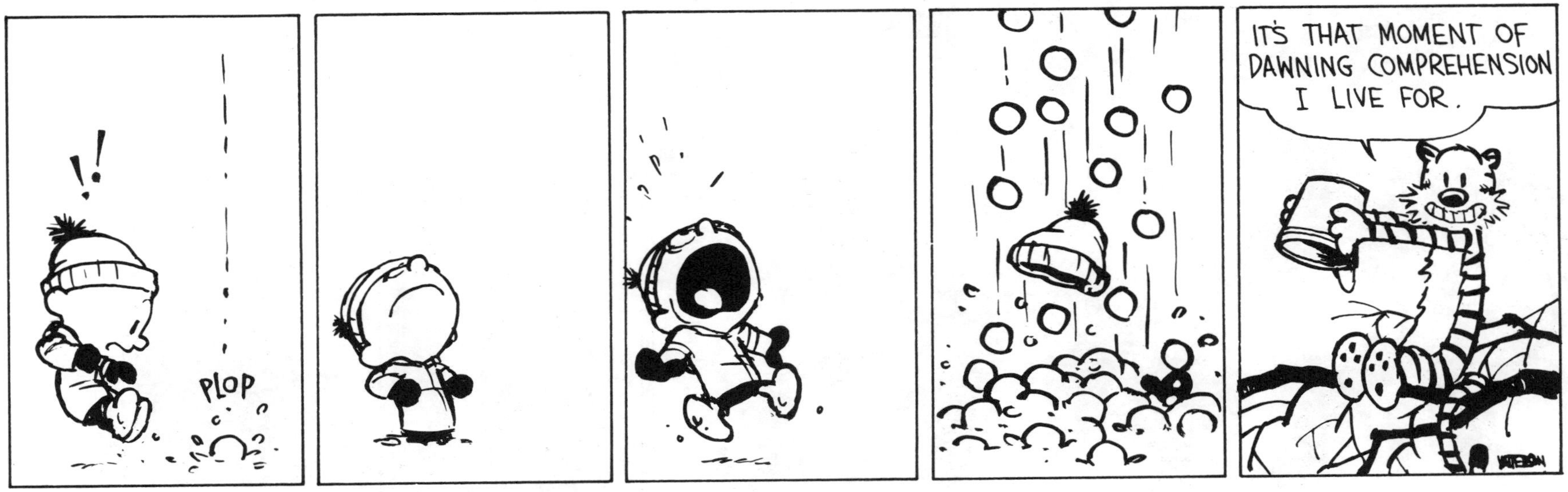
!!
PLOP
IT'S THAT MOMENT OF DAWNING COMPREHENSION I LIVE FOR.

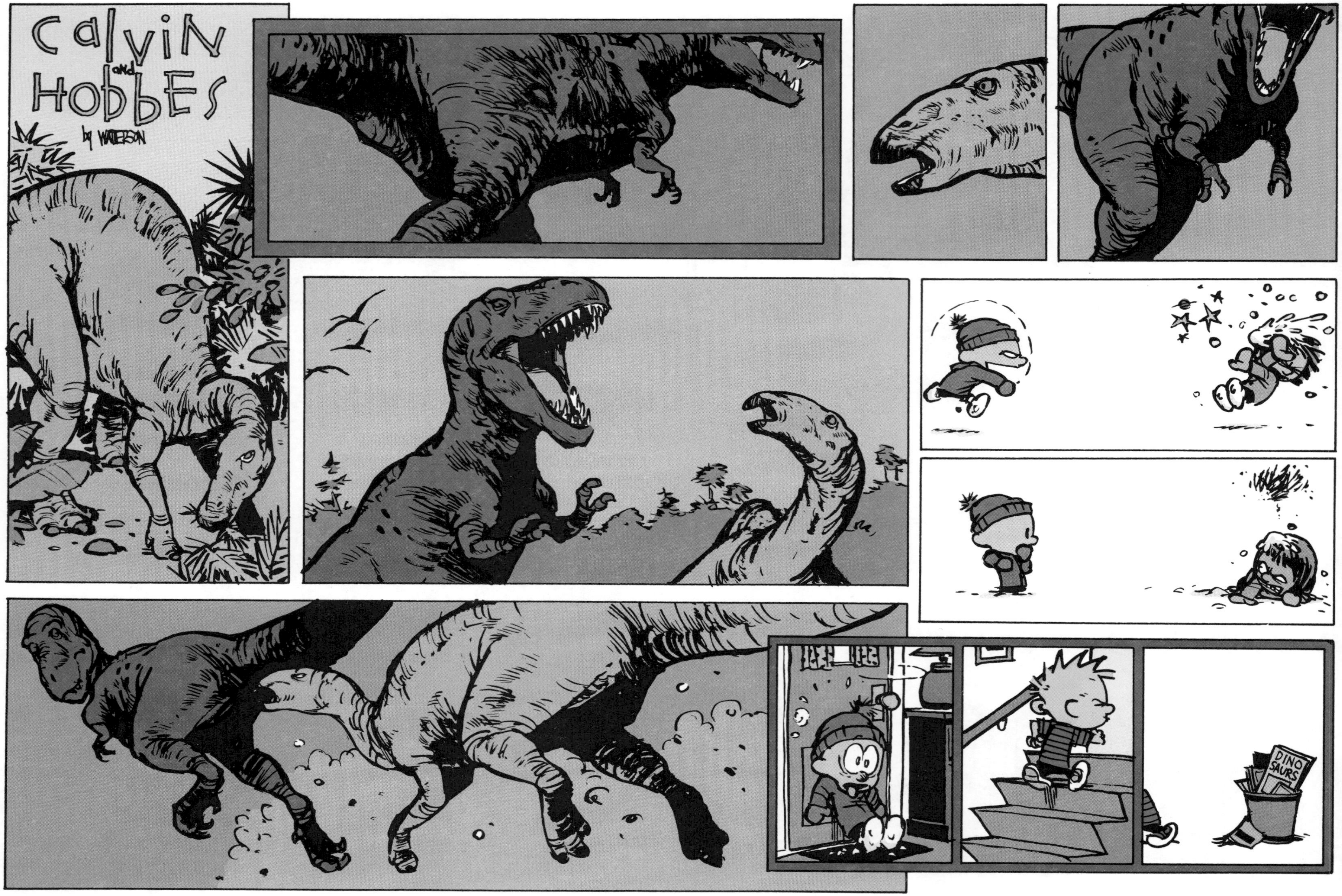
Calvin and HOBBES
by WATTERSON
DINO SAURS

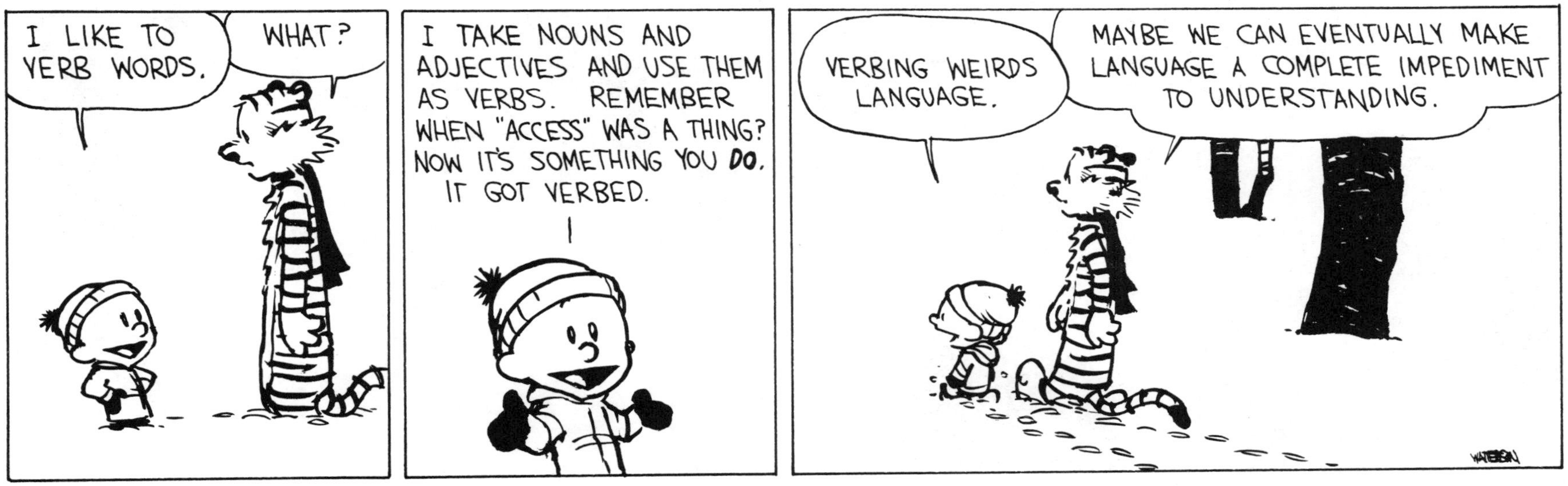
I LIKE TO VERB WORDS.
WHAT?
I TAKE NOUNS AND ADJECTIVES AND USE THEM AS VERBS. REMEMBER WHEN "ACCESS" WAS A THING? NOW IT'S SOMETHING YOU **DO**. IT GOT VERBED.
VERBING WEIRDS LANGUAGE.
MAYBE WE CAN EVENTUALLY MAKE LANGUAGE A COMPLETE IMPEDIMENT TO UNDERSTANDING.
WATTERSON

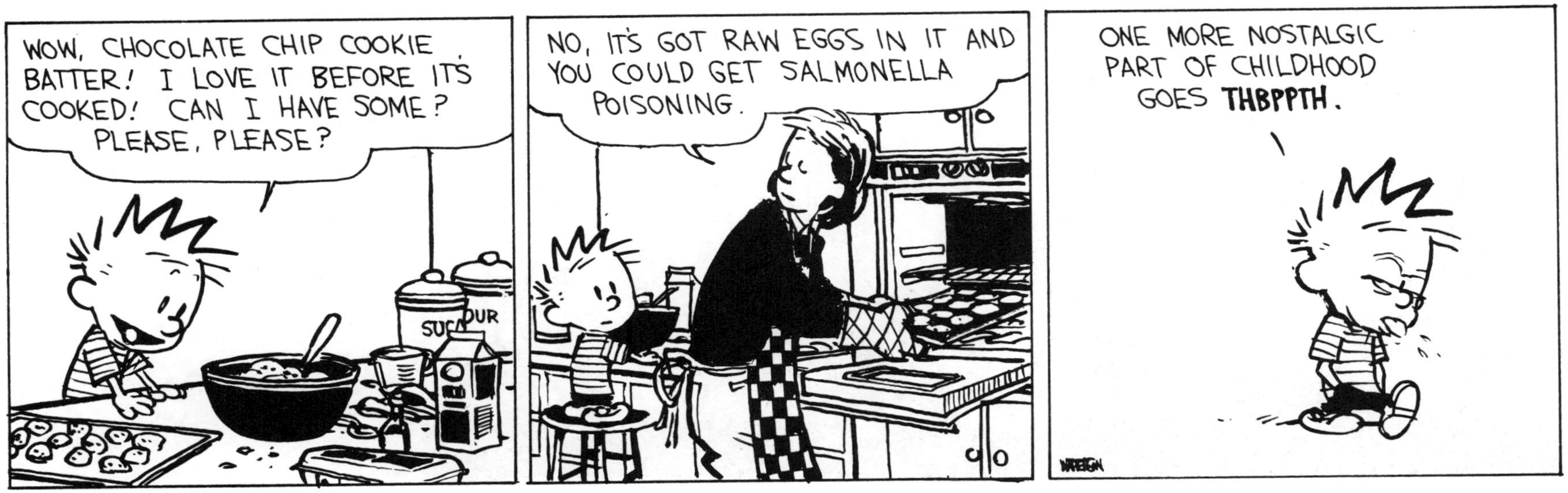
WOW, CHOCOLATE CHIP COOKIE BATTER! I LOVE IT BEFORE IT'S COOKED! CAN I HAVE SOME? PLEASE, PLEASE?
NO, IT'S GOT RAW EGGS IN IT AND YOU COULD GET SALMONELLA POISONING.
ONE MORE NOSTALGIC PART OF CHILDHOOD GOES **THBPPTH**.
WATTERSON

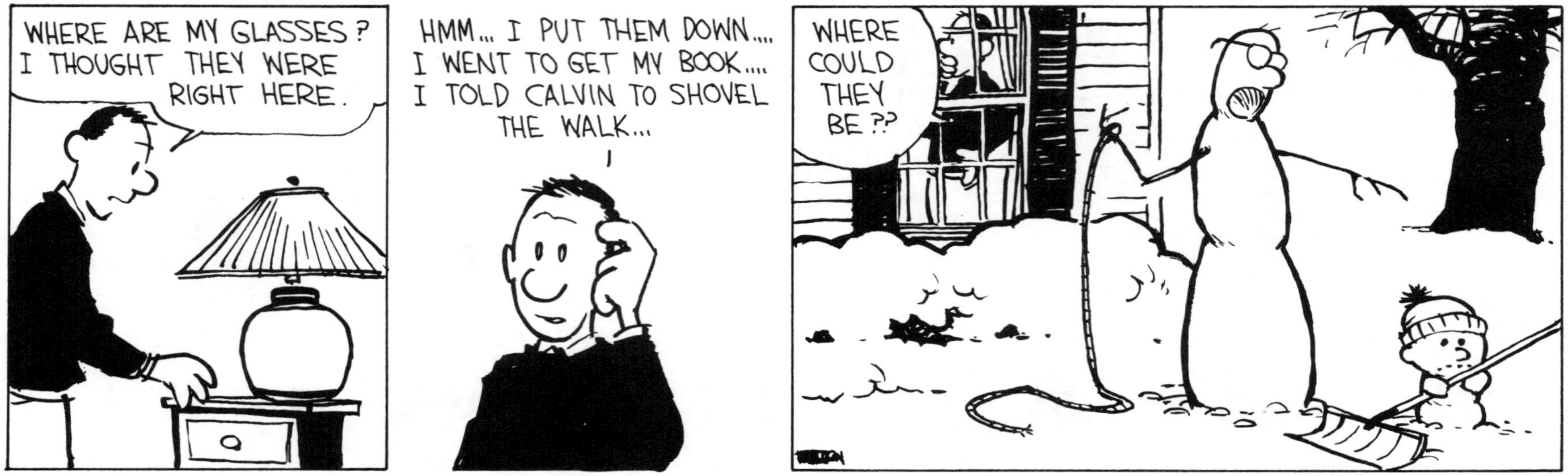
WHERE ARE MY GLASSES? I THOUGHT THEY WERE RIGHT HERE.
HMM... I PUT THEM DOWN.... I WENT TO GET MY BOOK.... I TOLD CALVIN TO SHOVEL THE WALK...
WHERE COULD THEY BE??

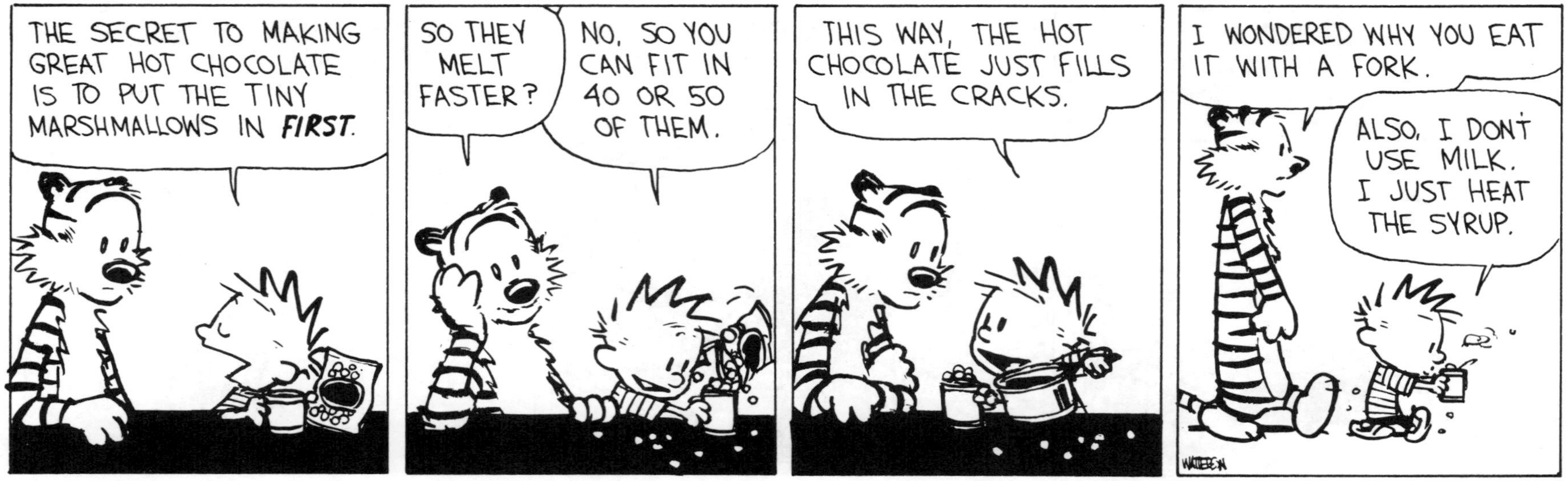
THE SECRET TO MAKING GREAT HOT CHOCOLATE IS TO PUT THE TINY MARSHMALLOWS IN FIRST.
SO THEY MELT FASTER?
NO, SO YOU CAN FIT IN 40 OR 50 OF THEM.
THIS WAY, THE HOT CHOCOLATE JUST FILLS IN THE CRACKS.
I WONDERED WHY YOU EAT IT WITH A FORK.
ALSO, I DON'T USE MILK. I JUST HEAT THE SYRUP.

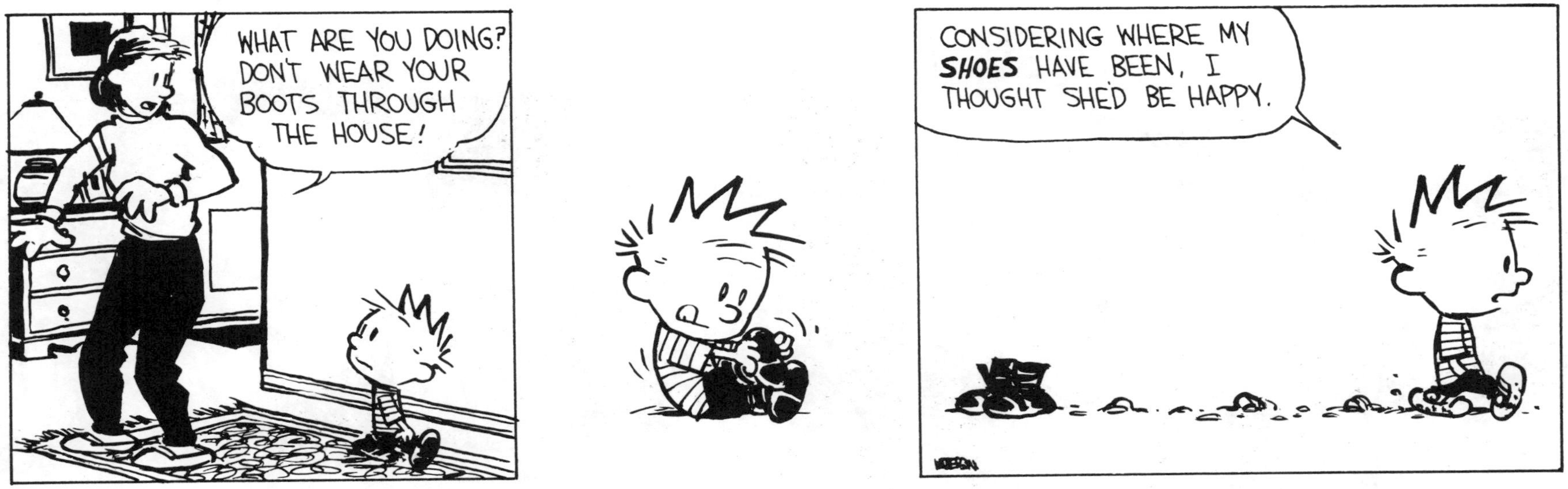
WHAT ARE YOU DOING? DON'T WEAR YOUR BOOTS THROUGH THE HOUSE!
CONSIDERING WHERE MY **SHOES** HAVE BEEN, I THOUGHT SHE'D BE HAPPY.

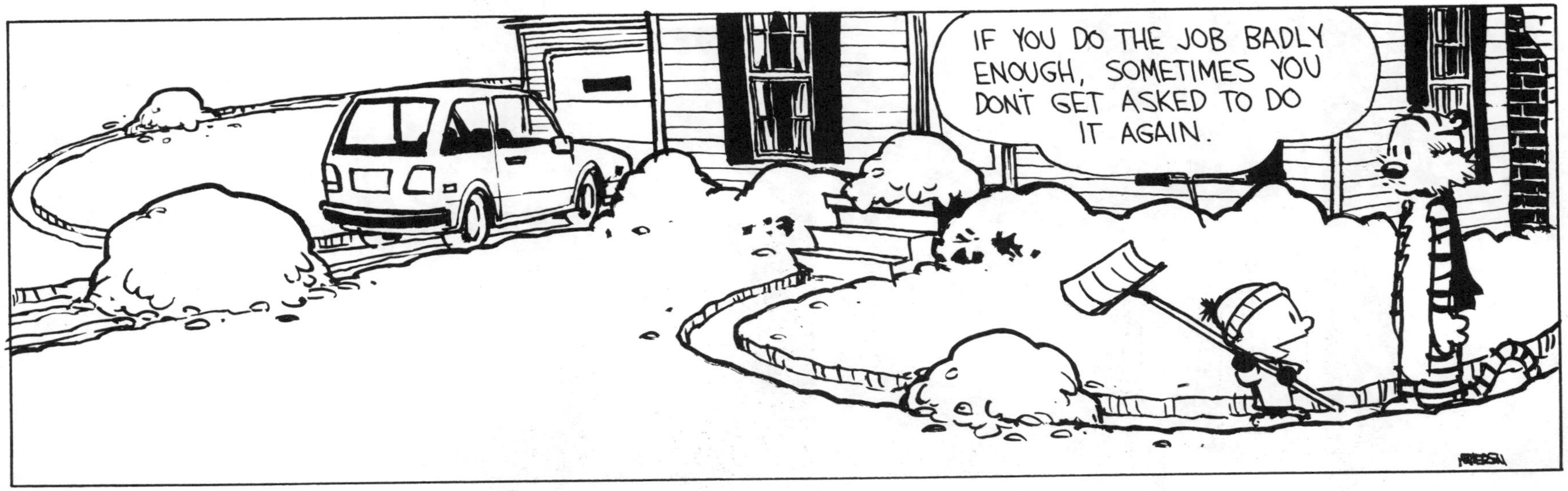
IF YOU DO THE JOB BADLY ENOUGH, SOMETIMES YOU DON'T GET ASKED TO DO IT AGAIN.

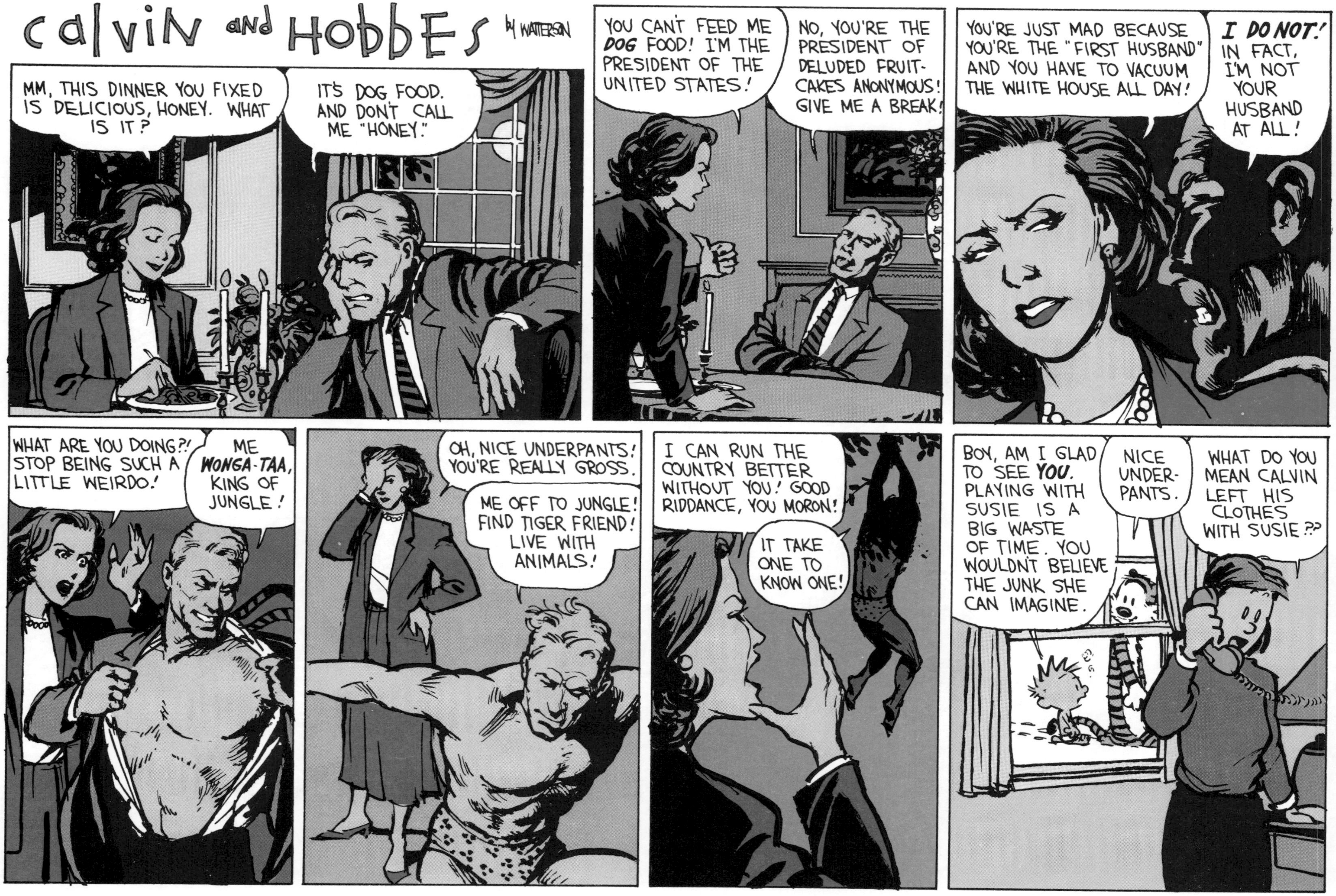

Calvin and Hobbes
by WATTERSON
MM, THIS DINNER YOU FIXED IS DELICIOUS, HONEY. WHAT IS IT?
IT'S DOG FOOD. AND DON'T CALL ME "HONEY."
YOU CAN'T FEED ME DOG FOOD! I'M THE PRESIDENT OF THE UNITED STATES!
NO, YOU'RE THE PRESIDENT OF DELUDED FRUIT-CAKES ANONYMOUS! GIVE ME A BREAK!
YOU'RE JUST MAD BECAUSE YOU'RE THE "FIRST HUSBAND" AND YOU HAVE TO VACUUM THE WHITE HOUSE ALL DAY!
I DO NOT! IN FACT, I'M NOT YOUR HUSBAND AT ALL!
WHAT ARE YOU DOING?! STOP BEING SUCH A LITTLE WEIRDO!
ME WONGA-TAA, KING OF JUNGLE!
OH, NICE UNDERPANTS! YOU'RE REALLY GROSS.
ME OFF TO JUNGLE! FIND TIGER FRIEND! LIVE WITH ANIMALS!
I CAN RUN THE COUNTRY BETTER WITHOUT YOU! GOOD RIDDANCE, YOU MORON!
IT TAKE ONE TO KNOW ONE!
BOY, AM I GLAD TO SEE YOU. PLAYING WITH SUSIE IS A BIG WASTE OF TIME. YOU WOULDN'T BELIEVE THE JUNK SHE CAN IMAGINE.
NICE UNDER-PANTS.
WHAT DO YOU MEAN CALVIN LEFT HIS CLOTHES WITH SUSIE??

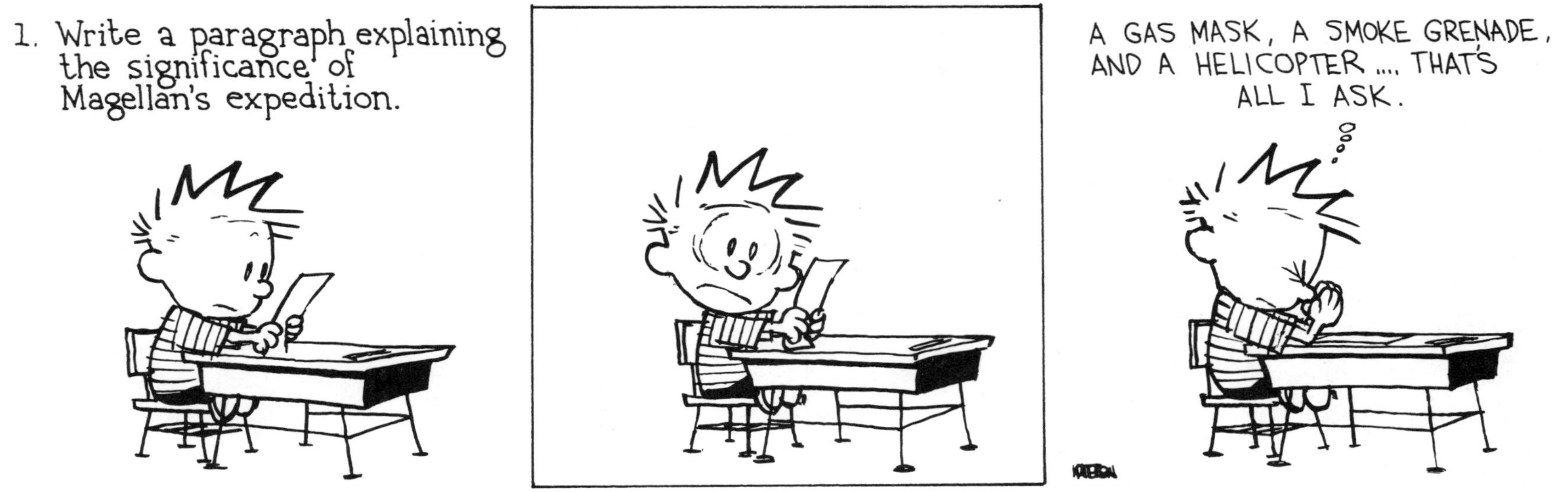
1. Write a paragraph explaining the significance of Magellan's expedition.
A GAS MASK, A SMOKE GRENADE, AND A HELICOPTER .... THAT'S ALL I ASK.
WATTERSON

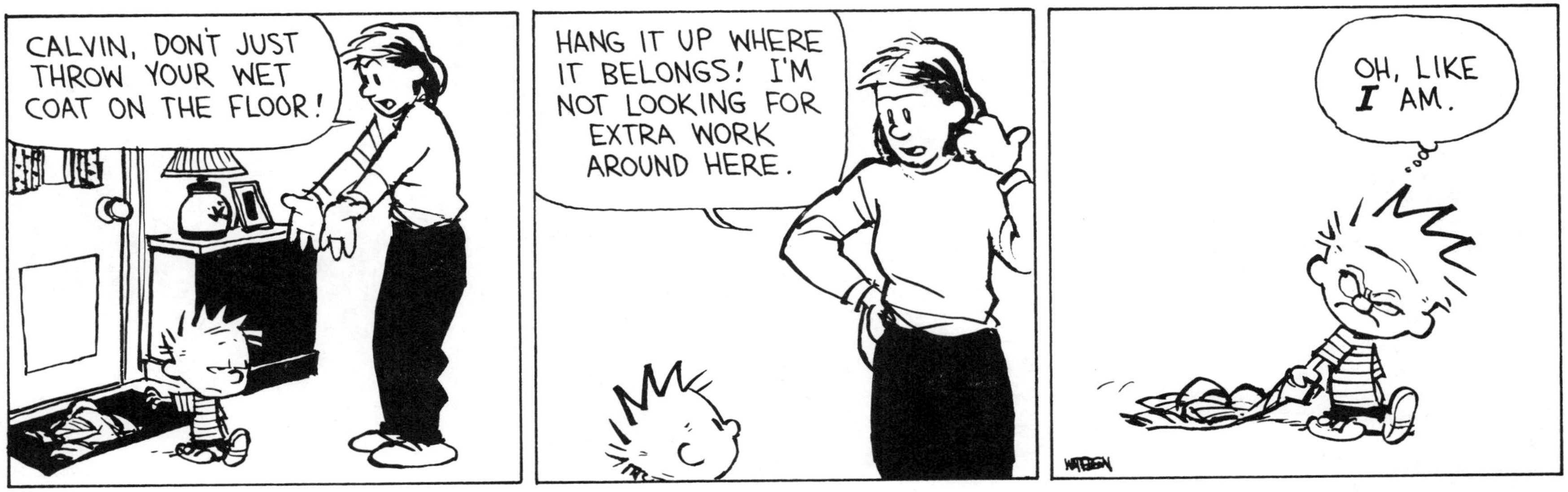
CALVIN, DON'T JUST THROW YOUR WET COAT ON THE FLOOR!
HANG IT UP WHERE IT BELONGS! I'M NOT LOOKING FOR EXTRA WORK AROUND HERE.
OH, LIKE *I* AM.
WATTERSON

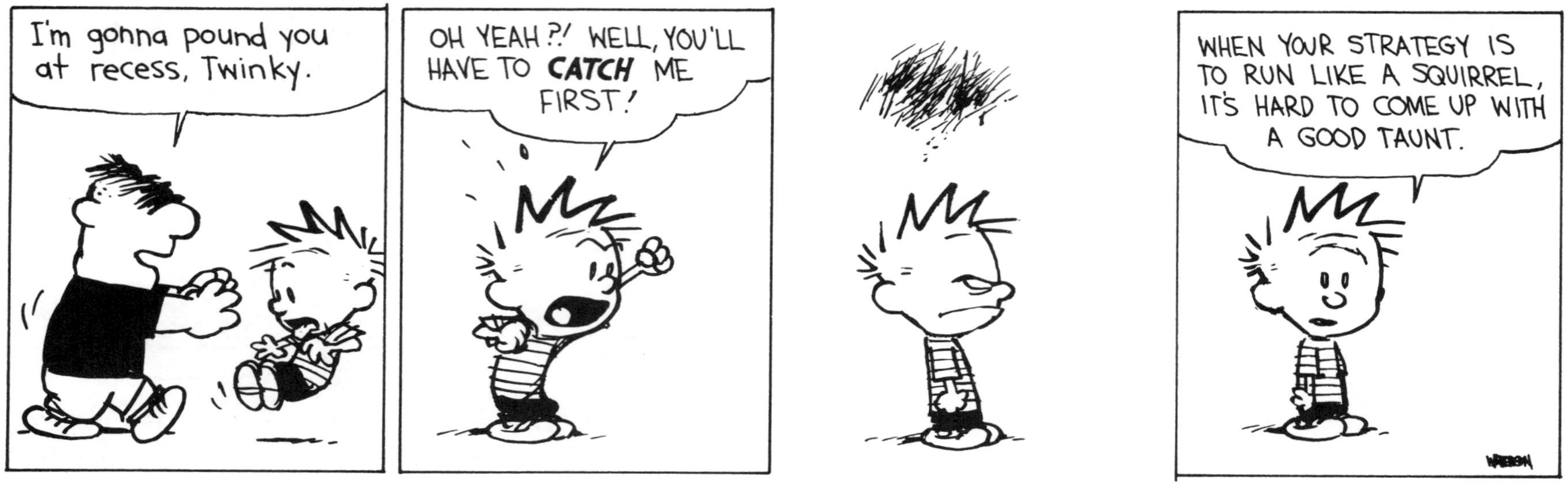
I'm gonna pound you at recess, Twinky.
OH YEAH ?! WELL, YOU'LL HAVE TO **CATCH** ME FIRST!
WHEN YOUR STRATEGY IS TO RUN LIKE A SQUIRREL, IT'S HARD TO COME UP WITH A GOOD TAUNT.

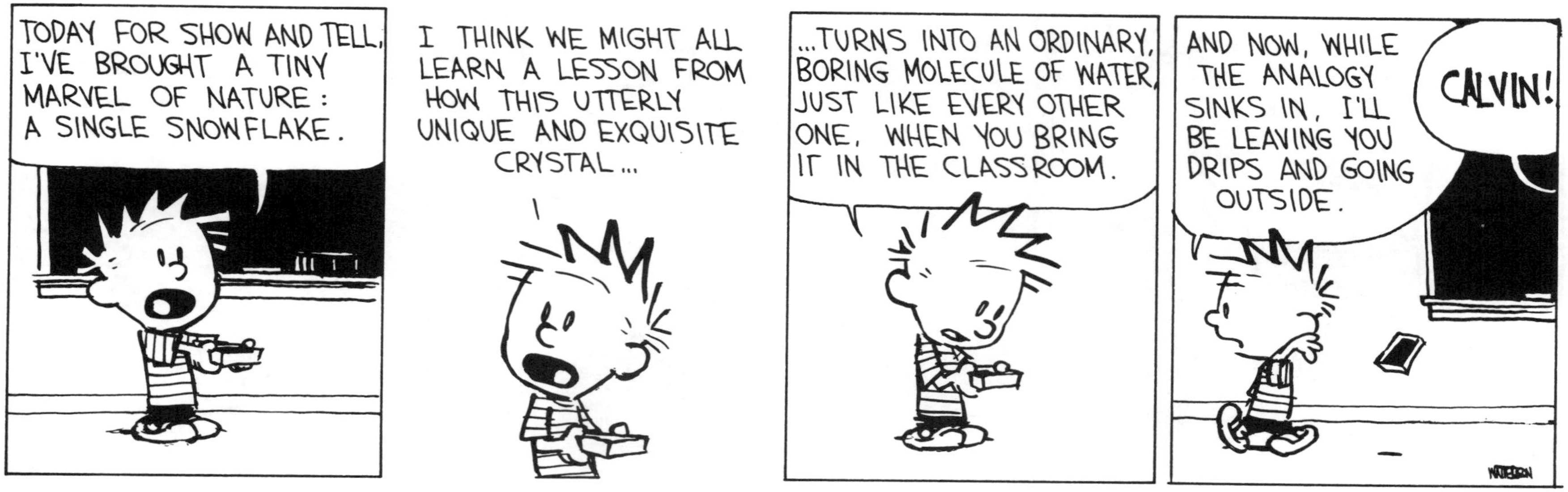
TODAY FOR SHOW AND TELL, I'VE BROUGHT A TINY MARVEL OF NATURE: A SINGLE SNOWFLAKE.
I THINK WE MIGHT ALL LEARN A LESSON FROM HOW THIS UTTERLY UNIQUE AND EXQUISITE CRYSTAL...
...TURNS INTO AN ORDINARY, BORING MOLECULE OF WATER, JUST LIKE EVERY OTHER ONE, WHEN YOU BRING IT IN THE CLASSROOM.
AND NOW, WHILE THE ANALOGY SINKS IN, I'LL BE LEAVING YOU DRIPS AND GOING OUTSIDE.
CALVIN!

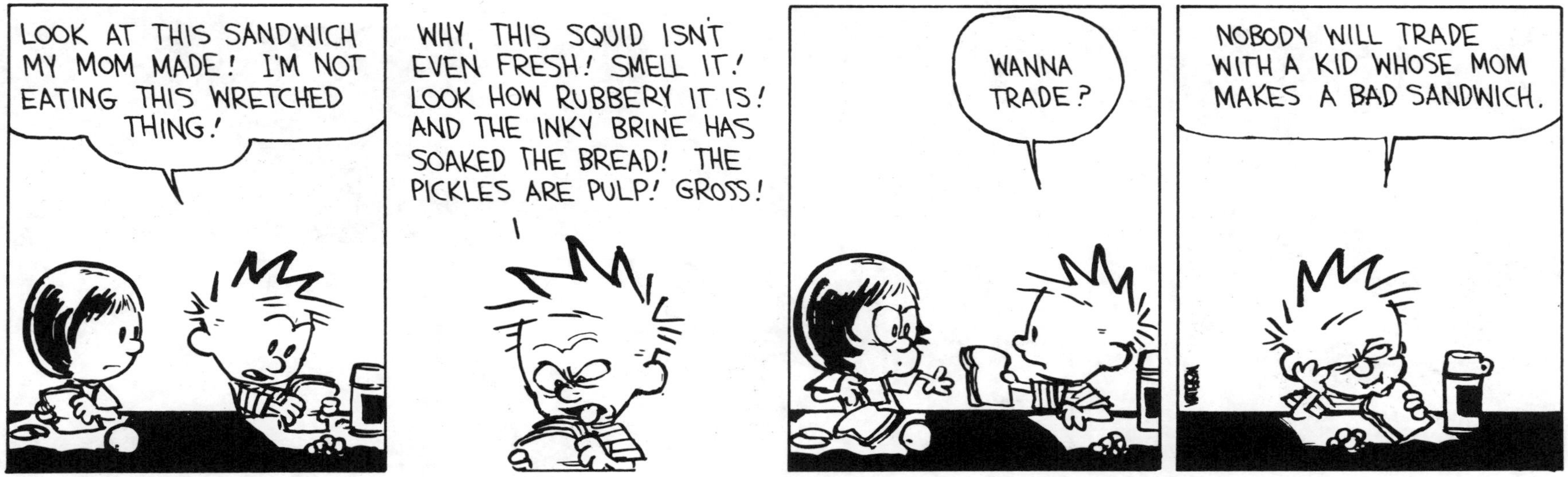
LOOK AT THIS SANDWICH MY MOM MADE! I'M NOT EATING THIS WRETCHED THING!
WHY, THIS SQUID ISN'T EVEN FRESH! SMELL IT! LOOK HOW RUBBERY IT IS! AND THE INKY BRINE HAS SOAKED THE BREAD! THE PICKLES ARE PULP! GROSS!
WANNA TRADE?
NOBODY WILL TRADE WITH A KID WHOSE MOM MAKES A BAD SANDWICH.

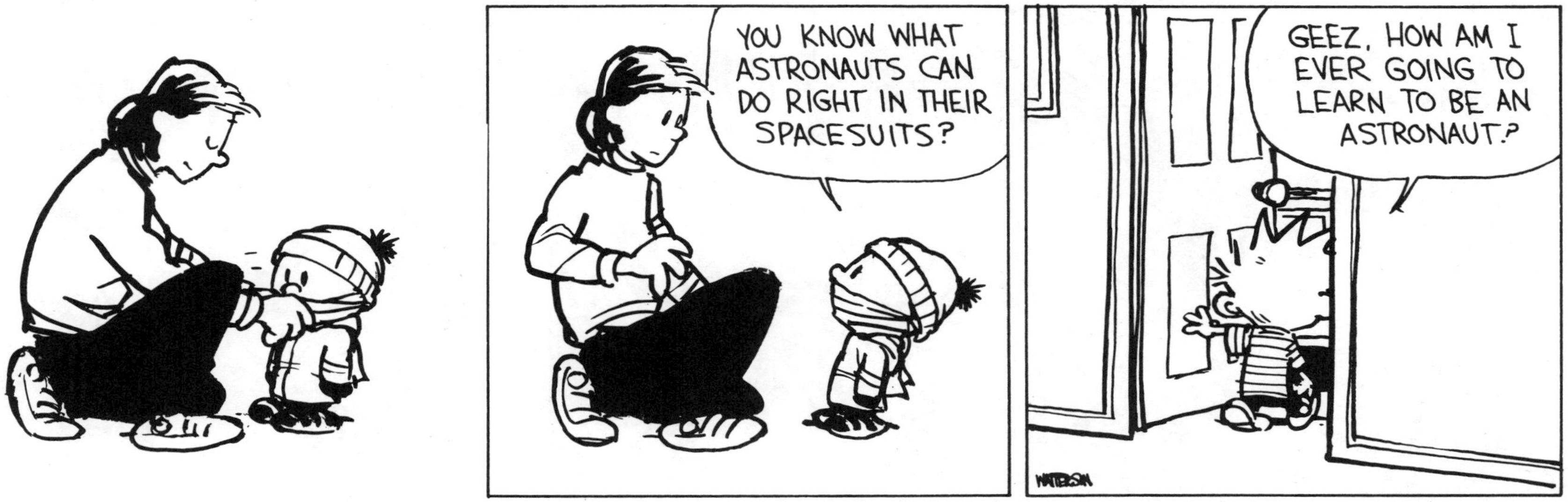
YOU KNOW WHAT ASTRONAUTS CAN DO RIGHT IN THEIR SPACESUITS?
GEEZ, HOW AM I EVER GOING TO LEARN TO BE AN ASTRONAUT?

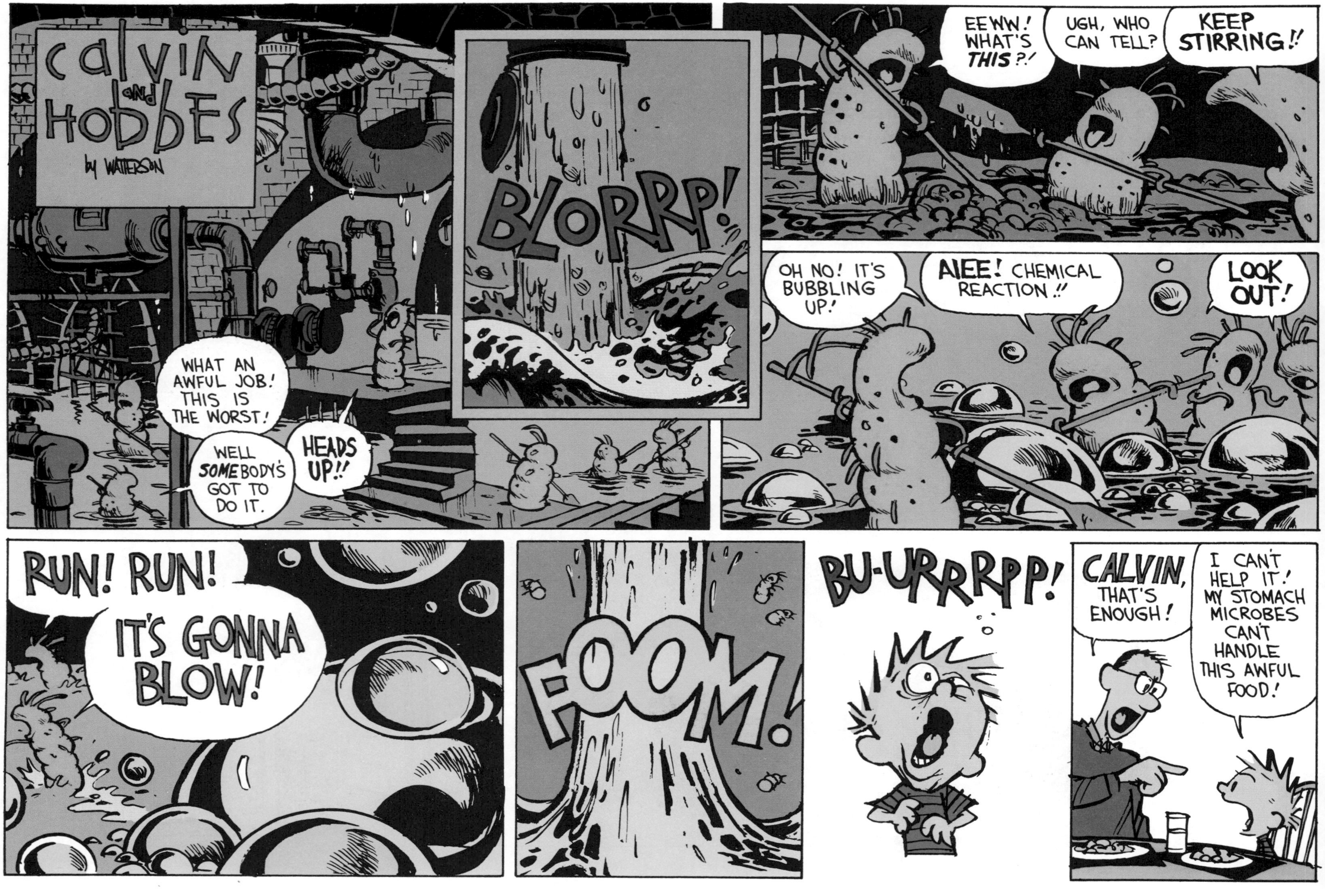
Calvin and Hobbes
by WATTERSON
WHAT AN AWFUL JOB! THIS IS THE WORST!
WELL SOMEBODY'S GOT TO DO IT.
HEADS UP!!
BLORRP!
EEWW! WHAT'S THIS?!
UGH, WHO CAN TELL?
KEEP STIRRING!!
OH NO! IT'S BUBBLING UP!
AIEE! CHEMICAL REACTION!!
LOOK OUT!
RUN! RUN!
IT'S GONNA BLOW!
FOOOM!
BU-URRRPP!
CALVIN, THAT'S ENOUGH!
I CAN'T HELP IT! MY STOMACH MICROBES CAN'T HANDLE THIS AWFUL FOOD!

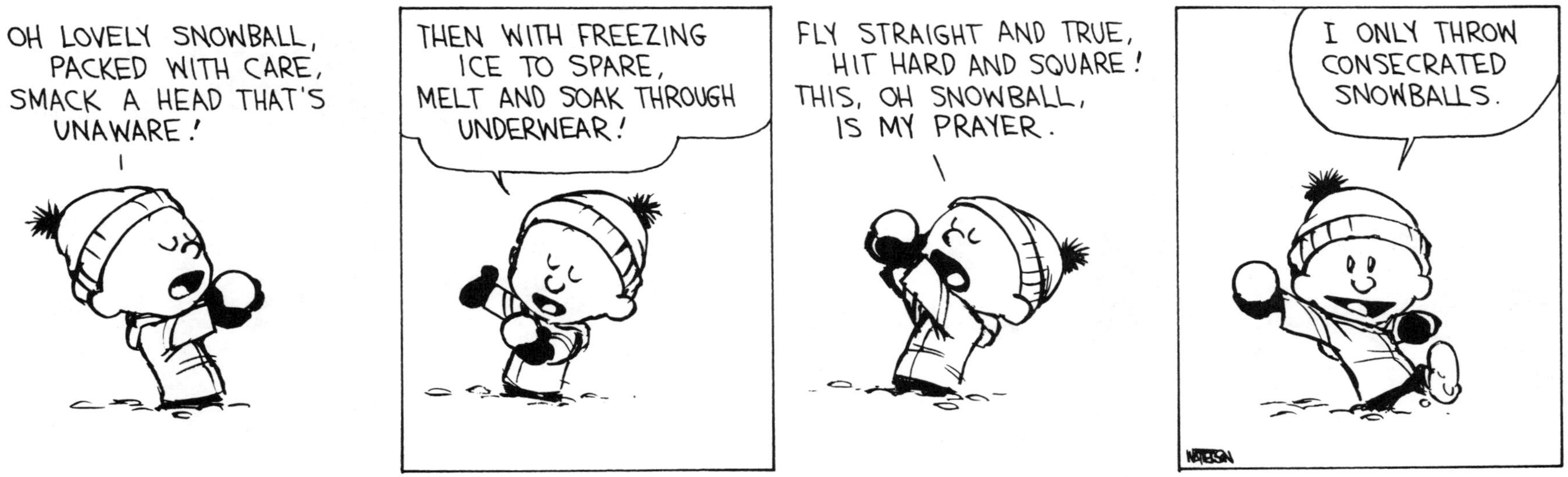
OH LOVELY SNOWBALL, PACKED WITH CARE, SMACK A HEAD THAT'S UNAWARE!
THEN WITH FREEZING ICE TO SPARE, MELT AND SOAK THROUGH UNDERWEAR!
FLY STRAIGHT AND TRUE, HIT HARD AND SQUARE! THIS, OH SNOWBALL, IS MY PRAYER.
I ONLY THROW CONSECRATED SNOWBALLS.

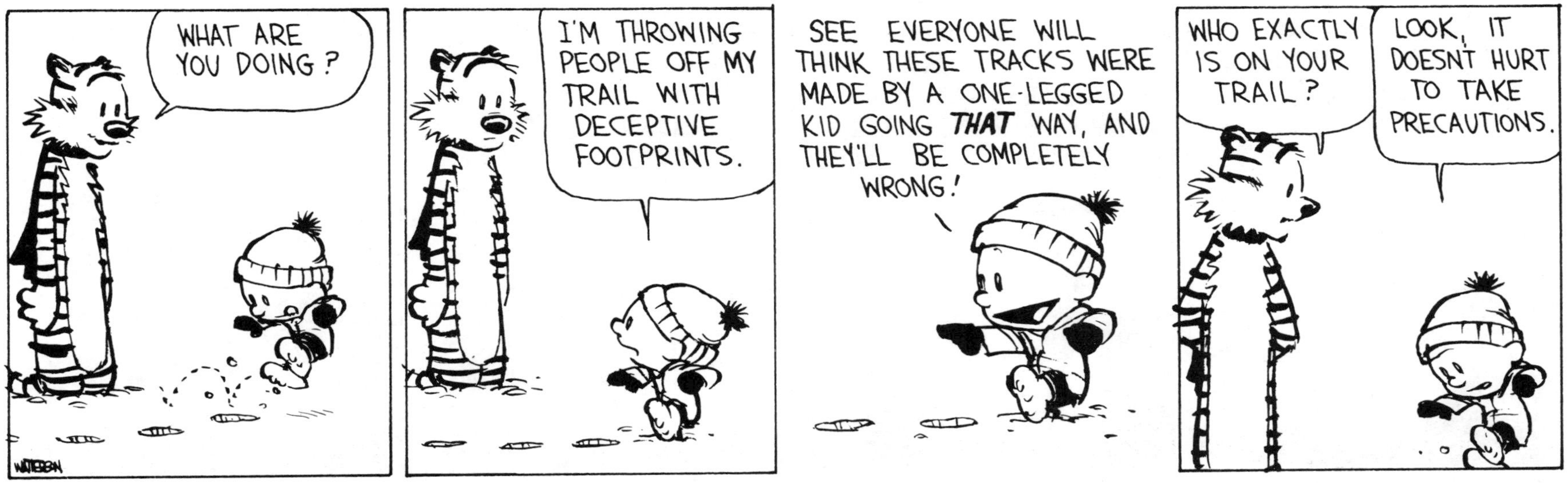
WHAT ARE YOU DOING?
I'M THROWING PEOPLE OFF MY TRAIL WITH DECEPTIVE FOOTPRINTS.
SEE EVERYONE WILL THINK THESE TRACKS WERE MADE BY A ONE-LEGGED KID GOING THAT WAY, AND THEY'LL BE COMPLETELY WRONG!
WHO EXACTLY IS ON YOUR TRAIL?
LOOK, IT DOESN'T HURT TO TAKE PRECAUTIONS.

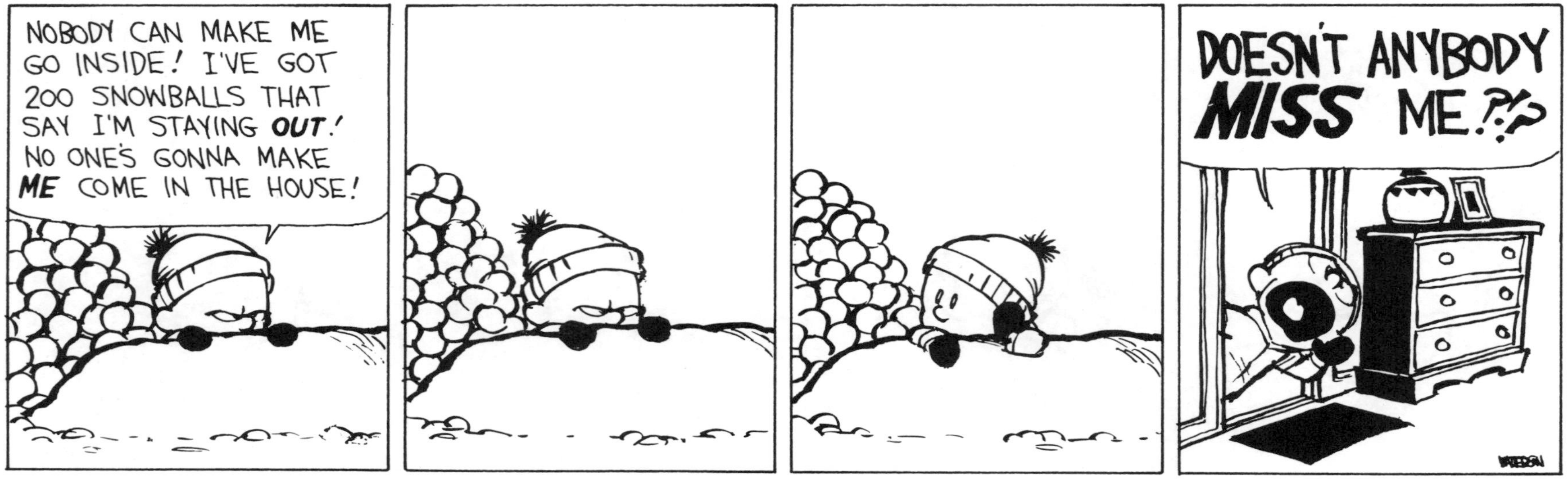
NOBODY CAN MAKE ME GO INSIDE! I'VE GOT 200 SNOWBALLS THAT SAY I'M STAYING **OUT**! NO ONE'S GONNA MAKE **ME** COME IN THE HOUSE!
DOESN'T ANYBODY **MISS** ME?!?
WATTERSON

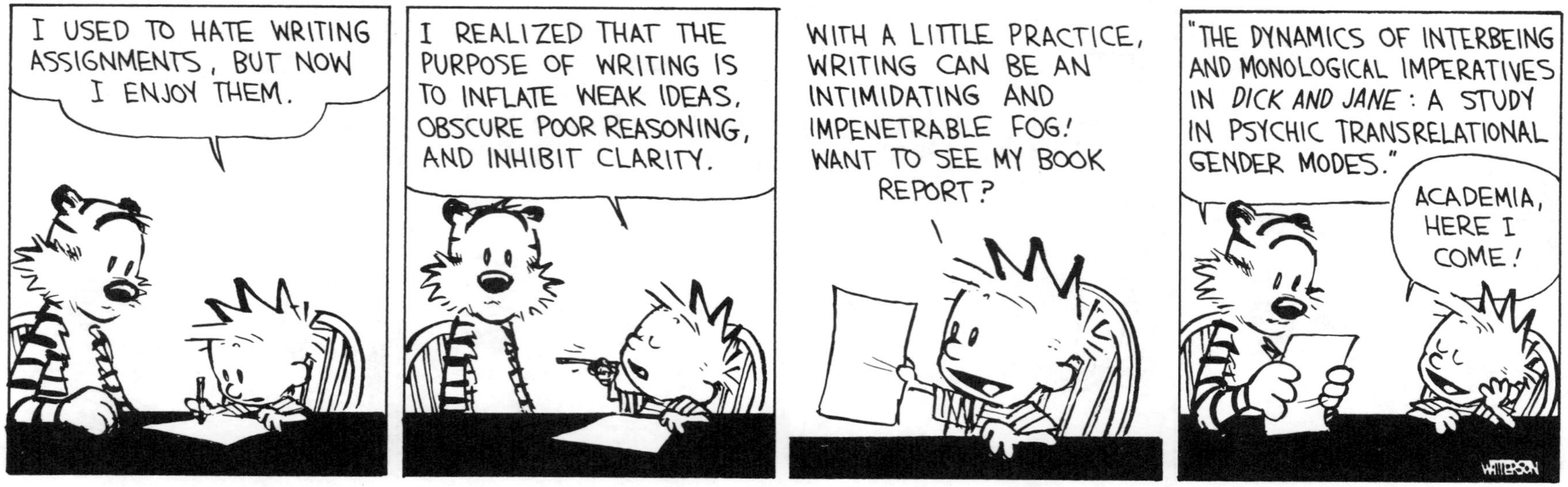
I USED TO HATE WRITING ASSIGNMENTS, BUT NOW I ENJOY THEM.
I REALIZED THAT THE PURPOSE OF WRITING IS TO INFLATE WEAK IDEAS, OBSCURE POOR REASONING, AND INHIBIT CLARITY.
WITH A LITTLE PRACTICE, WRITING CAN BE AN INTIMIDATING AND IMPENETRABLE FOG! WANT TO SEE MY BOOK REPORT?
"THE DYNAMICS OF INTERBEING AND MONOLOGICAL IMPERATIVES IN *DICK AND JANE*: A STUDY IN PSYCHIC TRANSRELATIONAL GENDER MODES."
ACADEMIA, HERE I COME!
WATTERSON

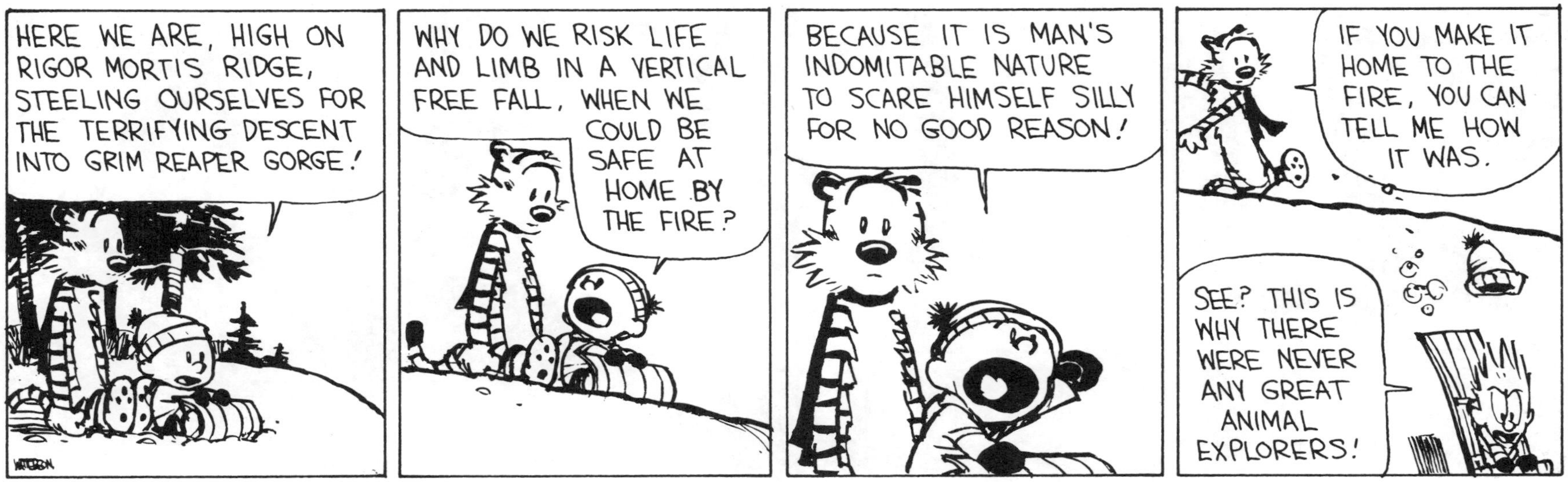
HERE WE ARE, HIGH ON RIGOR MORTIS RIDGE, STEELING OURSELVES FOR THE TERRIFYING DESCENT INTO GRIM REAPER GORGE!
WHY DO WE RISK LIFE AND LIMB IN A VERTICAL FREE FALL, WHEN WE COULD BE SAFE AT HOME BY THE FIRE?
BECAUSE IT IS MAN'S INDOMITABLE NATURE TO SCARE HIMSELF SILLY FOR NO GOOD REASON!
IF YOU MAKE IT HOME TO THE FIRE, YOU CAN TELL ME HOW IT WAS.
SEE? THIS IS WHY THERE WERE NEVER ANY GREAT ANIMAL EXPLORERS!

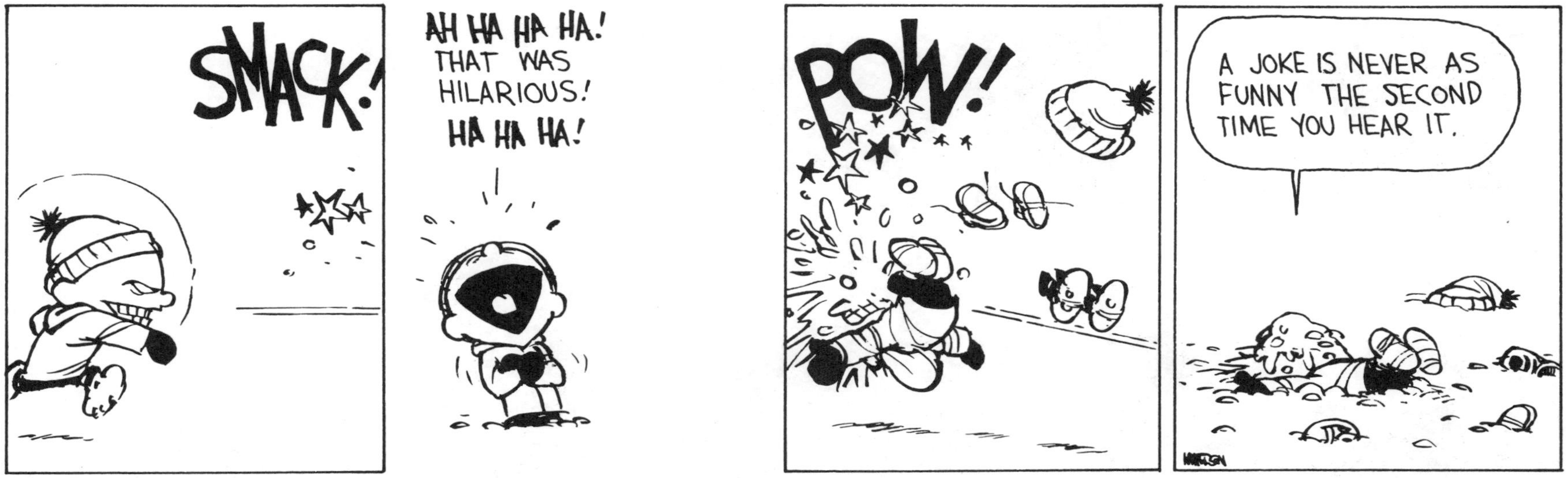
SMACK!
AH HA HA HA! THAT WAS HILARIOUS! HA HA HA!
POW!
A JOKE IS NEVER AS FUNNY THE SECOND TIME YOU HEAR IT.

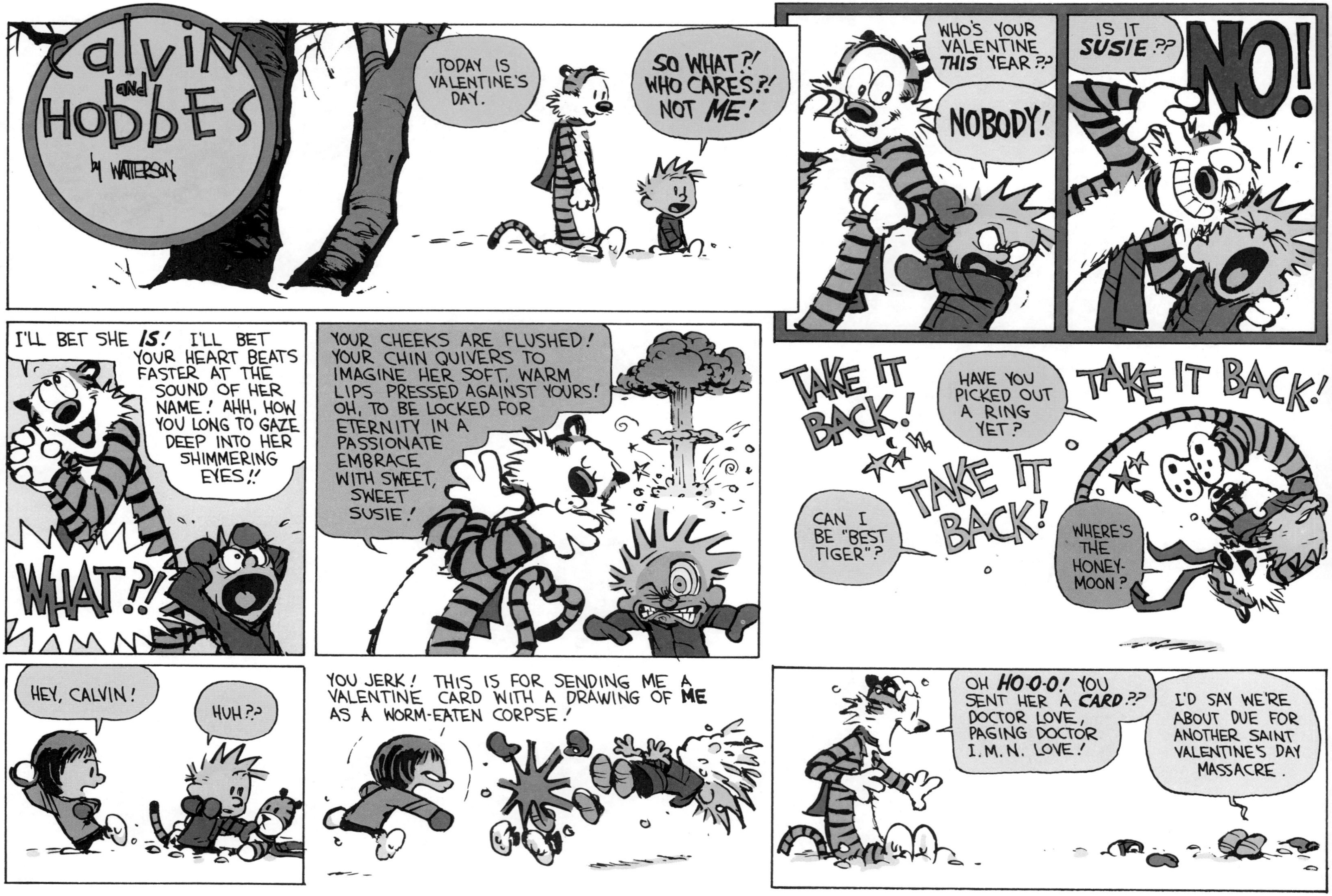
Calvin and Hobbes
by WATTERSON
TODAY IS VALENTINE'S DAY.
SO WHAT?! WHO CARES?! NOT ME!
WHO'S YOUR VALENTINE THIS YEAR??
NOBODY!
IS IT SUSIE??
NO!
I'LL BET SHE IS! I'LL BET YOUR HEART BEATS FASTER AT THE SOUND OF HER NAME! AHH, HOW YOU LONG TO GAZE DEEP INTO HER SHIMMERING EYES!!
WHAT?!
YOUR CHEEKS ARE FLUSHED! YOUR CHIN QUIVERS TO IMAGINE HER SOFT, WARM LIPS PRESSED AGAINST YOURS! OH, TO BE LOCKED FOR ETERNITY IN A PASSIONATE EMBRACE WITH SWEET, SWEET SUSIE!
TAKE IT BACK!
HAVE YOU PICKED OUT A RING YET?
TAKE IT BACK!
TAKE IT BACK!
CAN I BE "BEST TIGER"?
WHERE'S THE HONEY-MOON?
HEY, CALVIN!
HUH??
YOU JERK! THIS IS FOR SENDING ME A VALENTINE CARD WITH A DRAWING OF ME AS A WORM-EATEN CORPSE!
OH HO-O-O! YOU SENT HER A CARD?? DOCTOR LOVE, PAGING DOCTOR I.M.N. LOVE!
I'D SAY WE'RE ABOUT DUE FOR ANOTHER SAINT VALENTINE'S DAY MASSACRE.

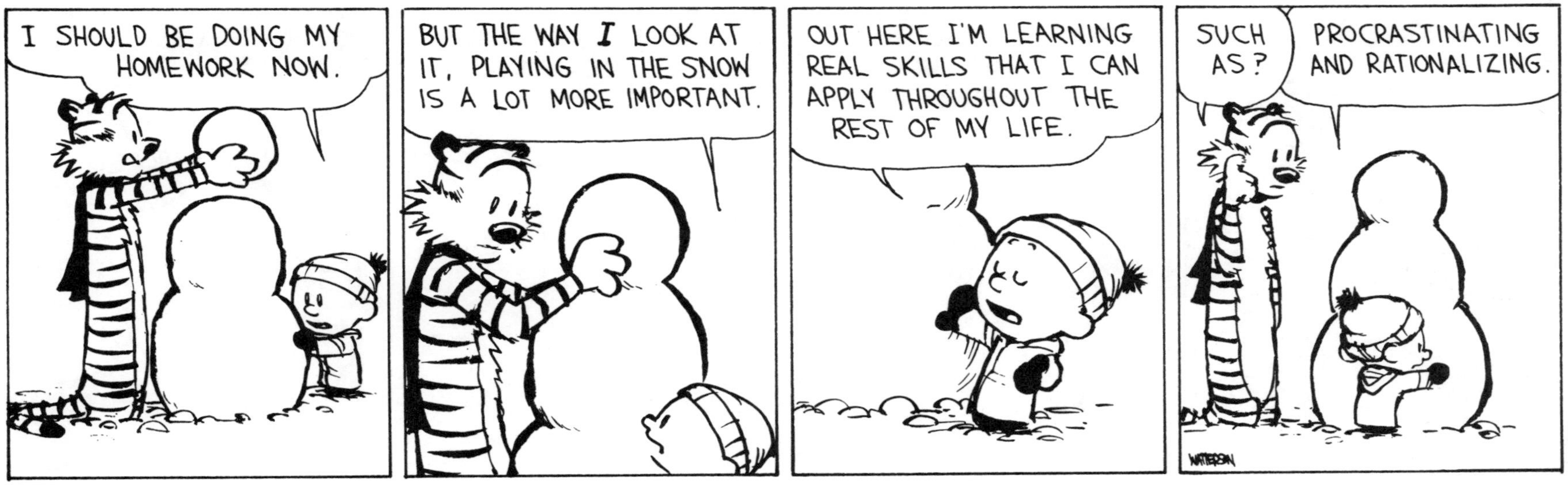
I SHOULD BE DOING MY HOMEWORK NOW.
BUT THE WAY *I* LOOK AT IT, PLAYING IN THE SNOW IS A LOT MORE IMPORTANT.
OUT HERE I'M LEARNING REAL SKILLS THAT I CAN APPLY THROUGHOUT THE REST OF MY LIFE.
SUCH AS?
PROCRASTINATING AND RATIONALIZING.

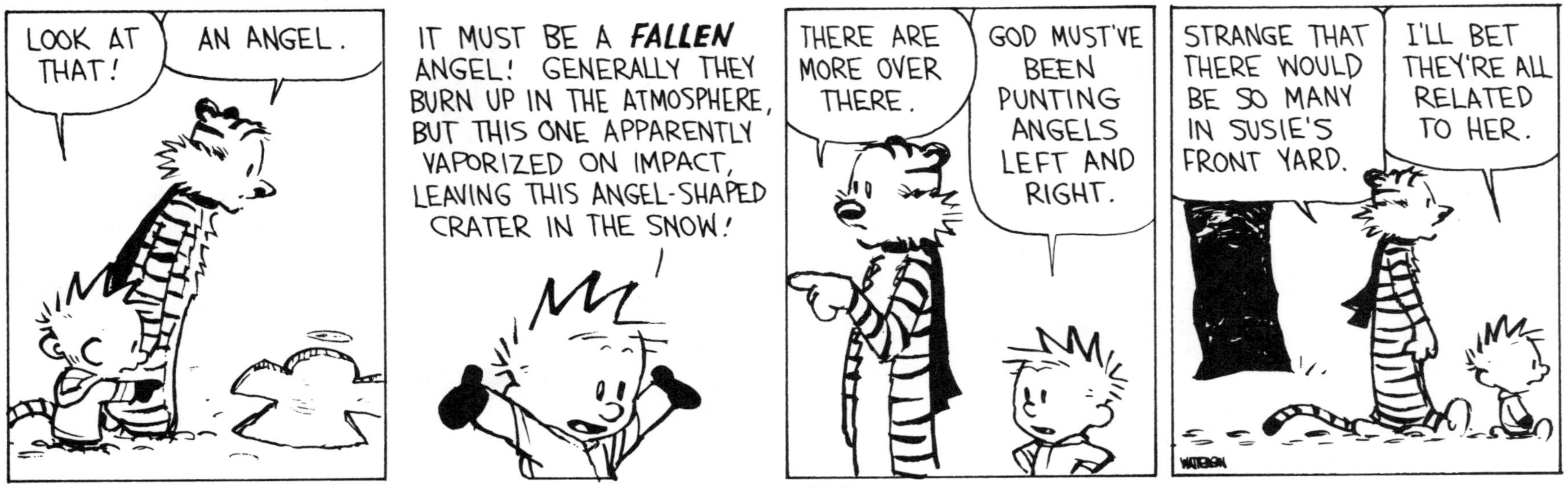
LOOK AT THAT!
AN ANGEL.
IT MUST BE A ***FALLEN*** ANGEL! GENERALLY THEY BURN UP IN THE ATMOSPHERE, BUT THIS ONE APPARENTLY VAPORIZED ON IMPACT, LEAVING THIS ANGEL-SHAPED CRATER IN THE SNOW!
THERE ARE MORE OVER THERE.
GOD MUST'VE BEEN PUNTING ANGELS LEFT AND RIGHT.
STRANGE THAT THERE WOULD BE SO MANY IN SUSIE'S FRONT YARD.
I'LL BET THEY'RE ALL RELATED TO HER.

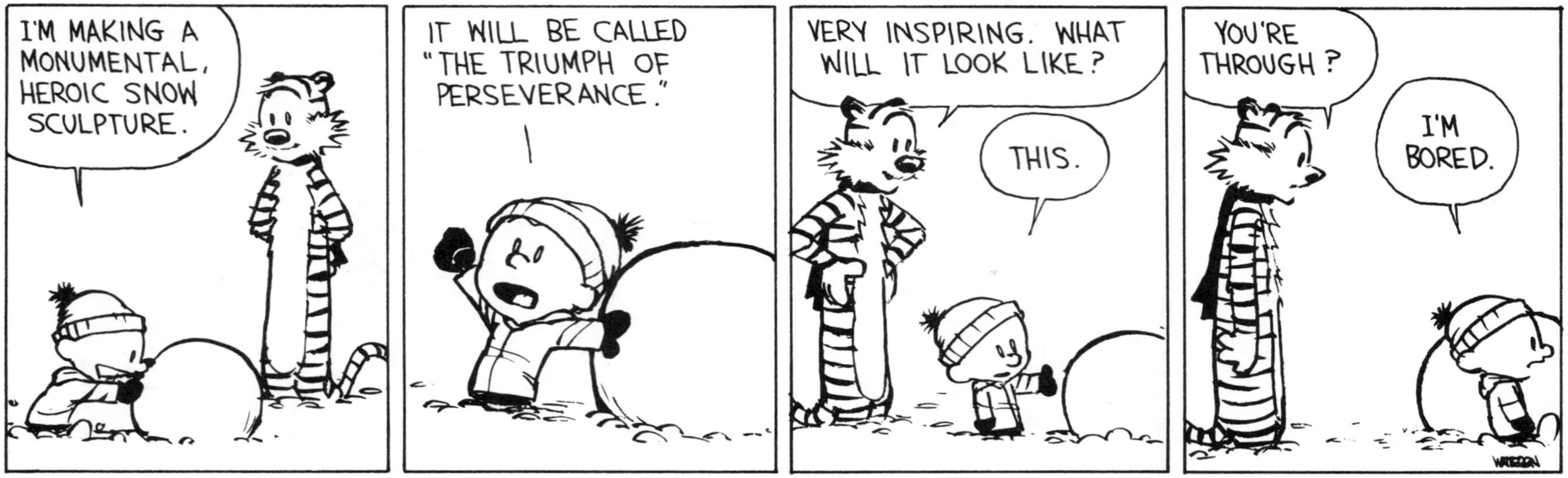
I'M MAKING A MONUMENTAL, HEROIC SNOW SCULPTURE.
IT WILL BE CALLED "THE TRIUMPH OF PERSEVERANCE."
VERY INSPIRING. WHAT WILL IT LOOK LIKE?
THIS.
YOU'RE THROUGH?
I'M BORED.

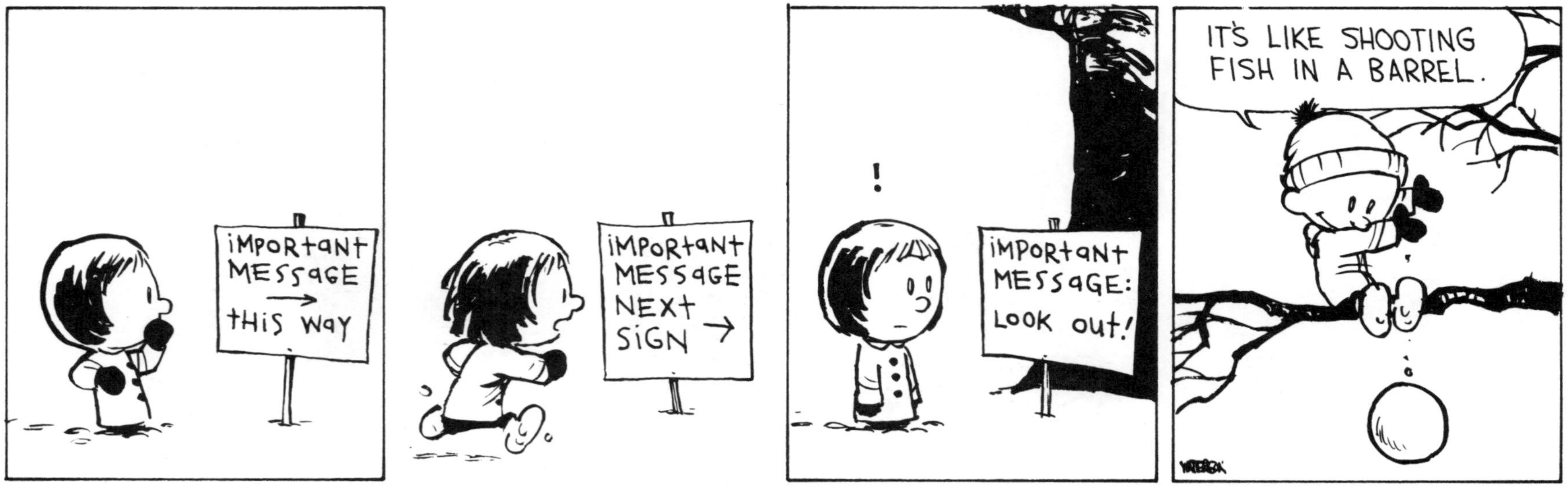
iMPORtaNt MESSaGE → tHiS Way
iMPORtaNt MESSaGE NExt SiGN →
!
iMPORtaNt MESSaGE: LOOk out!
IT'S LIKE SHOOTING FISH IN A BARREL.

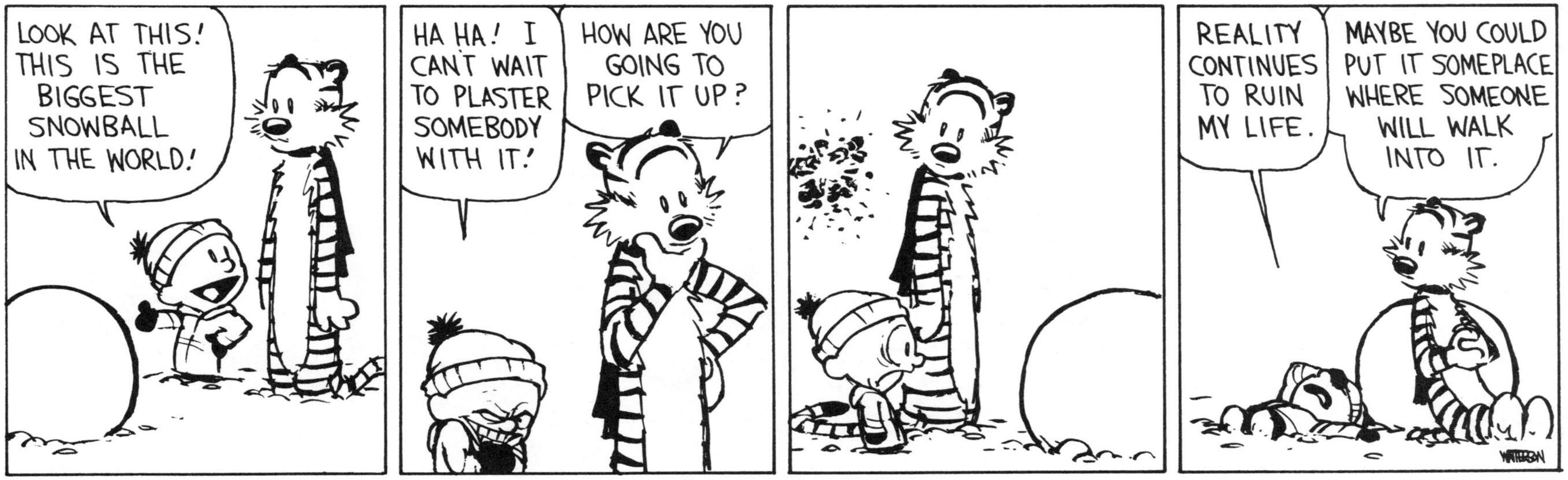
LOOK AT THIS! THIS IS THE BIGGEST SNOWBALL IN THE WORLD!
HA HA! I CAN'T WAIT TO PLASTER SOMEBODY WITH IT!
HOW ARE YOU GOING TO PICK IT UP?
REALITY CONTINUES TO RUIN MY LIFE.
MAYBE YOU COULD PUT IT SOMEPLACE WHERE SOMEONE WILL WALK INTO IT.

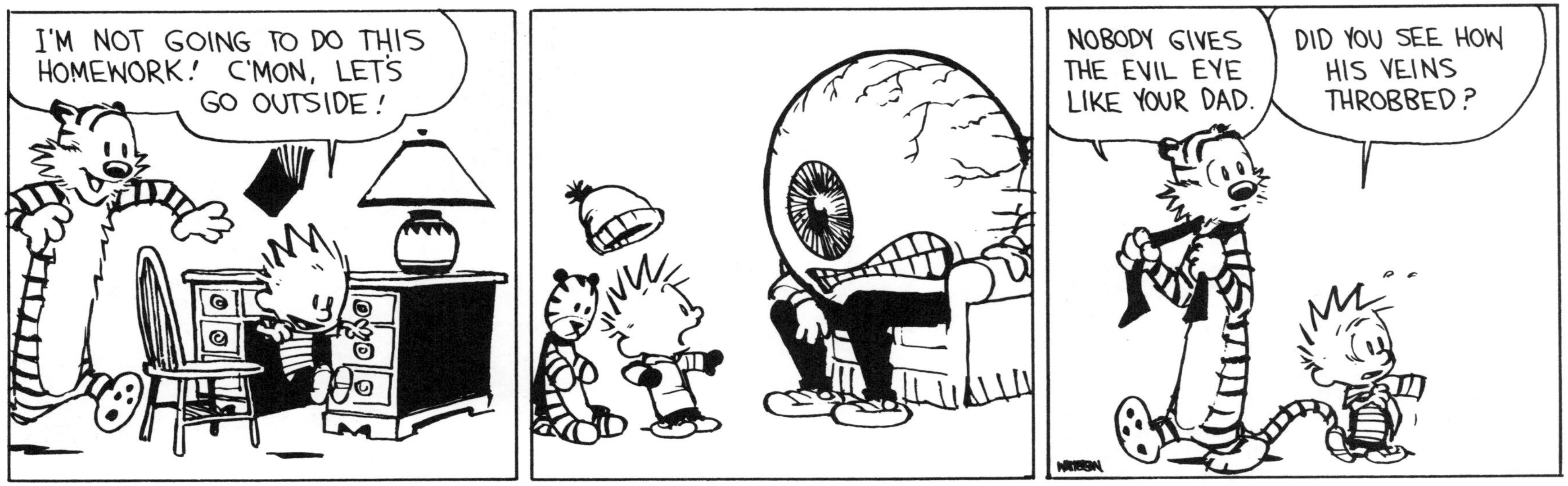
I'M NOT GOING TO DO THIS HOMEWORK! C'MON, LET'S GO OUTSIDE!
NOBODY GIVES THE EVIL EYE LIKE YOUR DAD.
DID YOU SEE HOW HIS VEINS THROBBED?

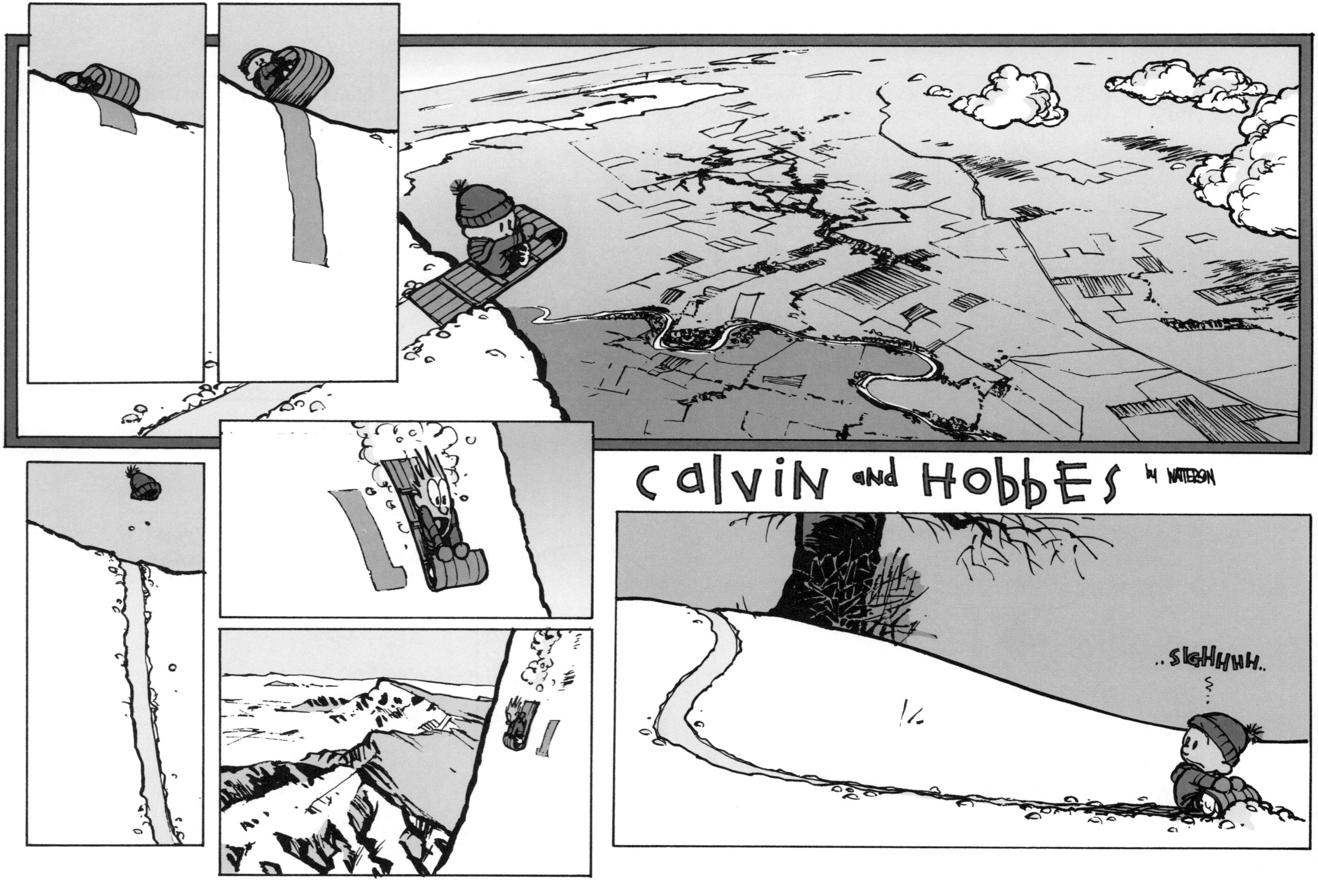
Calvin and HOBBES by WATERSON
..SIGHHHH..

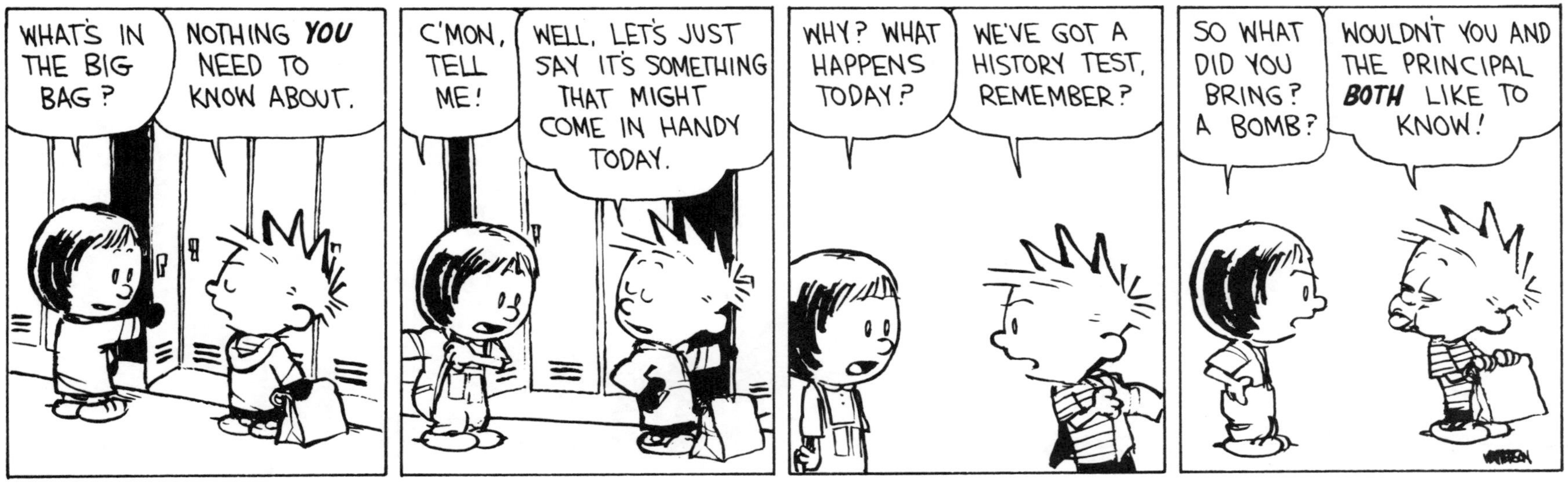
WHAT'S IN THE BIG BAG?
NOTHING **YOU** NEED TO KNOW ABOUT.
C'MON, TELL ME!
WELL, LET'S JUST SAY IT'S SOMETHING THAT MIGHT COME IN HANDY TODAY.
WHY? WHAT HAPPENS TODAY?
WE'VE GOT A HISTORY TEST, REMEMBER?
SO WHAT DID YOU BRING? A BOMB?
WOULDN'T YOU AND THE PRINCIPAL **BOTH** LIKE TO KNOW!

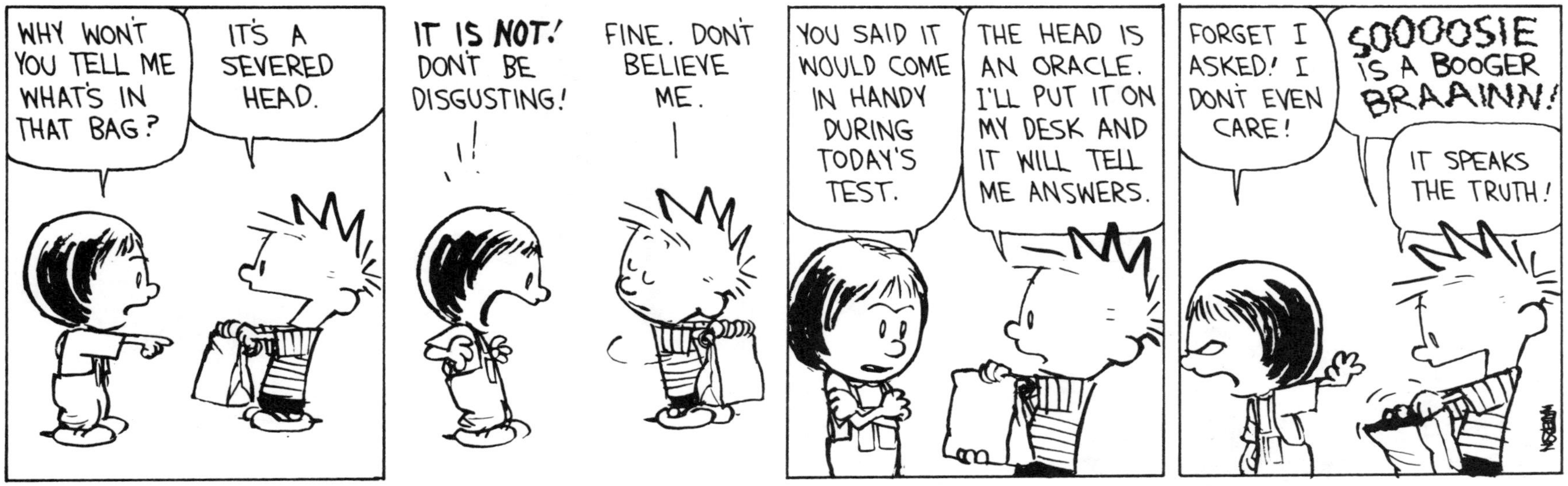
WHY WON'T YOU TELL ME WHAT'S IN THAT BAG?
IT'S A SEVERED HEAD.
IT IS **NOT**! DON'T BE DISGUSTING!
FINE. DON'T BELIEVE ME.
YOU SAID IT WOULD COME IN HANDY DURING TODAY'S TEST.
THE HEAD IS AN ORACLE. I'LL PUT IT ON MY DESK AND IT WILL TELL ME ANSWERS.
FORGET I ASKED! I DON'T EVEN CARE!
SOOOOSIE IS A BOOGER BRAAINN!
IT SPEAKS THE TRUTH!

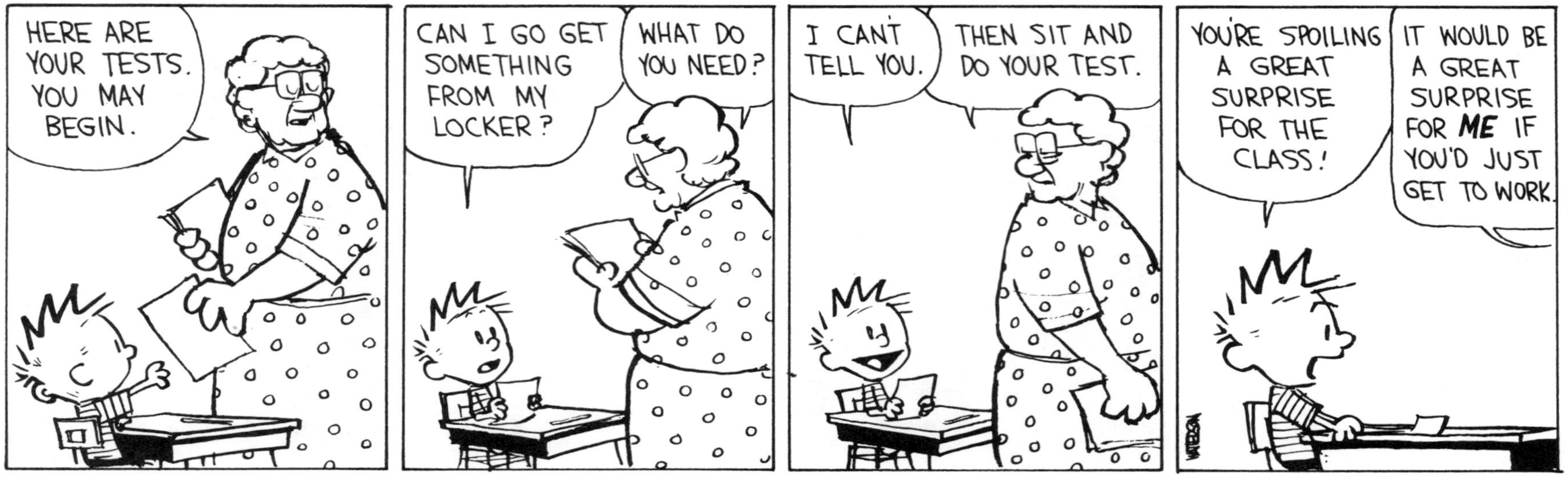
HERE ARE YOUR TESTS. YOU MAY BEGIN.
CAN I GO GET SOMETHING FROM MY LOCKER?
WHAT DO YOU NEED?
I CAN'T TELL YOU.
THEN SIT AND DO YOUR TEST.
YOU'RE SPOILING A GREAT SURPRISE FOR THE CLASS!
IT WOULD BE A GREAT SURPRISE FOR **ME** IF YOU'D JUST GET TO WORK.

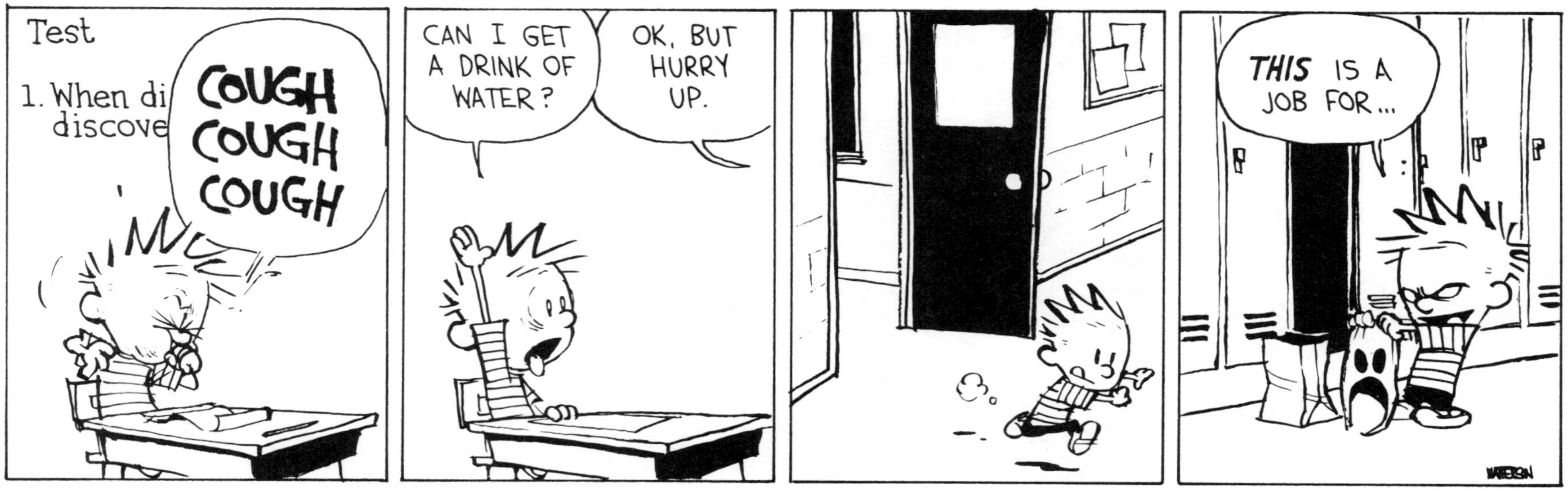
Test
1. When di
discove
COUGH COUGH COUGH
CAN I GET A DRINK OF WATER?
OK, BUT HURRY UP.
THIS IS A JOB FOR...

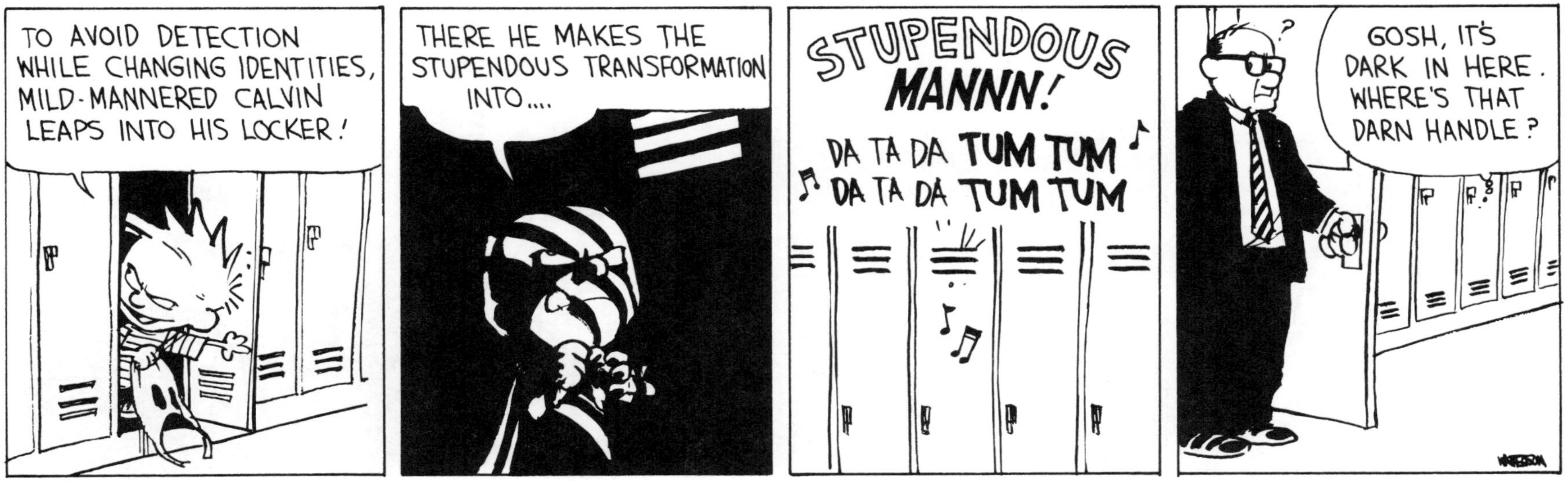
TO AVOID DETECTION WHILE CHANGING IDENTITIES, MILD-MANNERED CALVIN LEAPS INTO HIS LOCKER!
THERE HE MAKES THE STUPENDOUS TRANSFORMATION INTO....
STUPENDOUS MANNN!
DA TA DA TUM TUM DA TA DA TUM TUM
GOSH, IT'S DARK IN HERE. WHERE'S THAT DARN HANDLE?

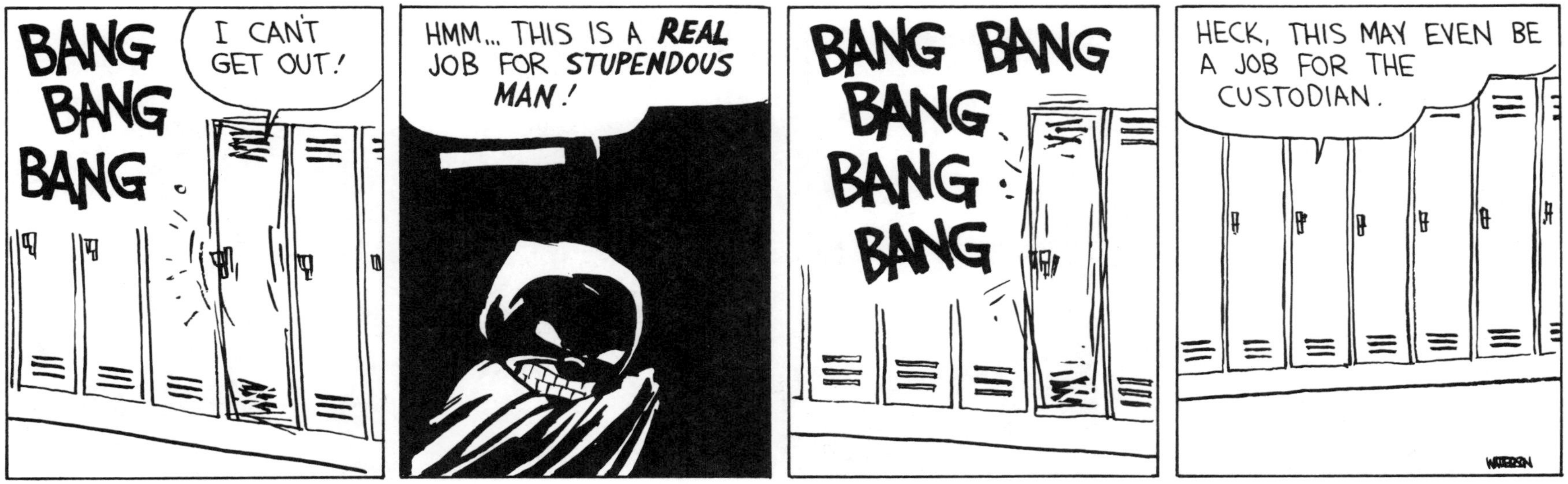
BANG BANG BANG
I CAN'T GET OUT!
HMM... THIS IS A REAL JOB FOR STUPENDOUS MAN!
BANG BANG BANG BANG BANG
HECK, THIS MAY EVEN BE A JOB FOR THE CUSTODIAN.

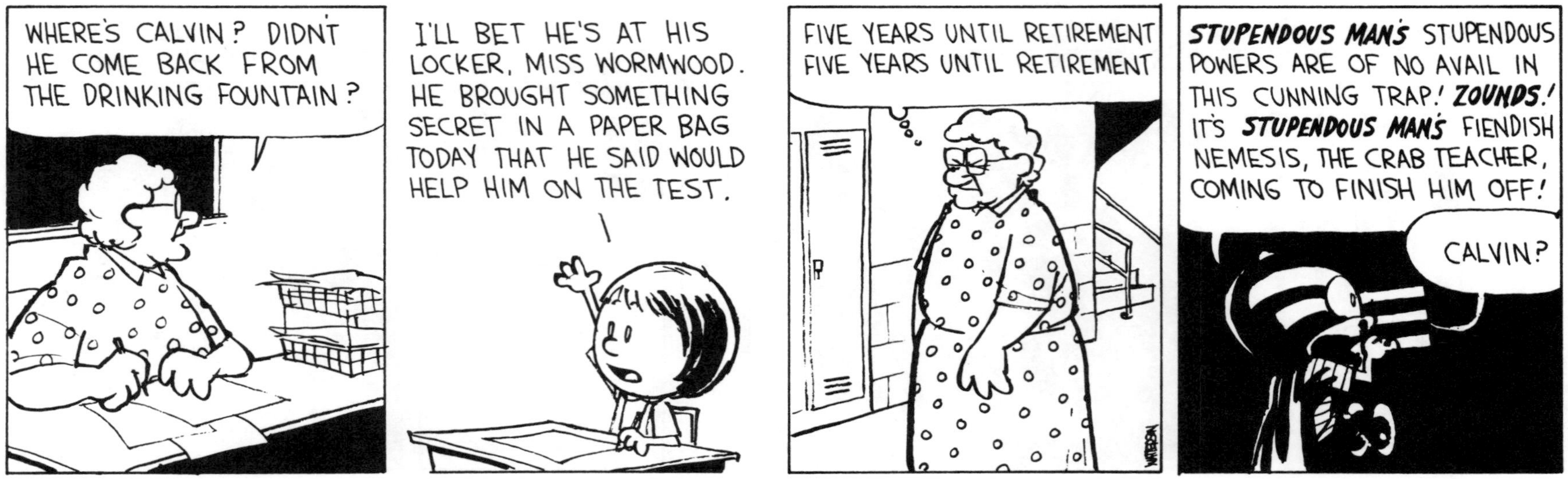
WHERE'S CALVIN? DIDN'T HE COME BACK FROM THE DRINKING FOUNTAIN?
I'LL BET HE'S AT HIS LOCKER, MISS WORMWOOD. HE BROUGHT SOMETHING SECRET IN A PAPER BAG TODAY THAT HE SAID WOULD HELP HIM ON THE TEST.
FIVE YEARS UNTIL RETIREMENT FIVE YEARS UNTIL RETIREMENT
STUPENDOUS MAN'S STUPENDOUS POWERS ARE OF NO AVAIL IN THIS CUNNING TRAP! ZOUNDS! IT'S STUPENDOUS MAN'S FIENDISH NEMESIS, THE CRAB TEACHER, COMING TO FINISH HIM OFF!
CALVIN?

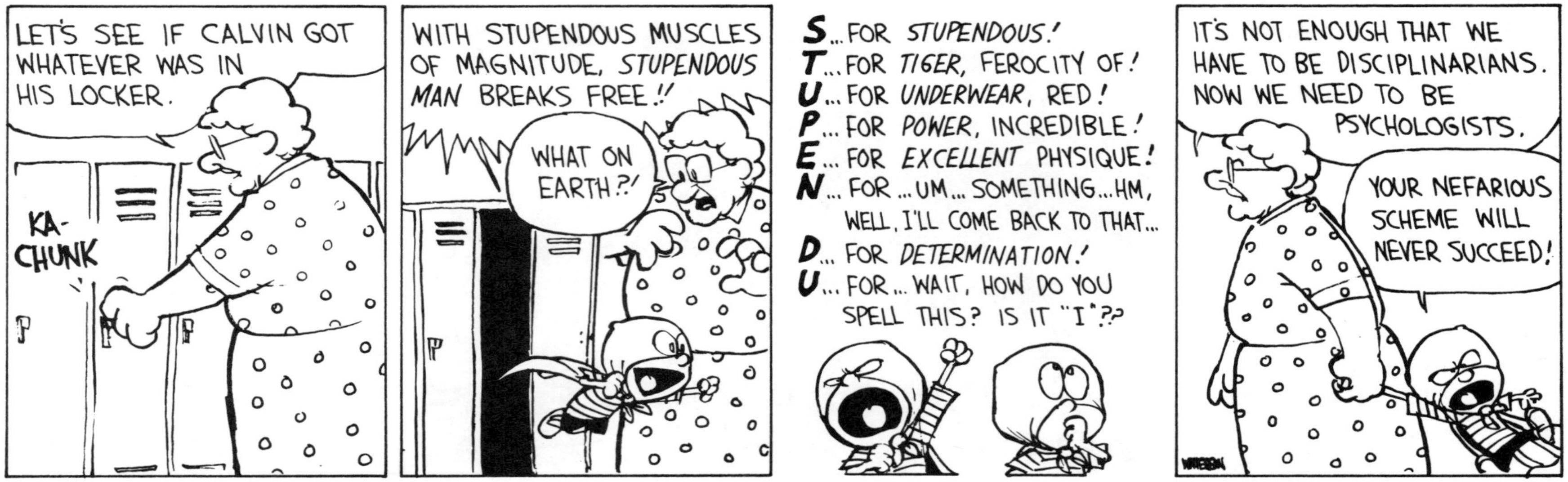
LET'S SEE IF CALVIN GOT WHATEVER WAS IN HIS LOCKER.
KA-CHUNK
WITH STUPENDOUS MUSCLES OF MAGNITUDE, STUPENDOUS MAN BREAKS FREE!!
WHAT ON EARTH?!
S... FOR STUPENDOUS!
T... FOR TIGER, FEROCITY OF!
U... FOR UNDERWEAR, RED!
P... FOR POWER, INCREDIBLE!
E... FOR EXCELLENT PHYSIQUE!
N... FOR ... UM ... SOMETHING ... HM, WELL, I'LL COME BACK TO THAT...
D... FOR DETERMINATION!
U... FOR ... WAIT, HOW DO YOU SPELL THIS? IS IT "I"??
IT'S NOT ENOUGH THAT WE HAVE TO BE DISCIPLINARIANS. NOW WE NEED TO BE PSYCHOLOGISTS.
YOUR NEFARIOUS SCHEME WILL NEVER SUCCEED!

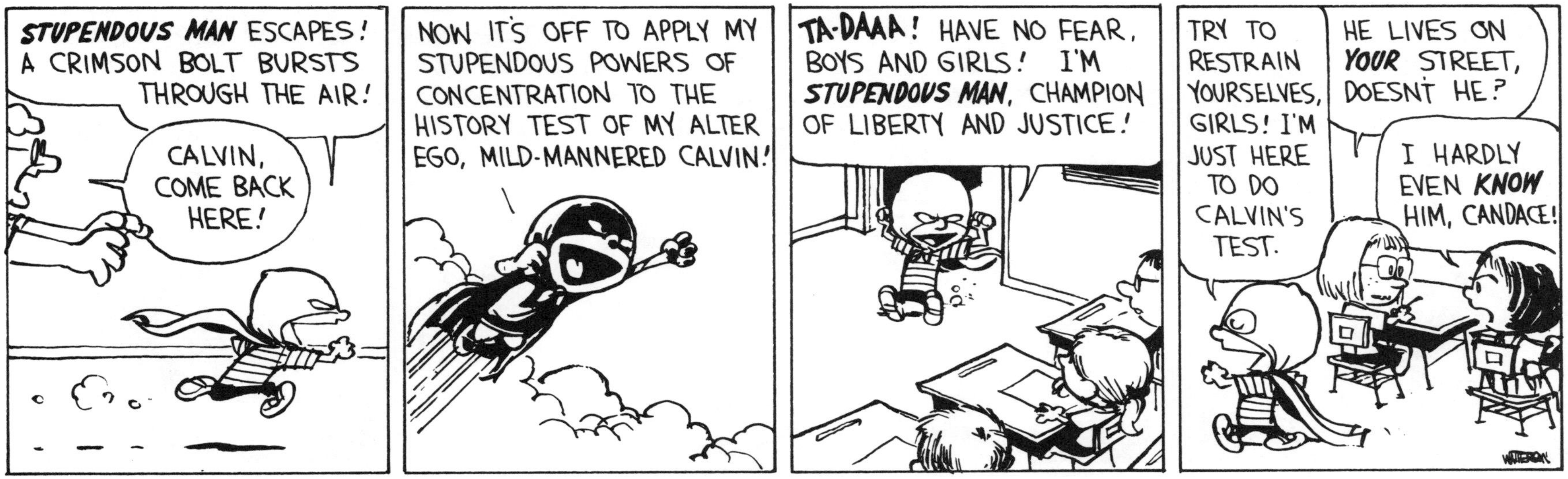
STUPENDOUS MAN ESCAPES! A CRIMSON BOLT BURSTS THROUGH THE AIR!
CALVIN, COME BACK HERE!
NOW IT'S OFF TO APPLY MY STUPENDOUS POWERS OF CONCENTRATION TO THE HISTORY TEST OF MY ALTER EGO, MILD-MANNERED CALVIN!
TA-DAAA! HAVE NO FEAR, BOYS AND GIRLS! I'M STUPENDOUS MAN, CHAMPION OF LIBERTY AND JUSTICE!
TRY TO RESTRAIN YOURSELVES, GIRLS! I'M JUST HERE TO DO CALVIN'S TEST.
HE LIVES ON YOUR STREET, DOESN'T HE?
I HARDLY EVEN KNOW HIM, CANDACE!

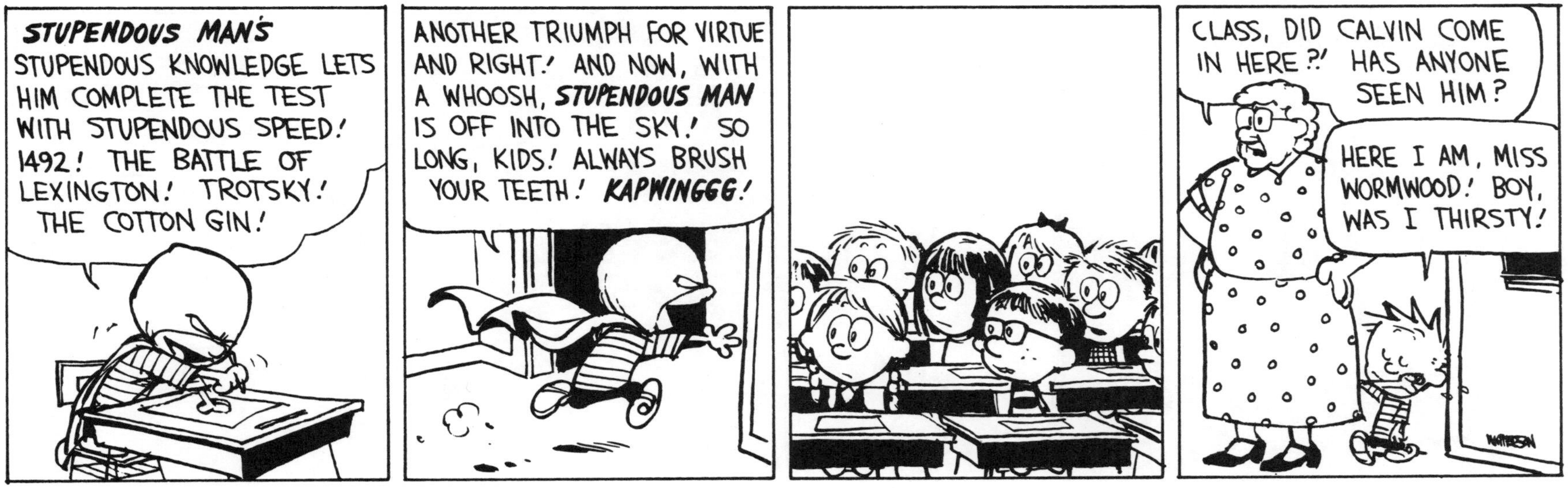
STUPENDOUS MAN'S STUPENDOUS KNOWLEDGE LETS HIM COMPLETE THE TEST WITH STUPENDOUS SPEED! 1492! THE BATTLE OF LEXINGTON! TROTSKY! THE COTTON GIN!
ANOTHER TRIUMPH FOR VIRTUE AND RIGHT! AND NOW, WITH A WHOOSH, STUPENDOUS MAN IS OFF INTO THE SKY! SO LONG, KIDS! ALWAYS BRUSH YOUR TEETH! KAPWINGGG!
CLASS, DID CALVIN COME IN HERE?! HAS ANYONE SEEN HIM?
HERE I AM, MISS WORMWOOD! BOY, WAS I THIRSTY!

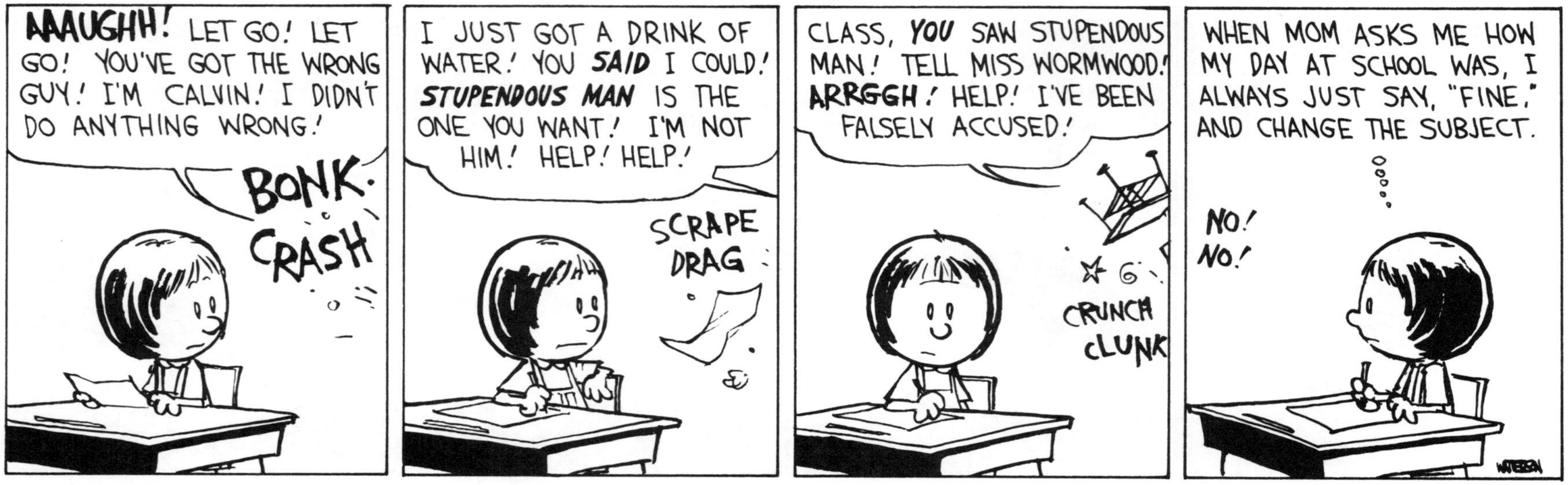
AAAUGHH! LET GO! LET GO! YOU'VE GOT THE WRONG GUY! I'M CALVIN! I DIDN'T DO ANYTHING WRONG!
BONK
CRASH
I JUST GOT A DRINK OF WATER! YOU SAID I COULD! STUPENDOUS MAN IS THE ONE YOU WANT! I'M NOT HIM! HELP! HELP!
SCRAPE
DRAG
CLASS, YOU SAW STUPENDOUS MAN! TELL MISS WORMWOOD! ARRGGH! HELP! I'VE BEEN FALSELY ACCUSED!
CRUNCH
CLUNK
WHEN MOM ASKS ME HOW MY DAY AT SCHOOL WAS, I ALWAYS JUST SAY, "FINE," AND CHANGE THE SUBJECT.
NO!
NO!

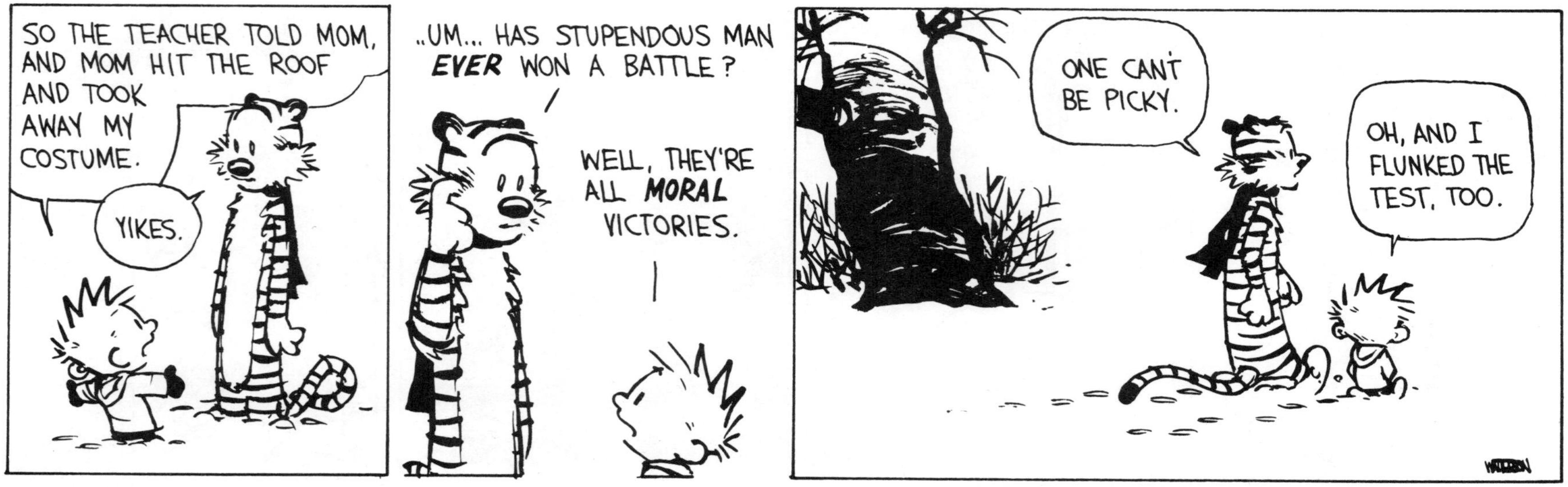
SO THE TEACHER TOLD MOM, AND MOM HIT THE ROOF AND TOOK AWAY MY COSTUME.
YIKES.
..UM... HAS STUPENDOUS MAN EVER WON A BATTLE?
WELL, THEY'RE ALL MORAL VICTORIES.
ONE CAN'T BE PICKY.
OH, AND I FLUNKED THE TEST, TOO.

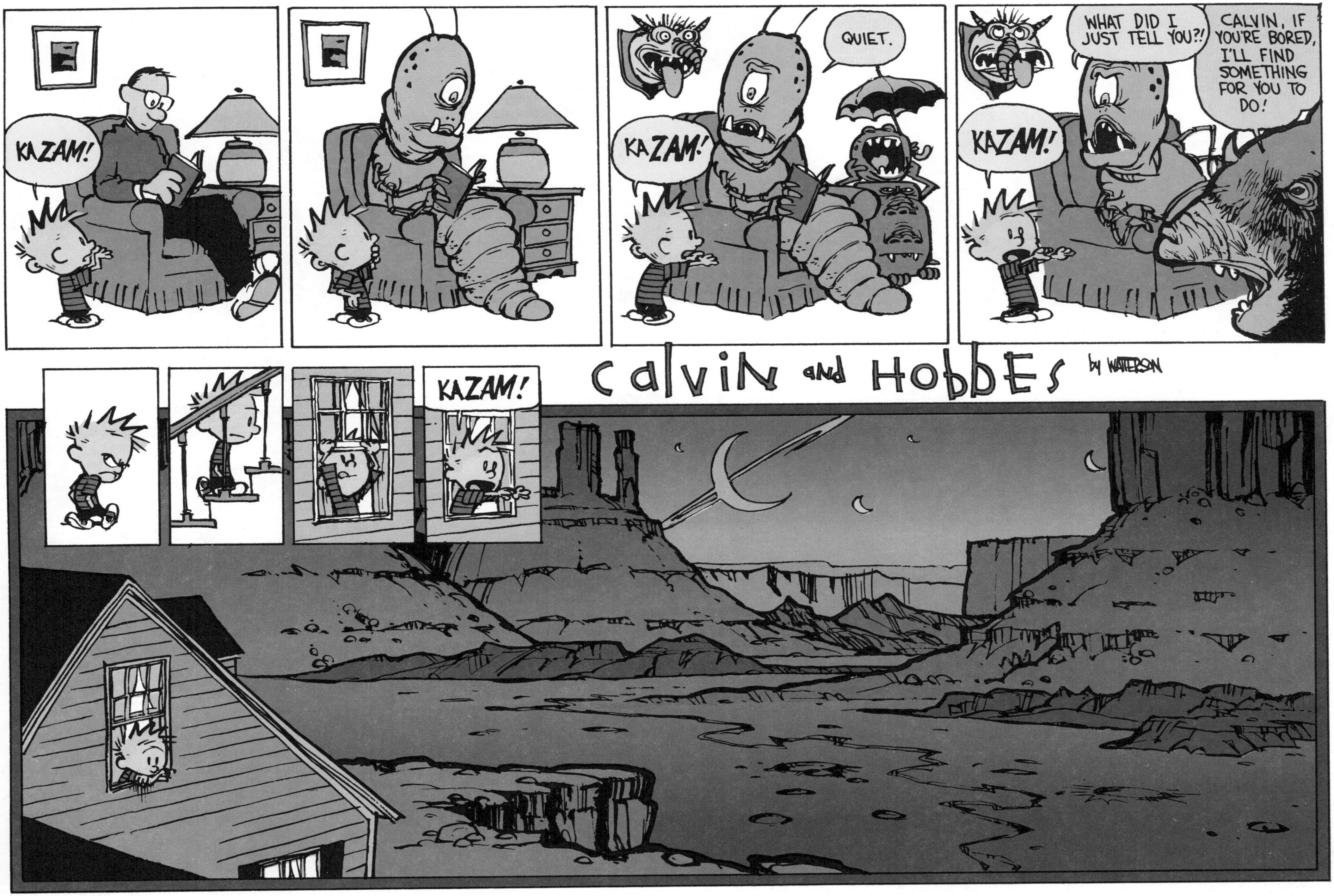
KAZAM!
KAZAM!
QUIET.
KAZAM!
WHAT DID I JUST TELL YOU?!
CALVIN, IF YOU'RE BORED, I'LL FIND SOMETHING FOR YOU TO DO!
calvin and HOBBES
by WATTERSON
KAZAM!

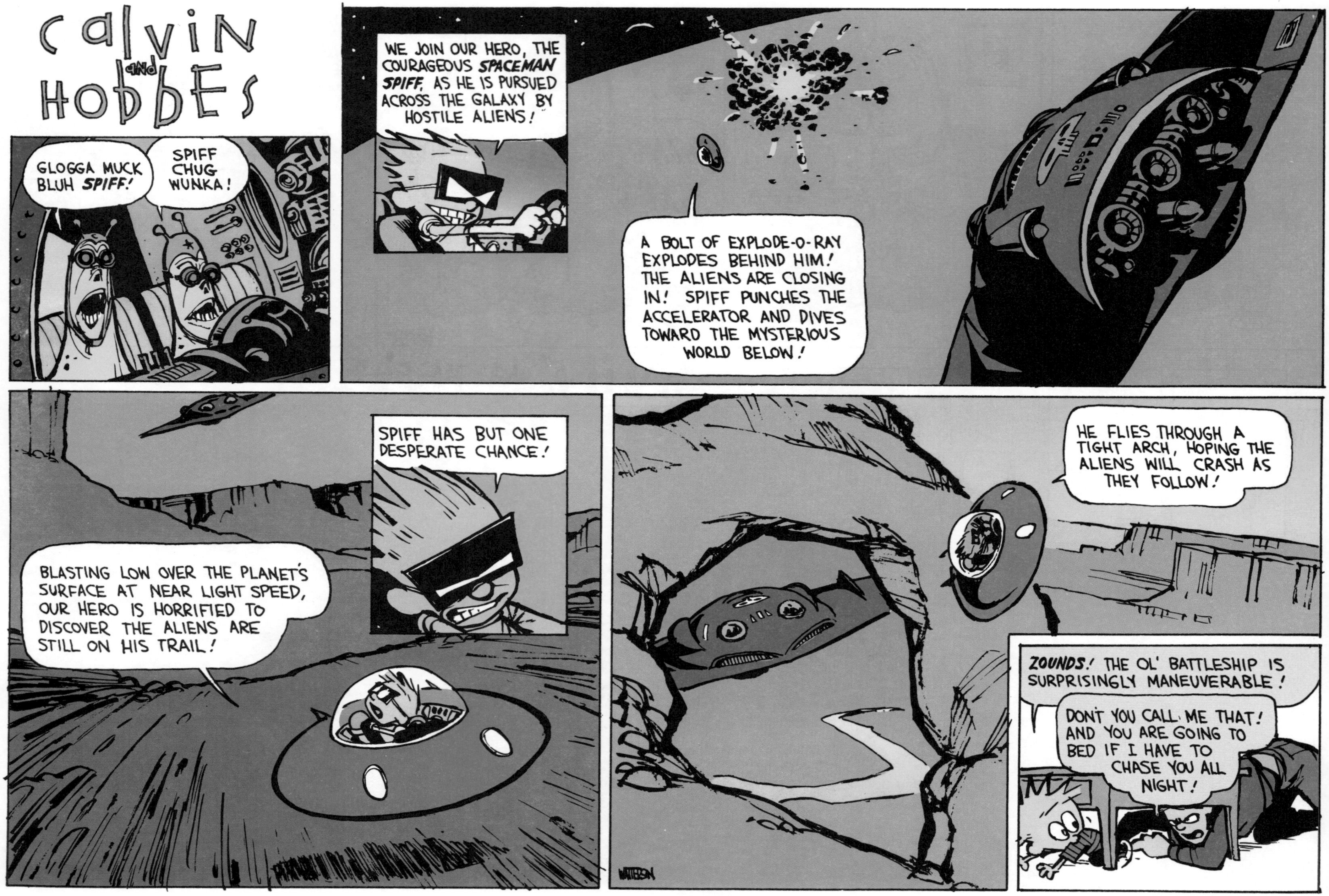

Calvin and Hobbes
GLOGGA MUCK BLUH SPIFF!
SPIFF CHUG WUNKA!
WE JOIN OUR HERO, THE COURAGEOUS SPACEMAN SPIFF, AS HE IS PURSUED ACROSS THE GALAXY BY HOSTILE ALIENS!
A BOLT OF EXPLODE-O-RAY EXPLODES BEHIND HIM! THE ALIENS ARE CLOSING IN! SPIFF PUNCHES THE ACCELERATOR AND DIVES TOWARD THE MYSTERIOUS WORLD BELOW!
SPIFF HAS BUT ONE DESPERATE CHANCE!
BLASTING LOW OVER THE PLANET'S SURFACE AT NEAR LIGHT SPEED, OUR HERO IS HORRIFIED TO DISCOVER THE ALIENS ARE STILL ON HIS TRAIL!
HE FLIES THROUGH A TIGHT ARCH, HOPING THE ALIENS WILL CRASH AS THEY FOLLOW!
ZOUNDS! THE OL' BATTLESHIP IS SURPRISINGLY MANEUVERABLE!
DON'T YOU CALL ME THAT! AND YOU ARE GOING TO BED IF I HAVE TO CHASE YOU ALL NIGHT!
WATTERSON

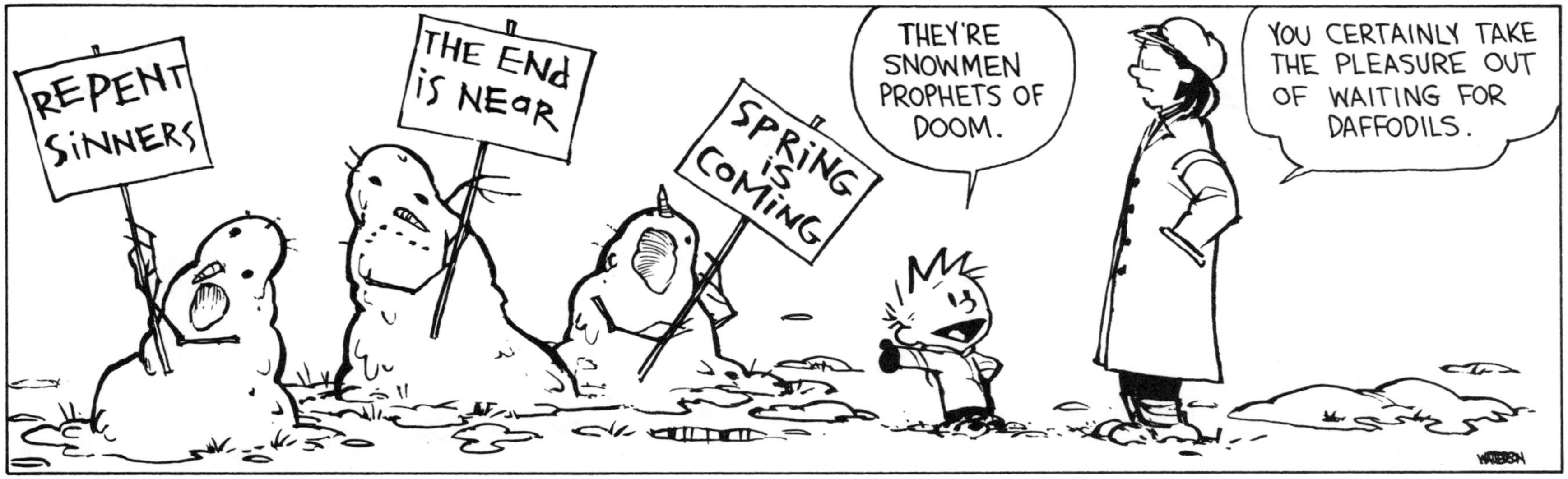
REPENT SINNERS
THE END IS NEAR
SPRING IS COMING
THEY'RE SNOWMEN PROPHETS OF DOOM.
YOU CERTAINLY TAKE THE PLEASURE OUT OF WAITING FOR DAFFODILS.

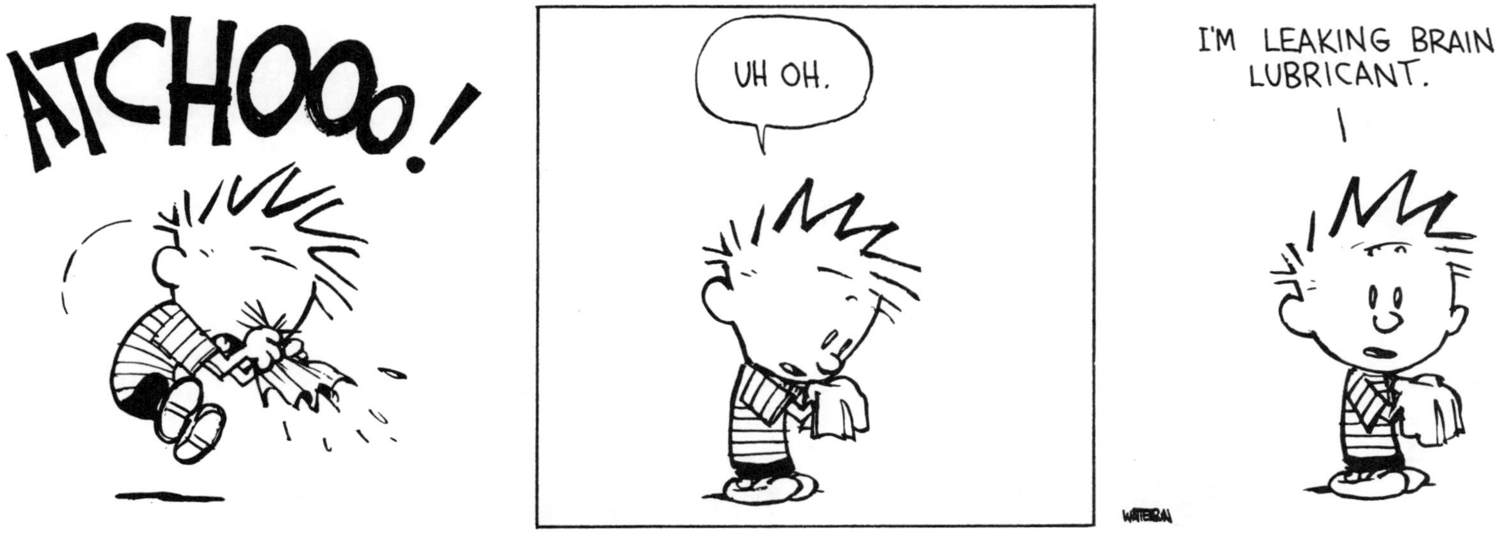
ATCHOOO!
UH OH.
I'M LEAKING BRAIN LUBRICANT.

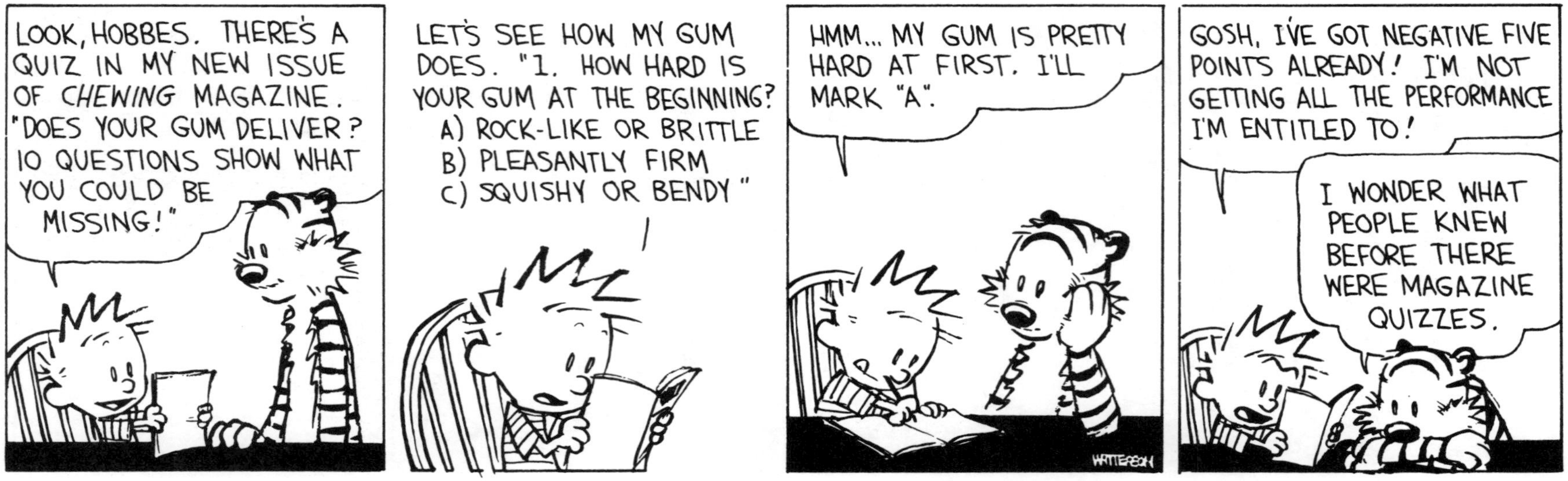
LOOK, HOBBES. THERE'S A QUIZ IN MY NEW ISSUE OF *CHEWING* MAGAZINE. "DOES YOUR GUM DELIVER? 10 QUESTIONS SHOW WHAT YOU COULD BE MISSING!"
LET'S SEE HOW MY GUM DOES. "1. HOW HARD IS YOUR GUM AT THE BEGINNING? A) ROCK-LIKE OR BRITTLE B) PLEASANTLY FIRM C) SQUISHY OR BENDY"
HMM... MY GUM IS PRETTY HARD AT FIRST. I'LL MARK "A".
GOSH, I'VE GOT NEGATIVE FIVE POINTS ALREADY! I'M NOT GETTING ALL THE PERFORMANCE I'M ENTITLED TO!
I WONDER WHAT PEOPLE KNEW BEFORE THERE WERE MAGAZINE QUIZZES.
WATTERSON

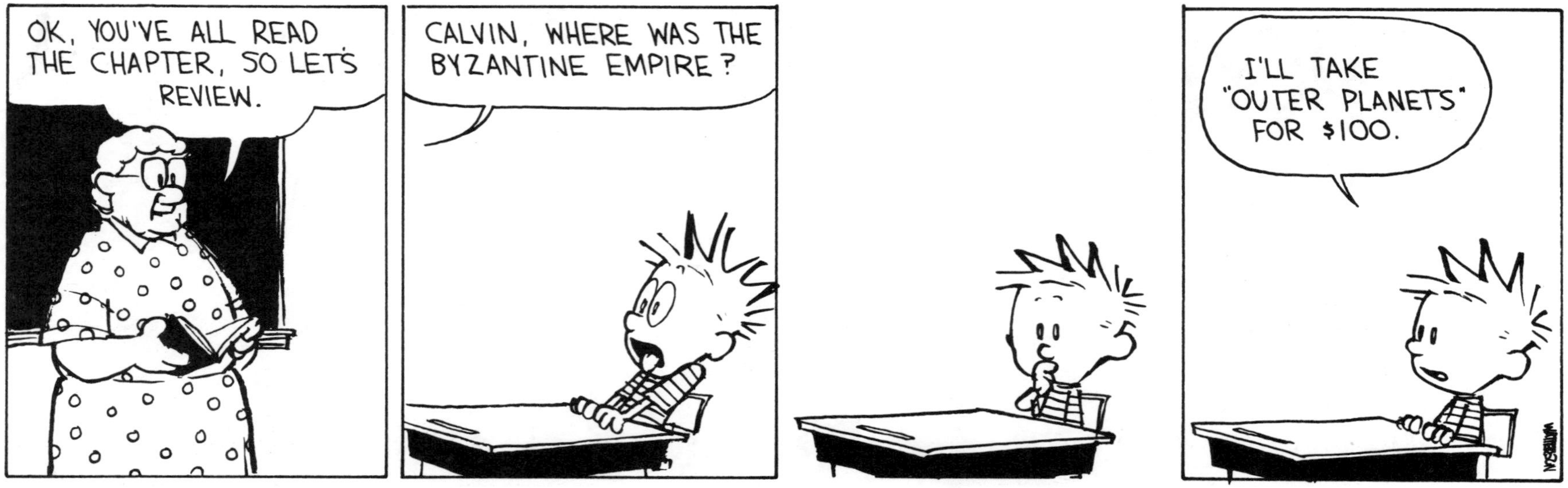
OK, YOU'VE ALL READ THE CHAPTER, SO LET'S REVIEW.
CALVIN, WHERE WAS THE BYZANTINE EMPIRE?
I'LL TAKE "OUTER PLANETS" FOR $100.
WATTERSON

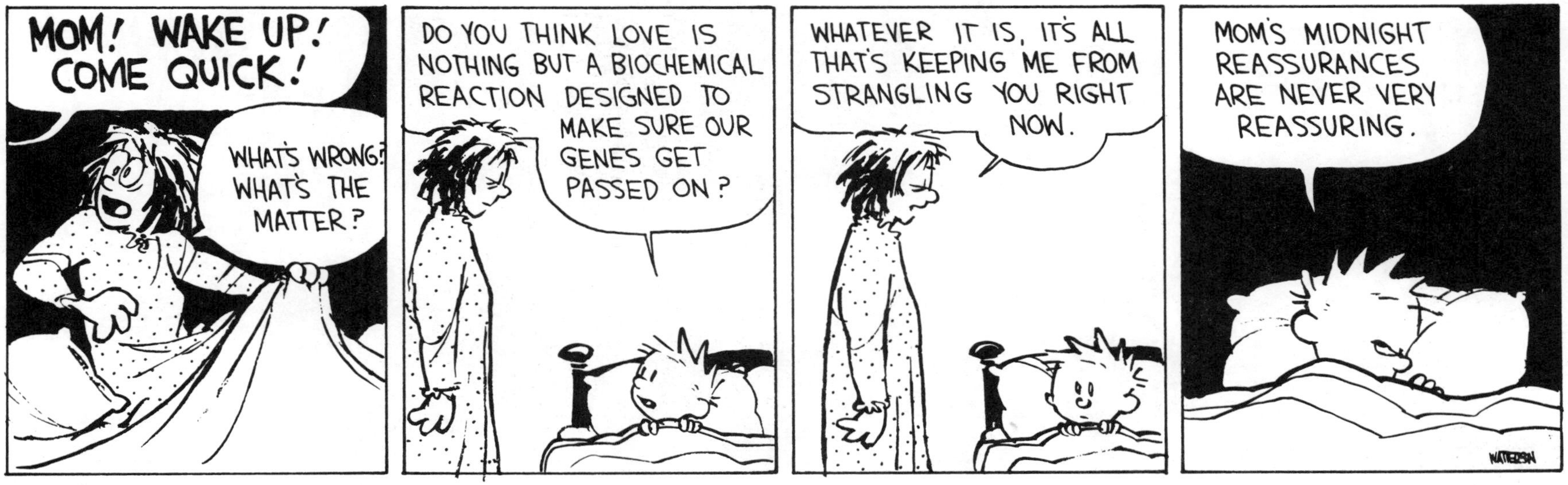
MOM! WAKE UP! COME QUICK!
WHAT'S WRONG? WHAT'S THE MATTER?
DO YOU THINK LOVE IS NOTHING BUT A BIOCHEMICAL REACTION DESIGNED TO MAKE SURE OUR GENES GET PASSED ON?
WHATEVER IT IS, IT'S ALL THAT'S KEEPING ME FROM STRANGLING YOU RIGHT NOW.
MOM'S MIDNIGHT REASSURANCES ARE NEVER VERY REASSURING.
WATTERSON

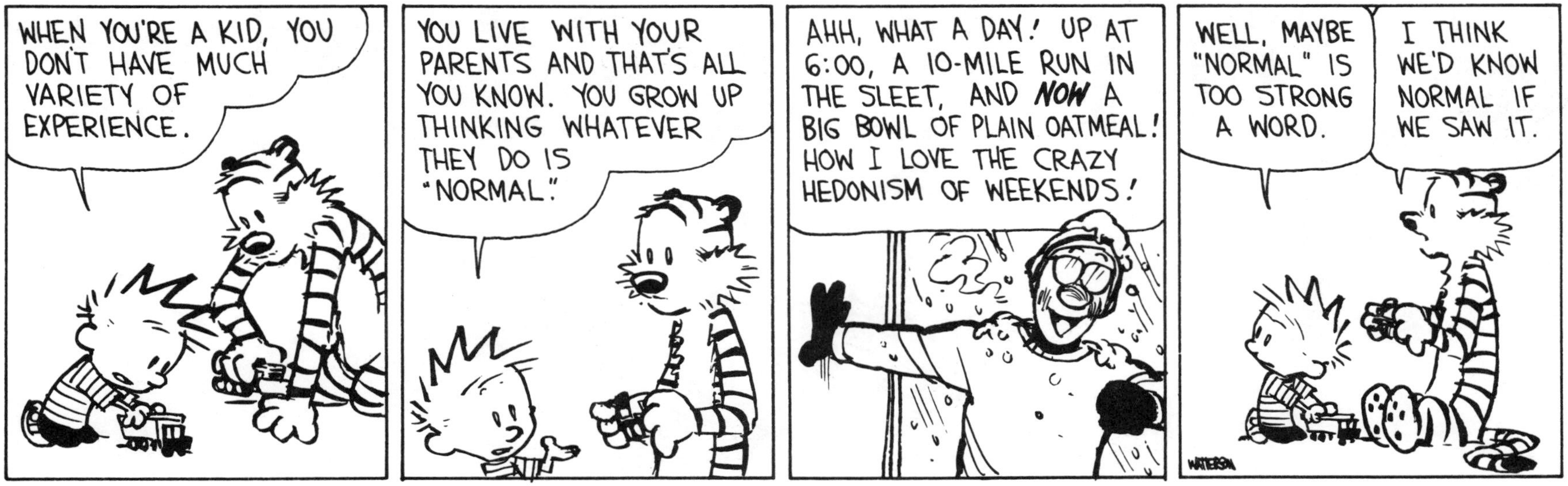
WHEN YOU'RE A KID, YOU DON'T HAVE MUCH VARIETY OF EXPERIENCE.
YOU LIVE WITH YOUR PARENTS AND THAT'S ALL YOU KNOW. YOU GROW UP THINKING WHATEVER THEY DO IS "NORMAL."
AHH, WHAT A DAY! UP AT 6:00, A 10-MILE RUN IN THE SLEET, AND NOW A BIG BOWL OF PLAIN OATMEAL! HOW I LOVE THE CRAZY HEDONISM OF WEEKENDS!
WELL, MAYBE "NORMAL" IS TOO STRONG A WORD.
I THINK WE'D KNOW NORMAL IF WE SAW IT.
WATTERSON

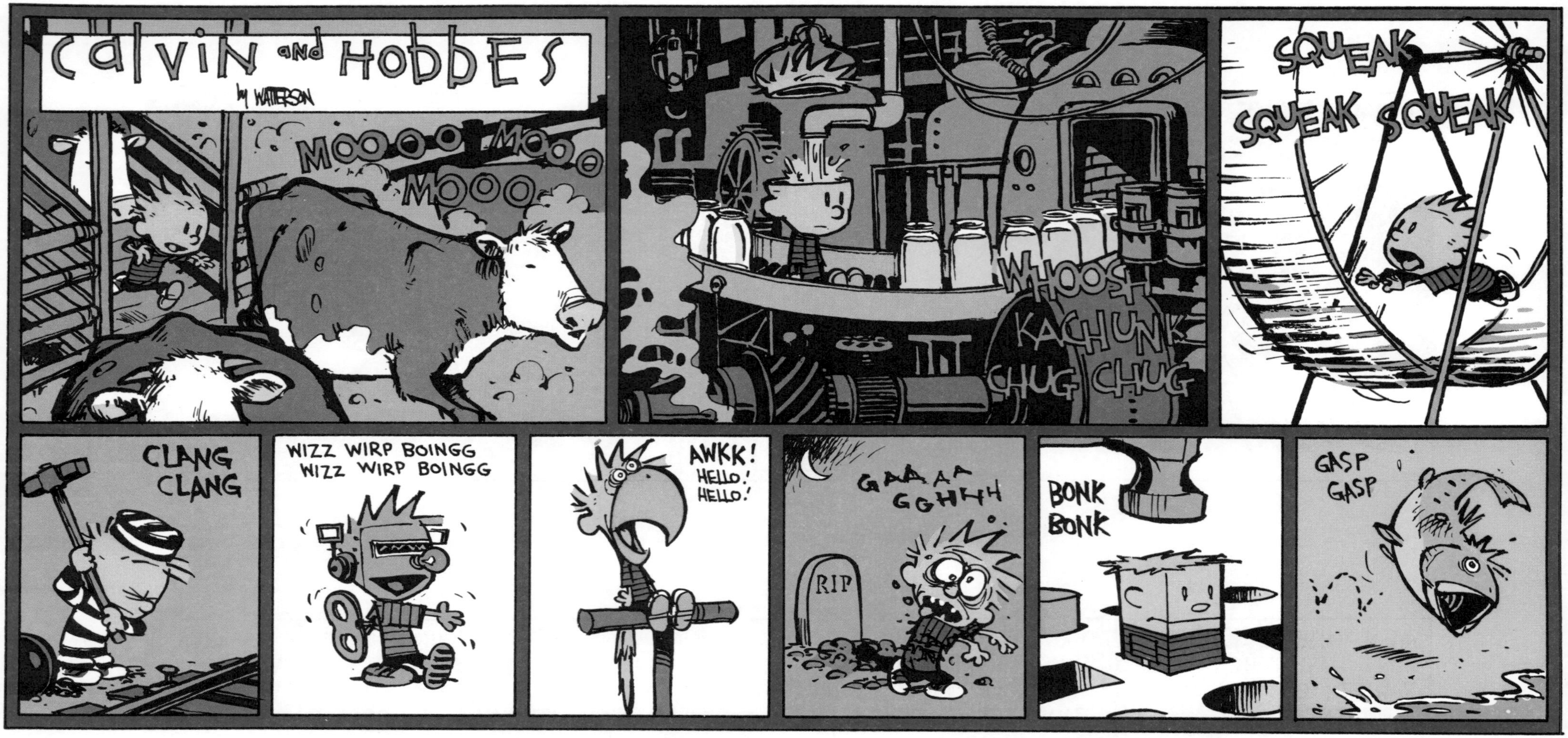
Calvin and HOBBES
by WATTERSON
MOOOO MOOOO
MOOOO
WHOOSH
KACHUNK
CHUG CHUG
SQUEAK
SQUEAK SQUEAK
CLANG
CLANG
WIZZ WIRP BOINGG
WIZZ WIRP BOINGG
AWKK!
HELLO!
HELLO!
RIP
GAAAA
GGHHHH
BONK
BONK
GASP
GASP

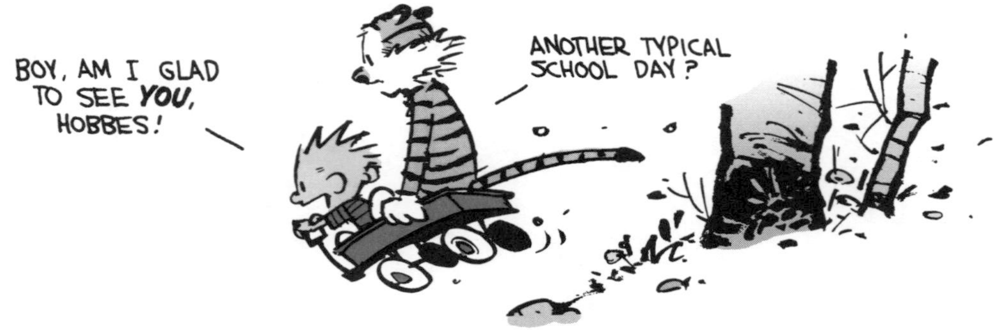
BOY, AM I GLAD TO SEE *YOU*, HOBBES!
ANOTHER TYPICAL SCHOOL DAY?

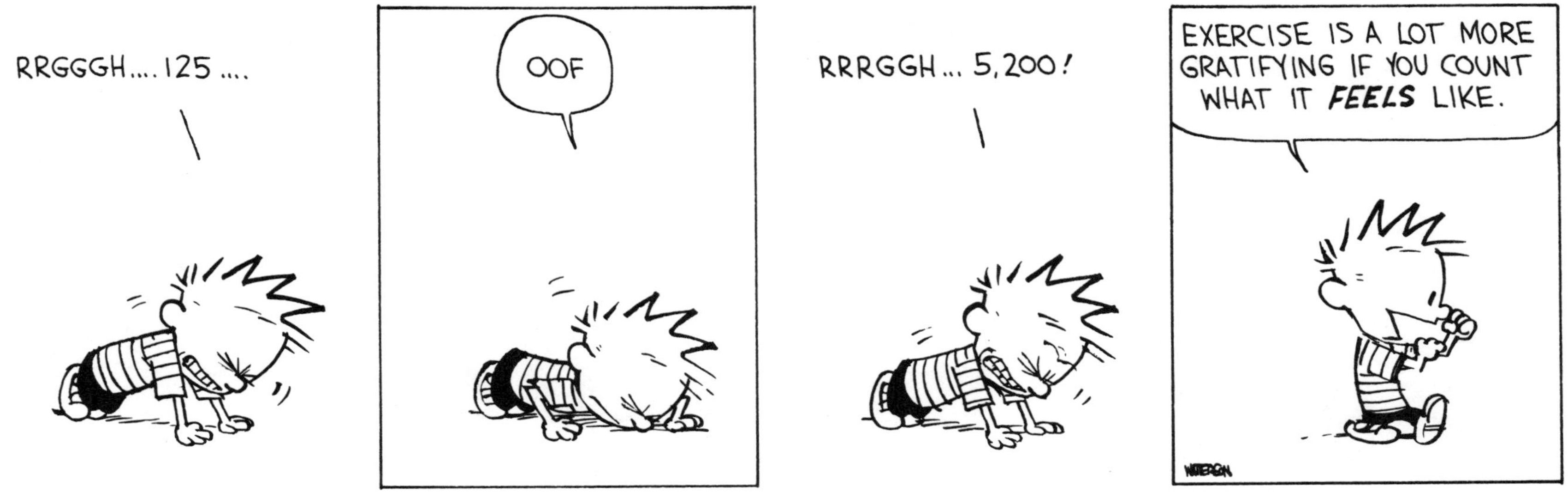
RRGGGH.... 125 ....
OOF
RRRGGH... 5,200!
EXERCISE IS A LOT MORE GRATIFYING IF YOU COUNT WHAT IT **FEELS** LIKE.

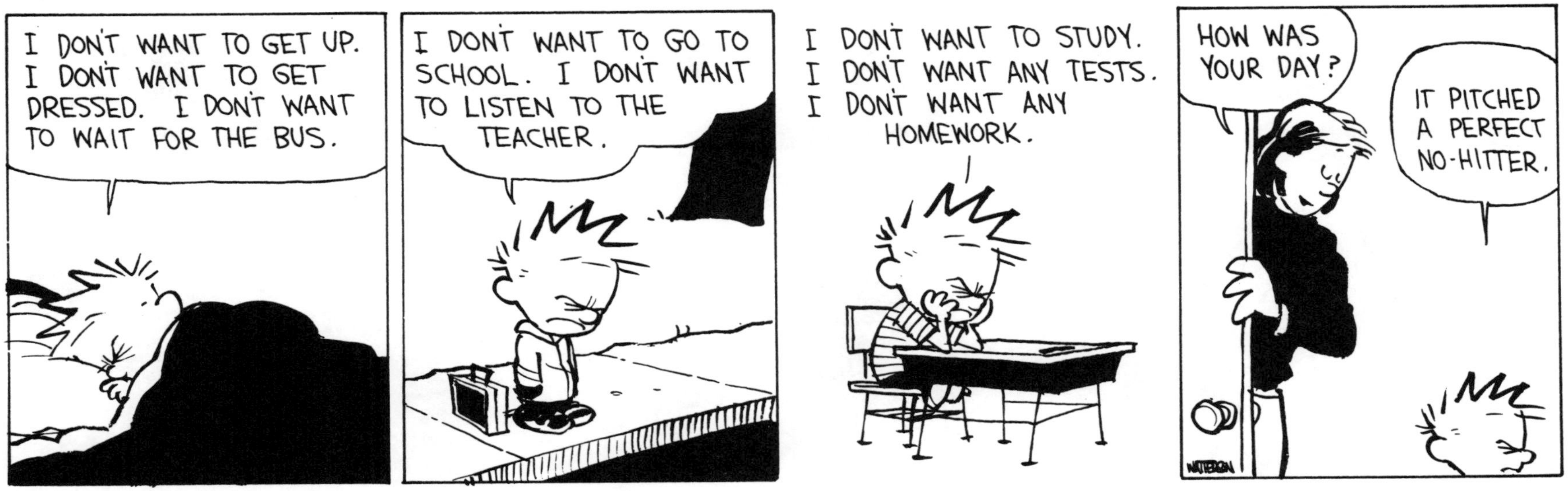
I DON'T WANT TO GET UP. I DON'T WANT TO GET DRESSED. I DON'T WANT TO WAIT FOR THE BUS.
I DON'T WANT TO GO TO SCHOOL. I DON'T WANT TO LISTEN TO THE TEACHER.
I DON'T WANT TO STUDY. I DON'T WANT ANY TESTS. I DON'T WANT ANY HOMEWORK.
HOW WAS YOUR DAY?
IT PITCHED A PERFECT NO-HITTER.

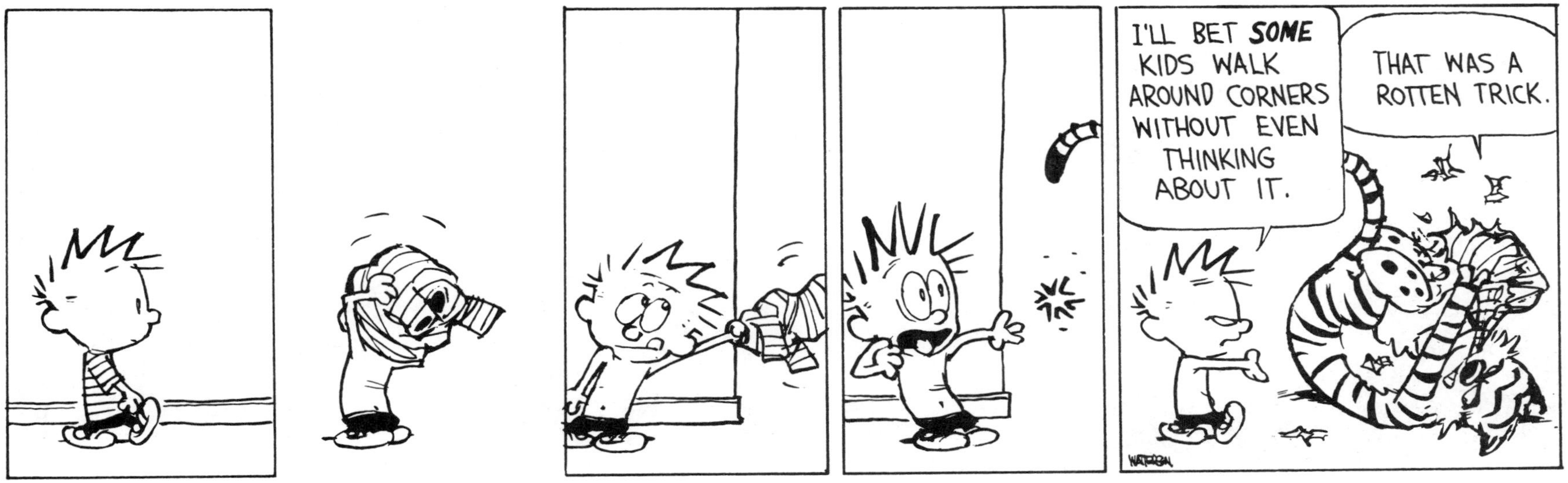
I'LL BET SOME KIDS WALK AROUND CORNERS WITHOUT EVEN THINKING ABOUT IT.
THAT WAS A ROTTEN TRICK.

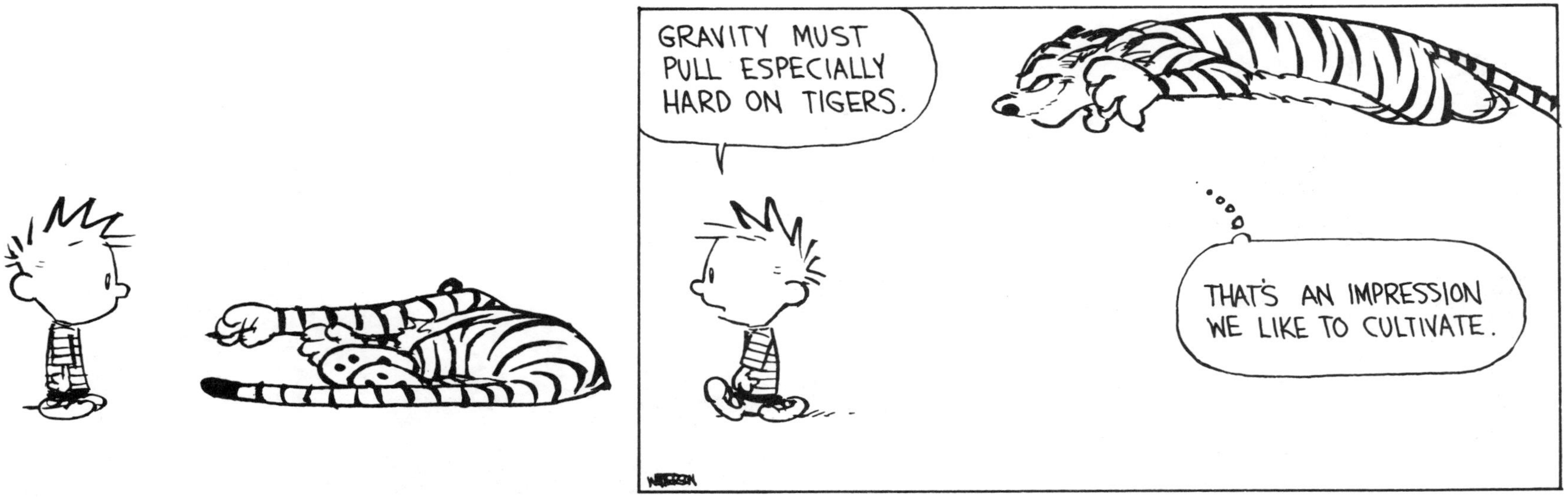
GRAVITY MUST PULL ESPECIALLY HARD ON TIGERS.
THAT'S AN IMPRESSION WE LIKE TO CULTIVATE.

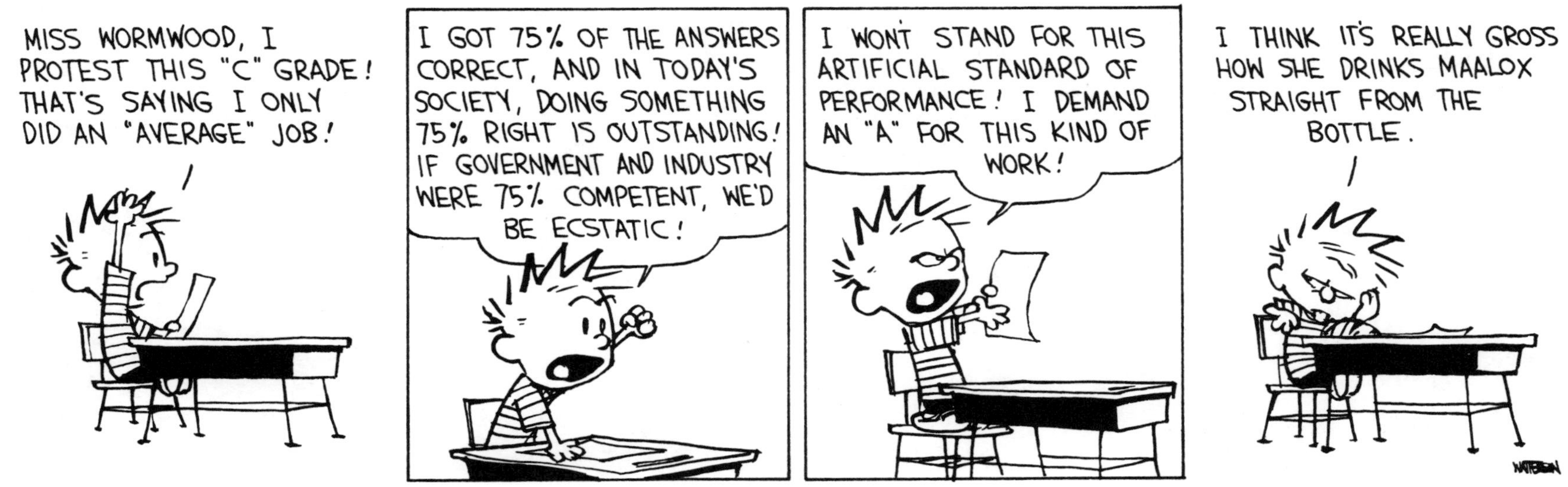
MISS WORMWOOD, I PROTEST THIS "C" GRADE! THAT'S SAYING I ONLY DID AN "AVERAGE" JOB!
I GOT 75% OF THE ANSWERS CORRECT, AND IN TODAY'S SOCIETY, DOING SOMETHING 75% RIGHT IS OUTSTANDING! IF GOVERNMENT AND INDUSTRY WERE 75% COMPETENT, WE'D BE ECSTATIC!
I WON'T STAND FOR THIS ARTIFICIAL STANDARD OF PERFORMANCE! I DEMAND AN "A" FOR THIS KIND OF WORK!
I THINK IT'S REALLY GROSS HOW SHE DRINKS MAALOX STRAIGHT FROM THE BOTTLE.

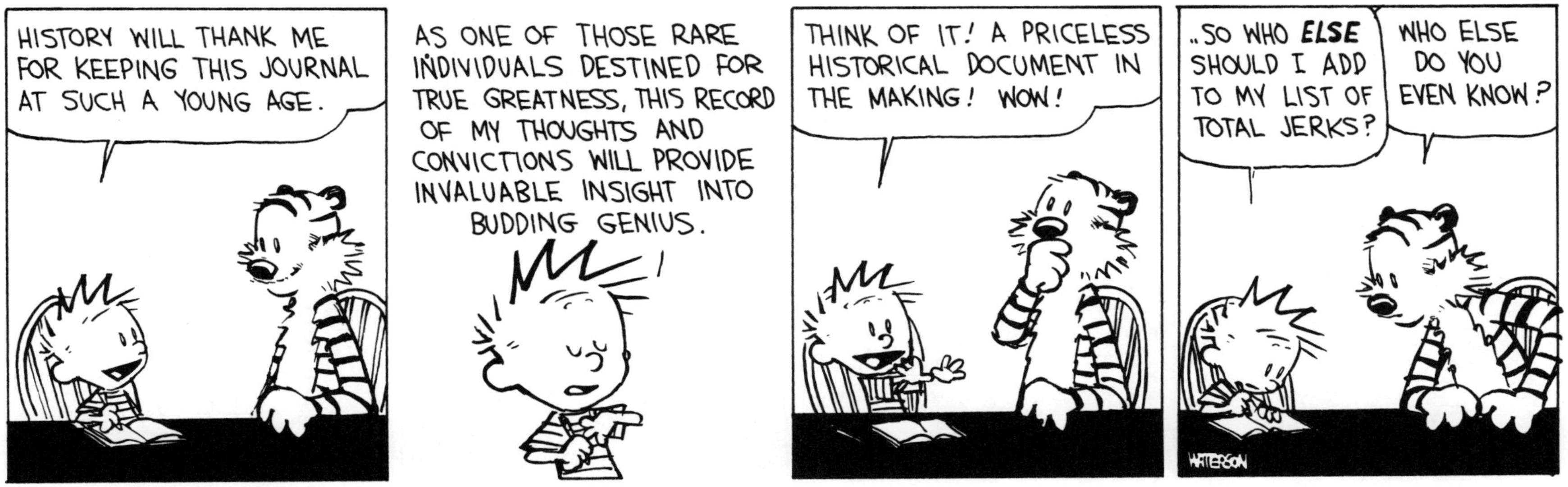
HISTORY WILL THANK ME FOR KEEPING THIS JOURNAL AT SUCH A YOUNG AGE.
AS ONE OF THOSE RARE INDIVIDUALS DESTINED FOR TRUE GREATNESS, THIS RECORD OF MY THOUGHTS AND CONVICTIONS WILL PROVIDE INVALUABLE INSIGHT INTO BUDDING GENIUS.
THINK OF IT! A PRICELESS HISTORICAL DOCUMENT IN THE MAKING! WOW!
..SO WHO ***ELSE*** SHOULD I ADD TO MY LIST OF TOTAL JERKS?
WHO ELSE DO YOU EVEN KNOW?
WATTERSON

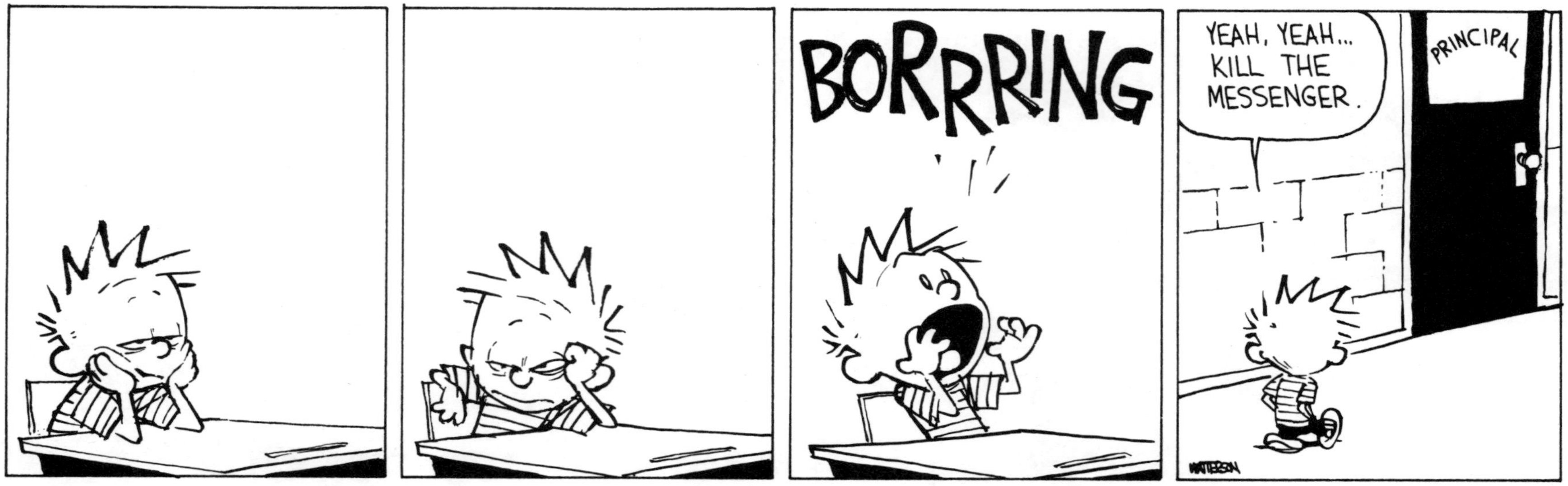
BORRRING
YEAH, YEAH... KILL THE MESSENGER.
PRINCIPAL

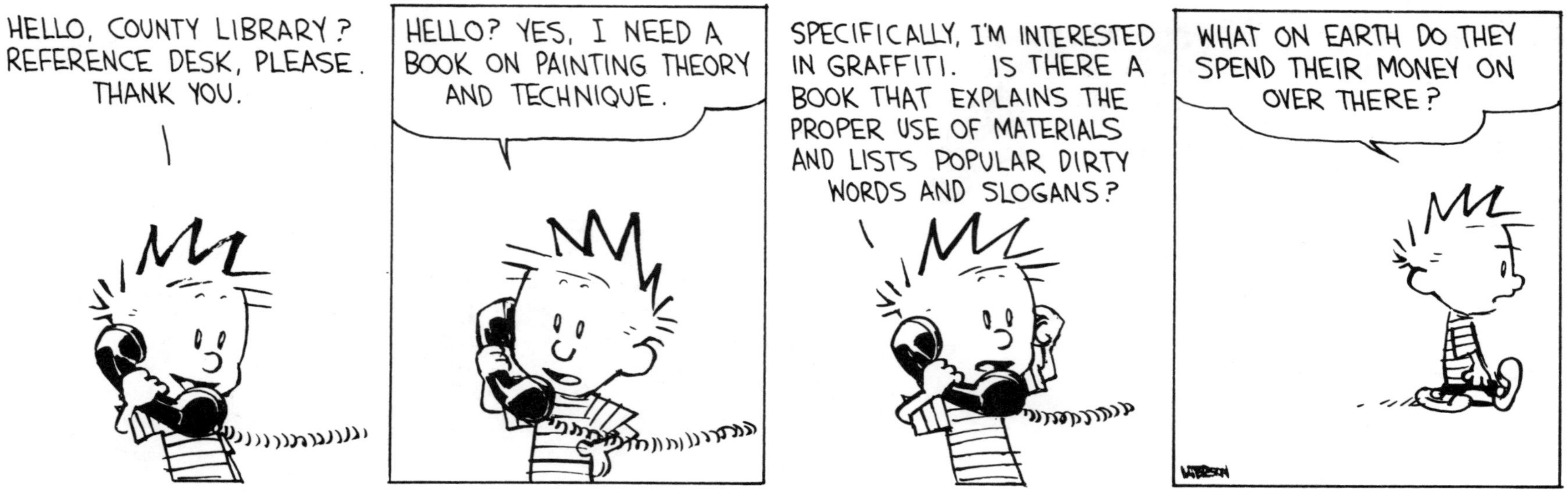
HELLO, COUNTY LIBRARY? REFERENCE DESK, PLEASE. THANK YOU.
HELLO? YES, I NEED A BOOK ON PAINTING THEORY AND TECHNIQUE.
SPECIFICALLY, I'M INTERESTED IN GRAFFITI. IS THERE A BOOK THAT EXPLAINS THE PROPER USE OF MATERIALS AND LISTS POPULAR DIRTY WORDS AND SLOGANS?
WHAT ON EARTH DO THEY SPEND THEIR MONEY ON OVER THERE?

93

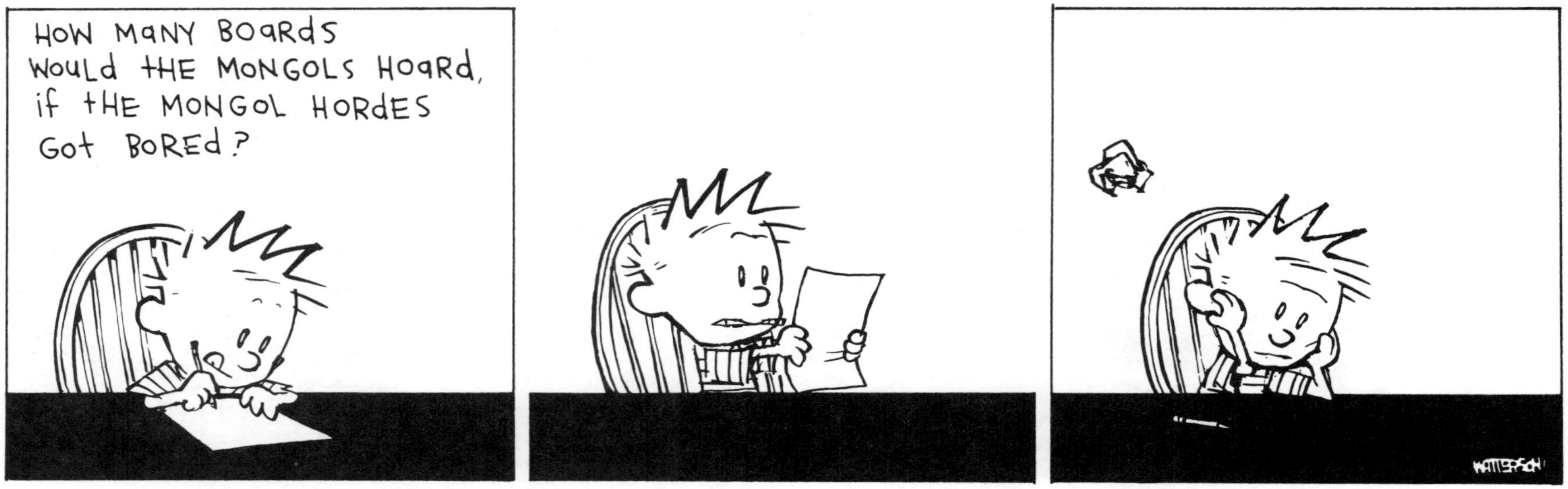
HOW MANY BOARDS WOULD THE MONGOLS HOARD, IF THE MONGOL HORDES GOT BORED?
WATTERSON

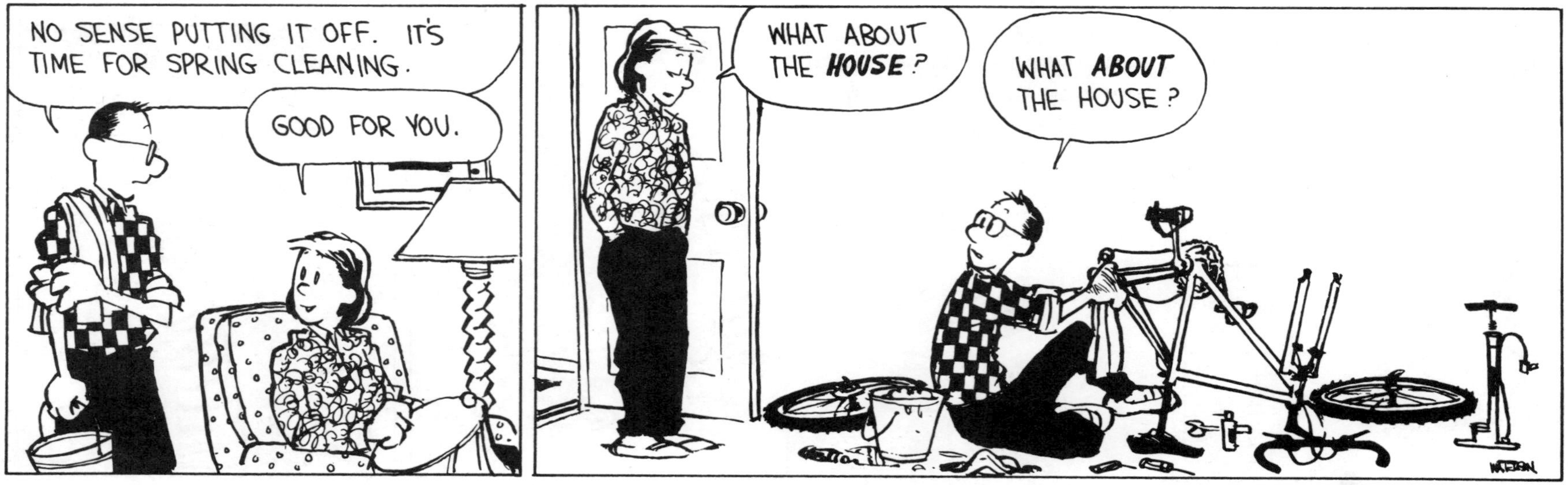
NO SENSE PUTTING IT OFF. IT'S TIME FOR SPRING CLEANING.
GOOD FOR YOU.
WHAT ABOUT THE **HOUSE**?
WHAT **ABOUT** THE HOUSE?
WATERSON

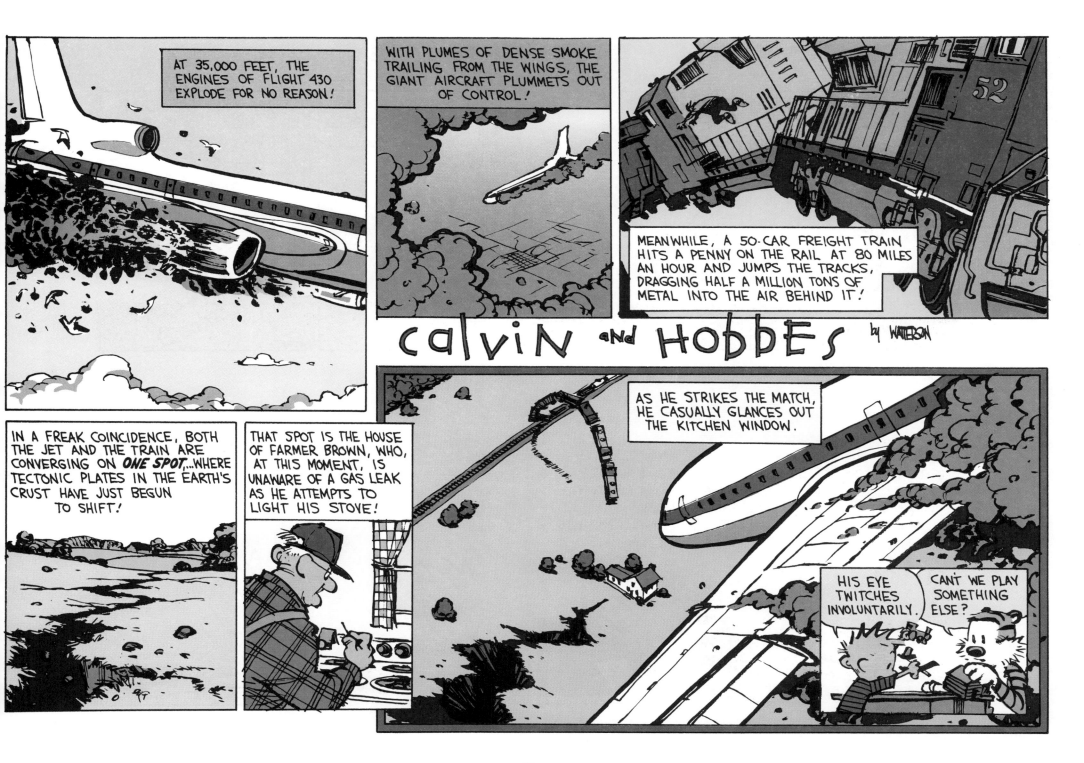

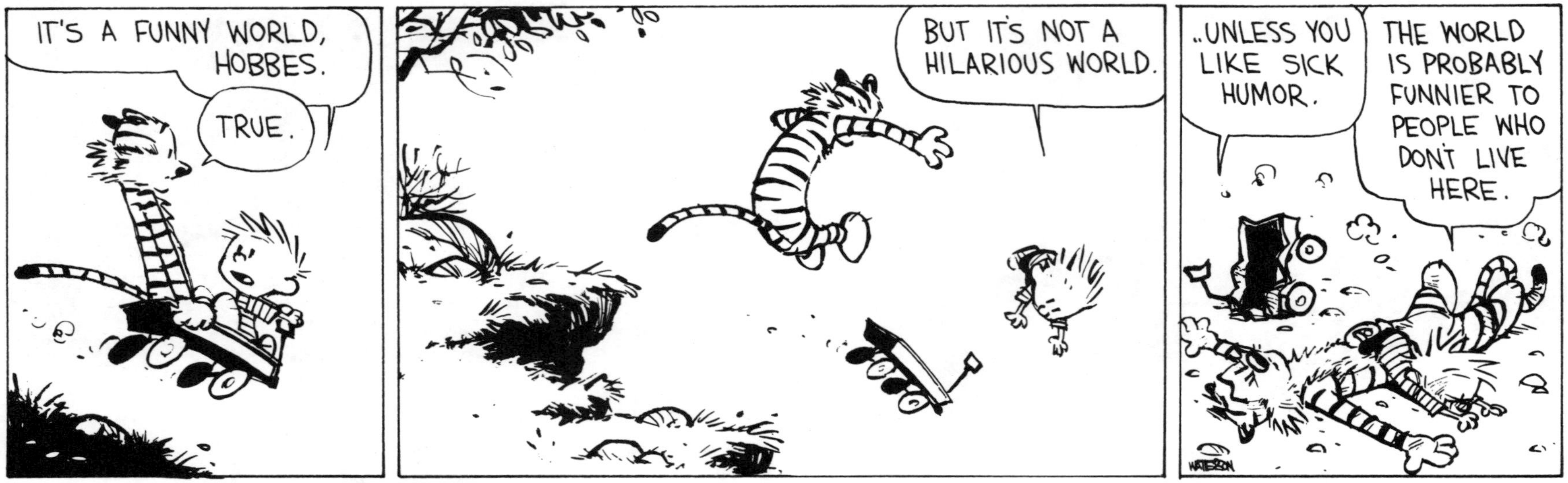
IT'S A FUNNY WORLD, HOBBES.
TRUE.
BUT IT'S NOT A HILARIOUS WORLD.
..UNLESS YOU LIKE SICK HUMOR.
THE WORLD IS PROBABLY FUNNIER TO PEOPLE WHO DON'T LIVE HERE.

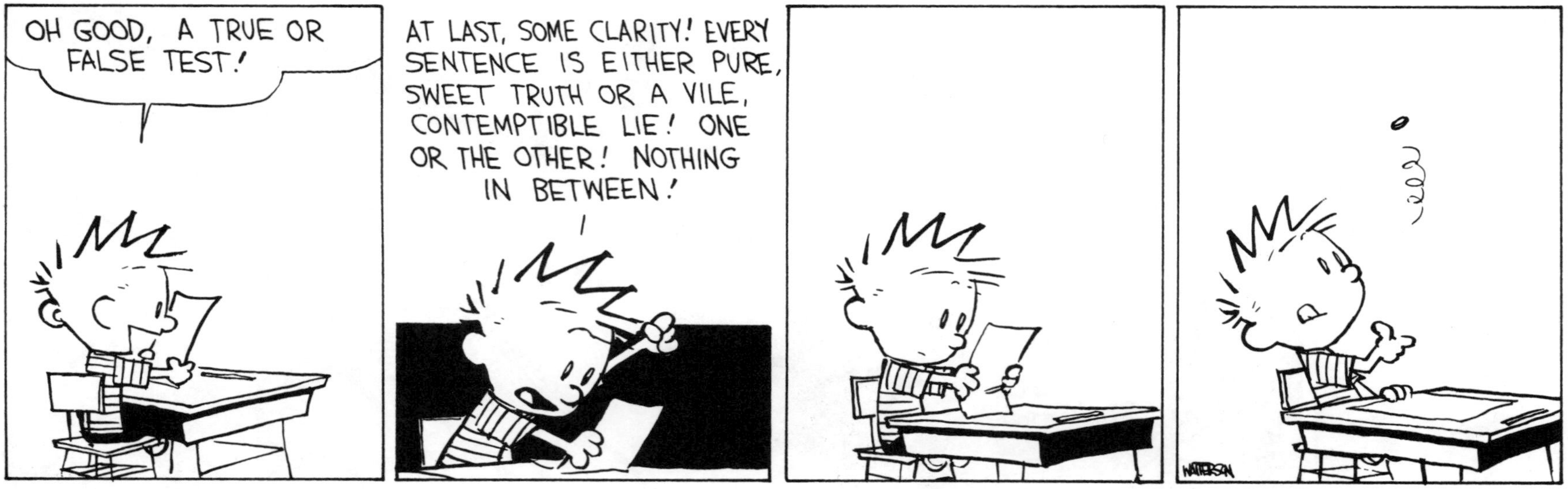
OH GOOD, A TRUE OR FALSE TEST!
AT LAST, SOME CLARITY! EVERY SENTENCE IS EITHER PURE, SWEET TRUTH OR A VILE, CONTEMPTIBLE LIE! ONE OR THE OTHER! NOTHING IN BETWEEN!

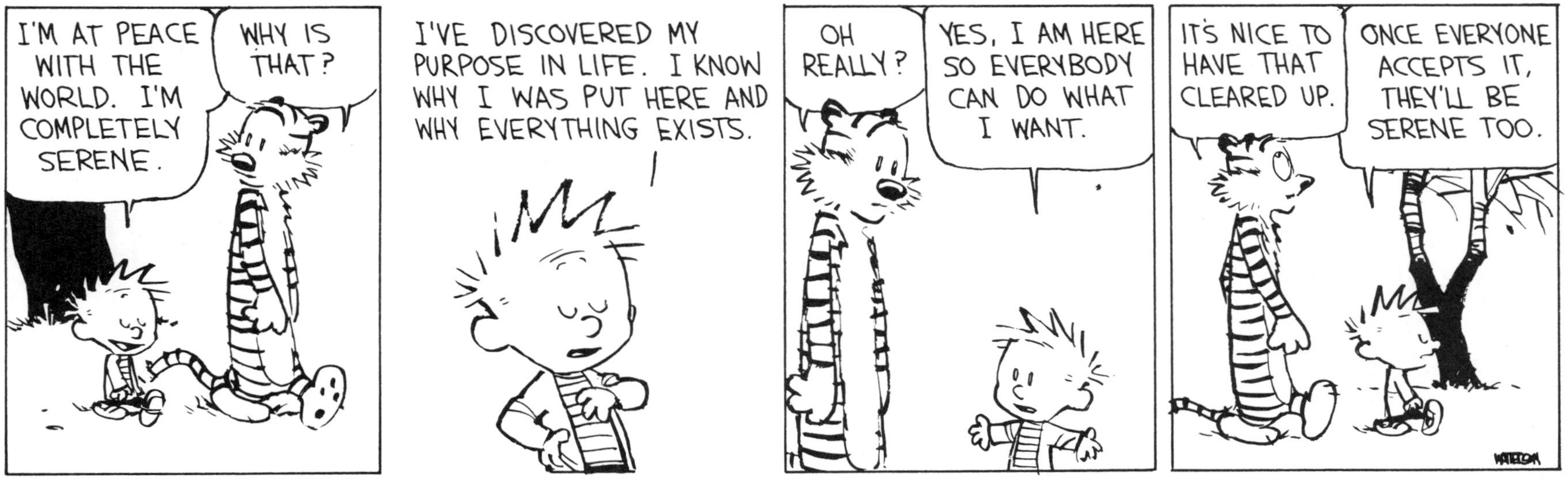
I'M AT PEACE WITH THE WORLD. I'M COMPLETELY SERENE.
WHY IS THAT?
I'VE DISCOVERED MY PURPOSE IN LIFE. I KNOW WHY I WAS PUT HERE AND WHY EVERYTHING EXISTS.
OH REALLY?
YES, I AM HERE SO EVERYBODY CAN DO WHAT I WANT.
IT'S NICE TO HAVE THAT CLEARED UP.
ONCE EVERYONE ACCEPTS IT, THEY'LL BE SERENE TOO.

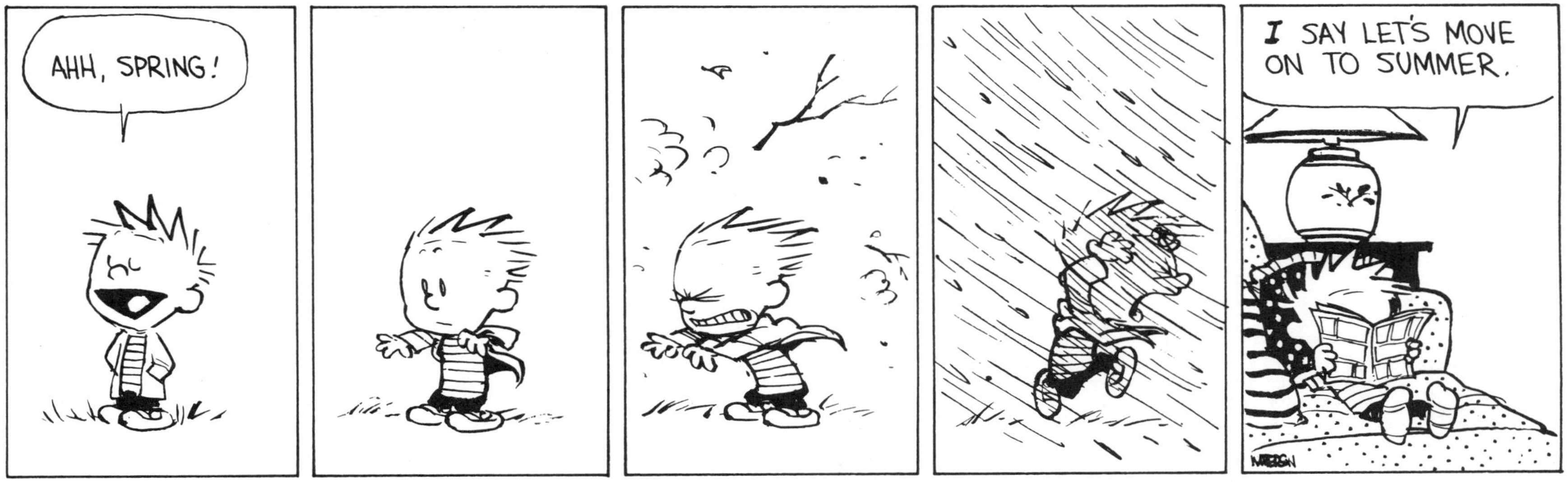
AHH, SPRING!
I SAY LET'S MOVE ON TO SUMMER.

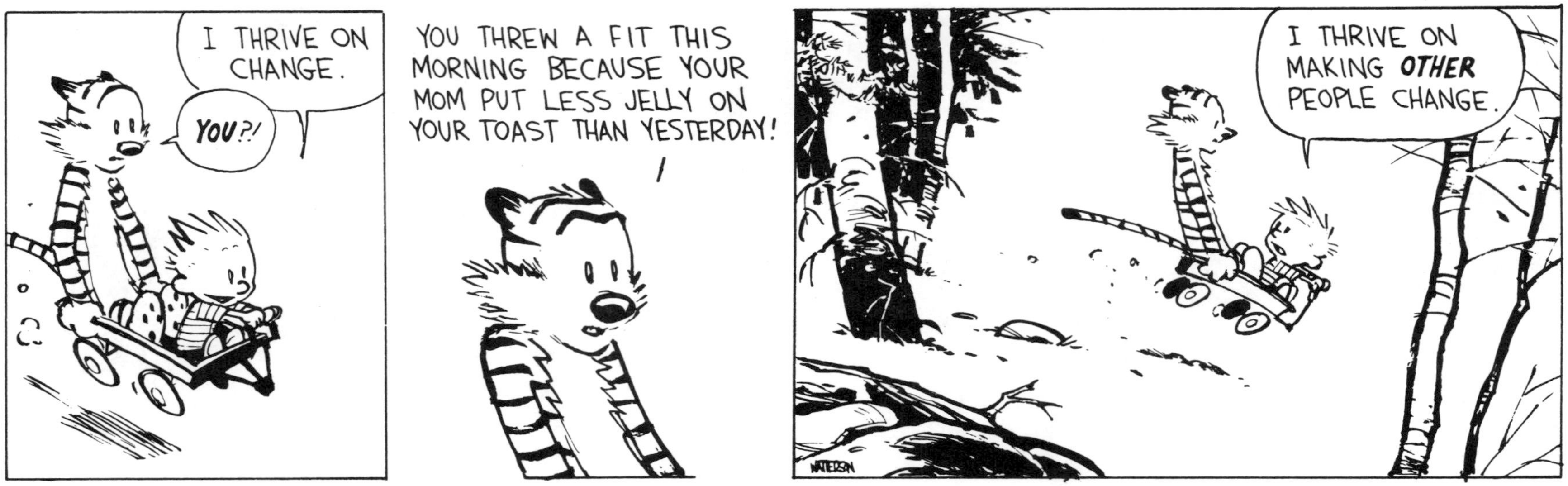
I THRIVE ON CHANGE.
YOU?!
YOU THREW A FIT THIS MORNING BECAUSE YOUR MOM PUT LESS JELLY ON YOUR TOAST THAN YESTERDAY!
I THRIVE ON MAKING OTHER PEOPLE CHANGE.

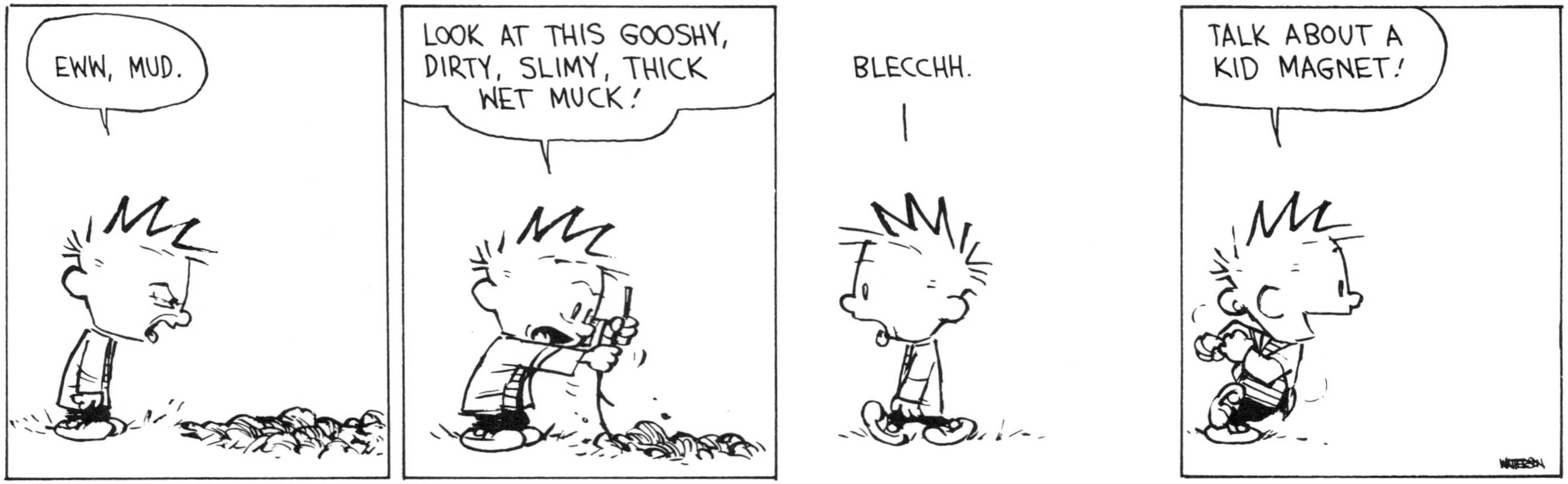
EWW, MUD.
LOOK AT THIS GOOSHY, DIRTY, SLIMY, THICK WET MUCK!
BLECCHH.
TALK ABOUT A KID MAGNET!

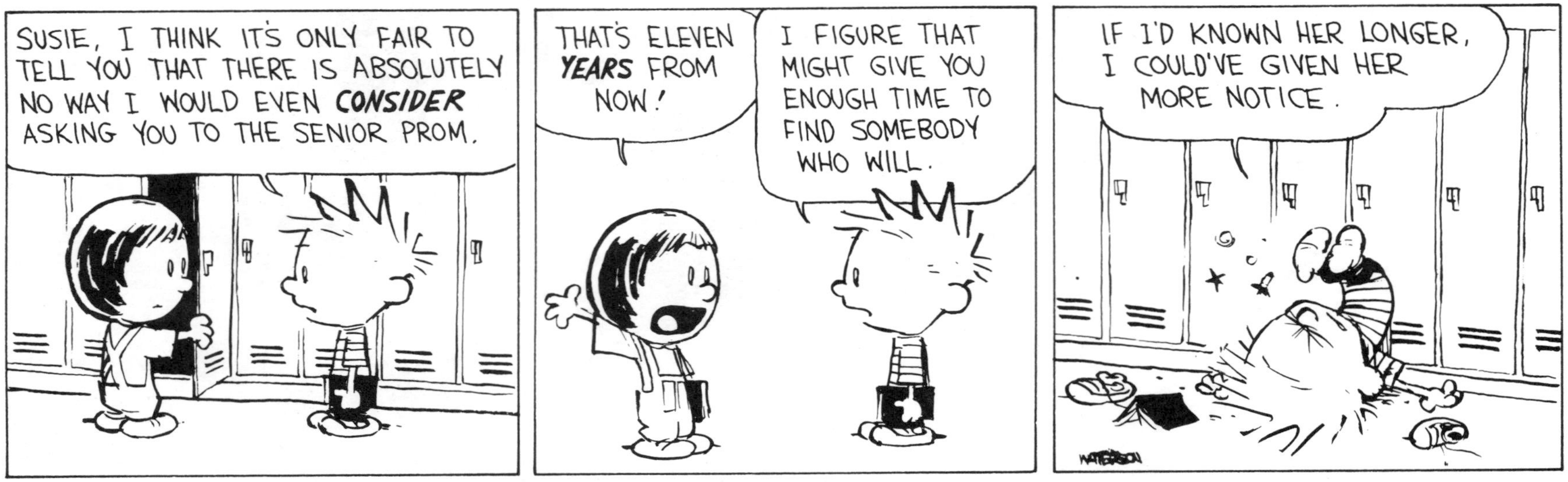
SUSIE, I THINK IT'S ONLY FAIR TO TELL YOU THAT THERE IS ABSOLUTELY NO WAY I WOULD EVEN **CONSIDER** ASKING YOU TO THE SENIOR PROM.
THAT'S ELEVEN **YEARS** FROM NOW!
I FIGURE THAT MIGHT GIVE YOU ENOUGH TIME TO FIND SOMEBODY WHO WILL.
IF I'D KNOWN HER LONGER, I COULD'VE GIVEN HER MORE NOTICE.
WATTERSON

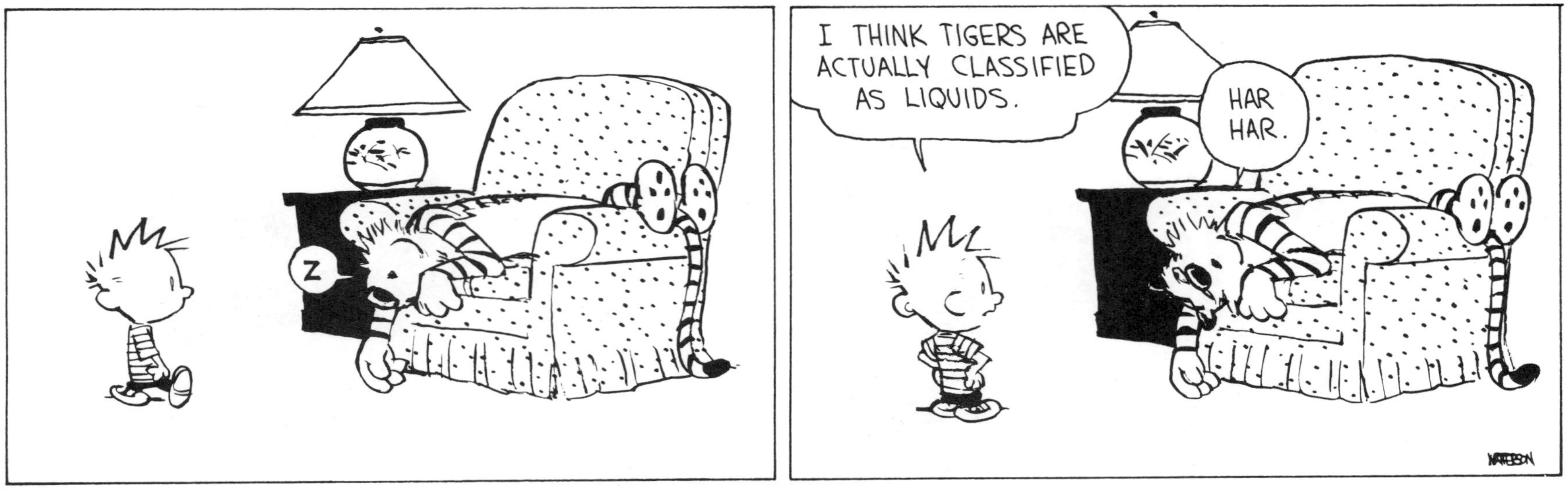
Z
I THINK TIGERS ARE ACTUALLY CLASSIFIED AS LIQUIDS.
HAR HAR.
WATTERSON

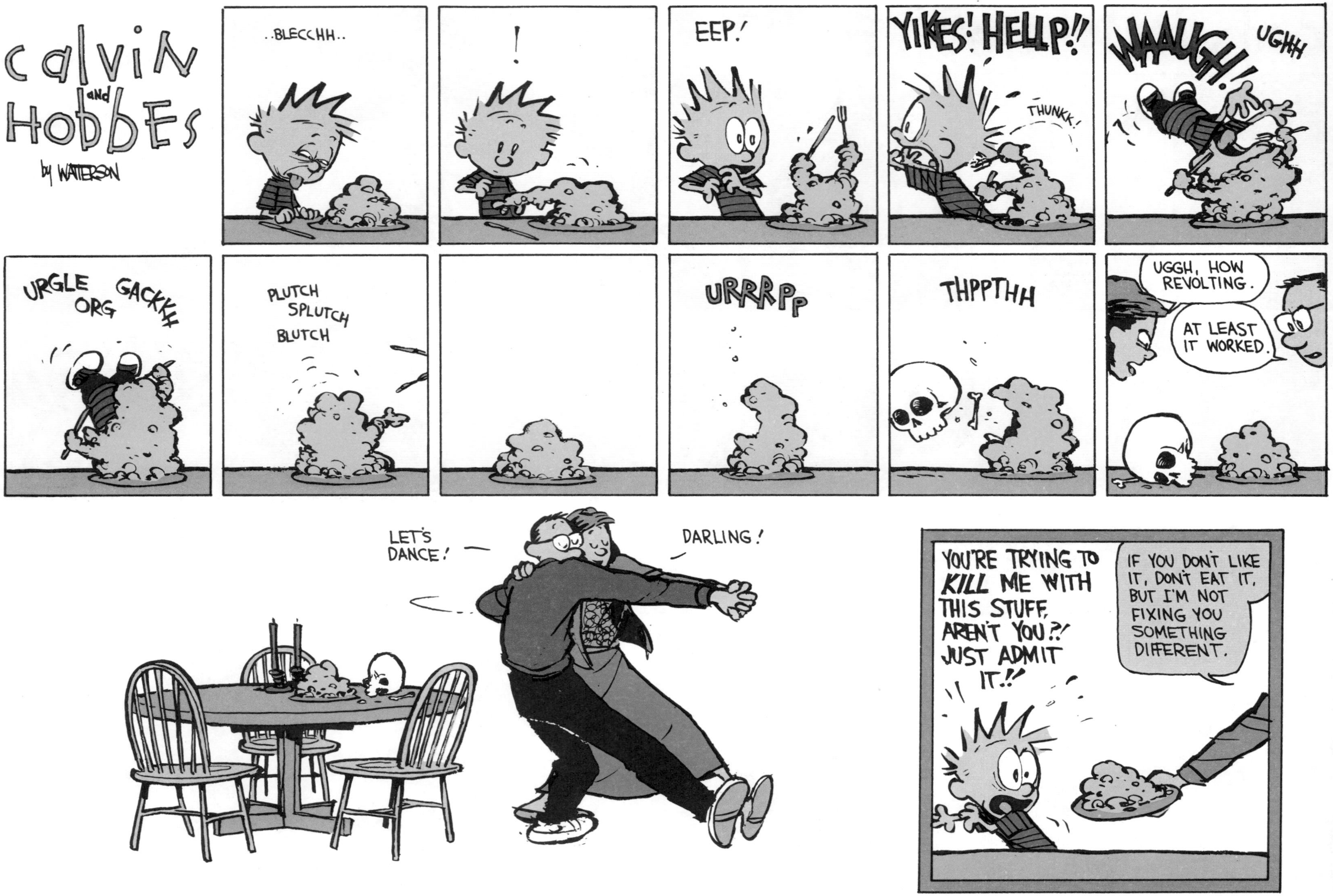

Calvin and Hobbes
by WATTERSON
..BLECCHH..
!
EEP!
YIKES! HELLP!!
THUNKK!
WAAUGH!!
UGHH
URGLE
ORG
GACKKH
PLUTCH
SPLUTCH
BLUTCH
URRRPP
THPPTHH
UGGH, HOW REVOLTING.
AT LEAST IT WORKED.
LET'S DANCE!
DARLING!
YOU'RE TRYING TO *KILL* ME WITH THIS STUFF, AREN'T YOU?! JUST ADMIT IT!!
IF YOU DON'T LIKE IT, DON'T EAT IT, BUT I'M NOT FIXING YOU SOMETHING DIFFERENT.

105

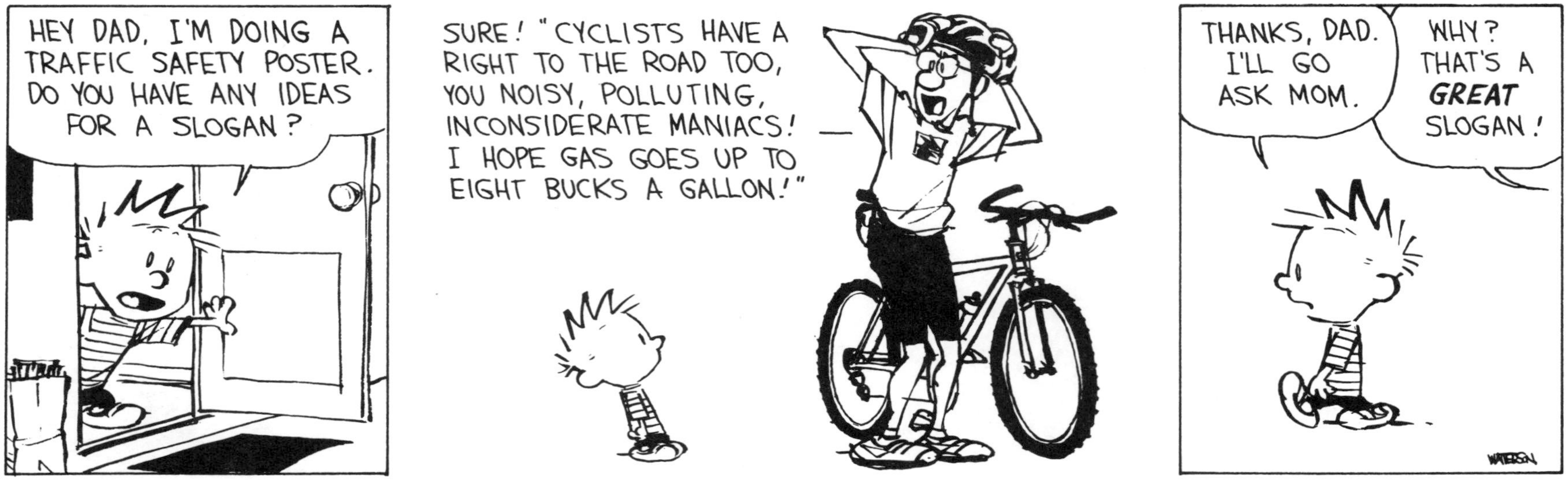
HEY DAD, I'M DOING A TRAFFIC SAFETY POSTER. DO YOU HAVE ANY IDEAS FOR A SLOGAN?
SURE! "CYCLISTS HAVE A RIGHT TO THE ROAD TOO, YOU NOISY, POLLUTING, INCONSIDERATE MANIACS! I HOPE GAS GOES UP TO EIGHT BUCKS A GALLON!"
THANKS, DAD. I'LL GO ASK MOM.
WHY? THAT'S A **GREAT** SLOGAN!

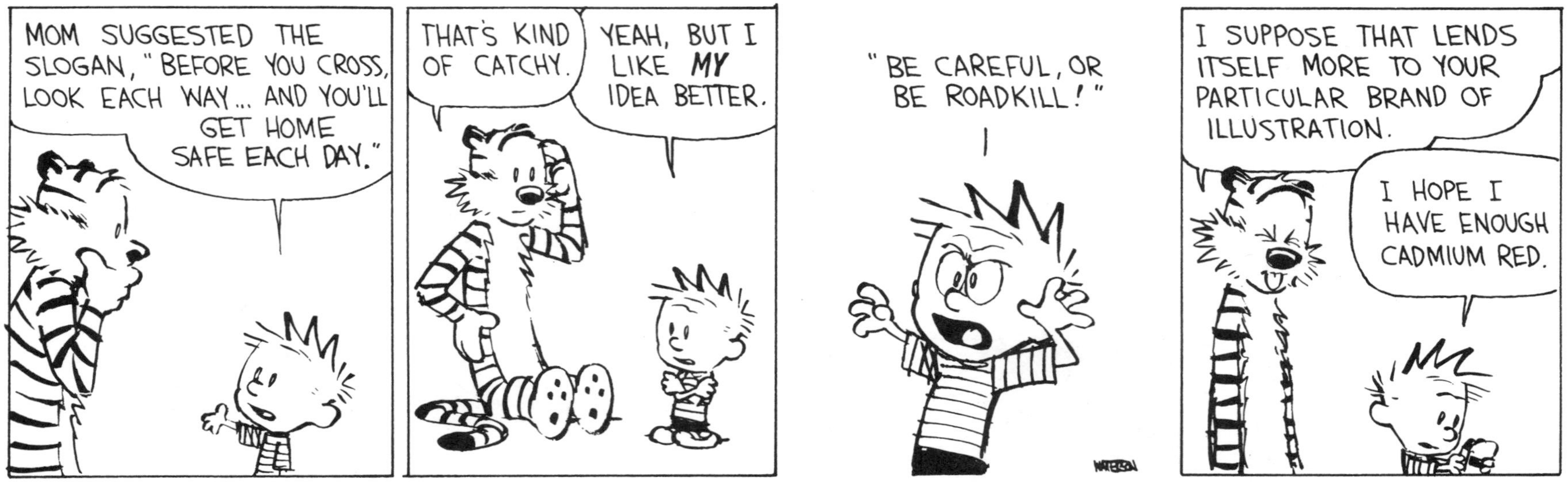
MOM SUGGESTED THE SLOGAN, "BEFORE YOU CROSS, LOOK EACH WAY... AND YOU'LL GET HOME SAFE EACH DAY."
THAT'S KIND OF CATCHY.
YEAH, BUT I LIKE **MY** IDEA BETTER.
"BE CAREFUL, OR BE ROADKILL!"
I SUPPOSE THAT LENDS ITSELF MORE TO YOUR PARTICULAR BRAND OF ILLUSTRATION.
I HOPE I HAVE ENOUGH CADMIUM RED.

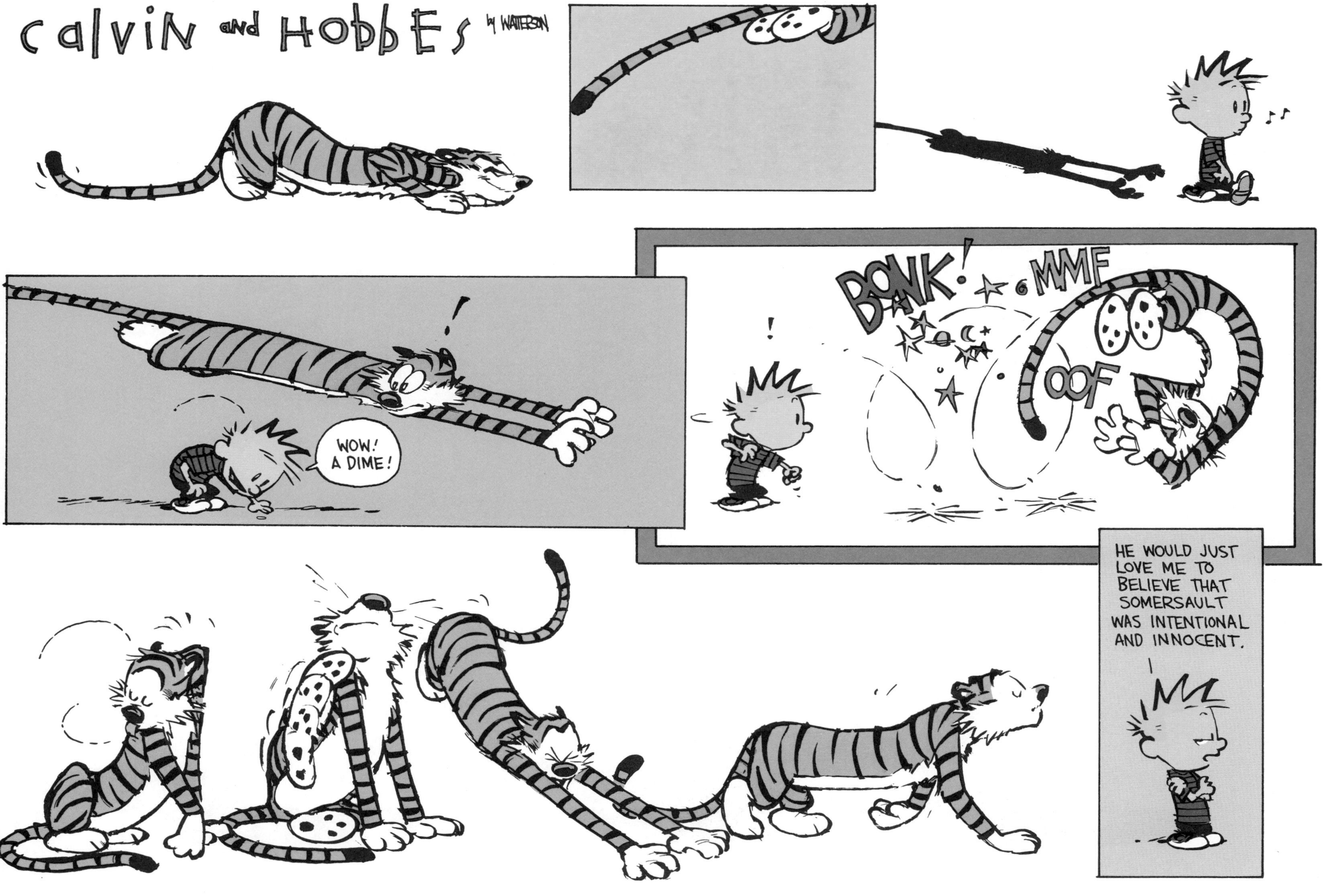
Calvin and Hobbes
by WATTERSON
WOW! A DIME!
BONK!
MMF
OOF
HE WOULD JUST LOVE ME TO BELIEVE THAT SOMERSAULT WAS INTENTIONAL AND INNOCENT.

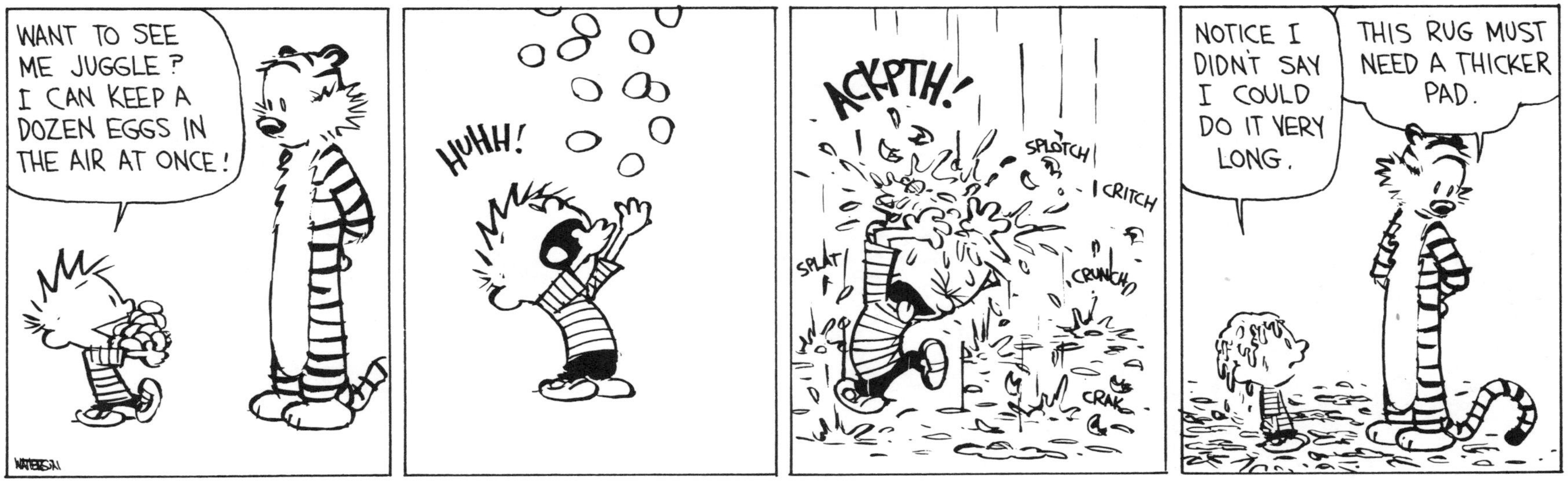
WANT TO SEE ME JUGGLE? I CAN KEEP A DOZEN EGGS IN THE AIR AT ONCE!
HUHH!
ACKPTH!
SPLOTCH
CRITCH
SPLAT
CRUNCH
CRAK
NOTICE I DIDN'T SAY I COULD DO IT VERY LONG.
THIS RUG MUST NEED A THICKER PAD.

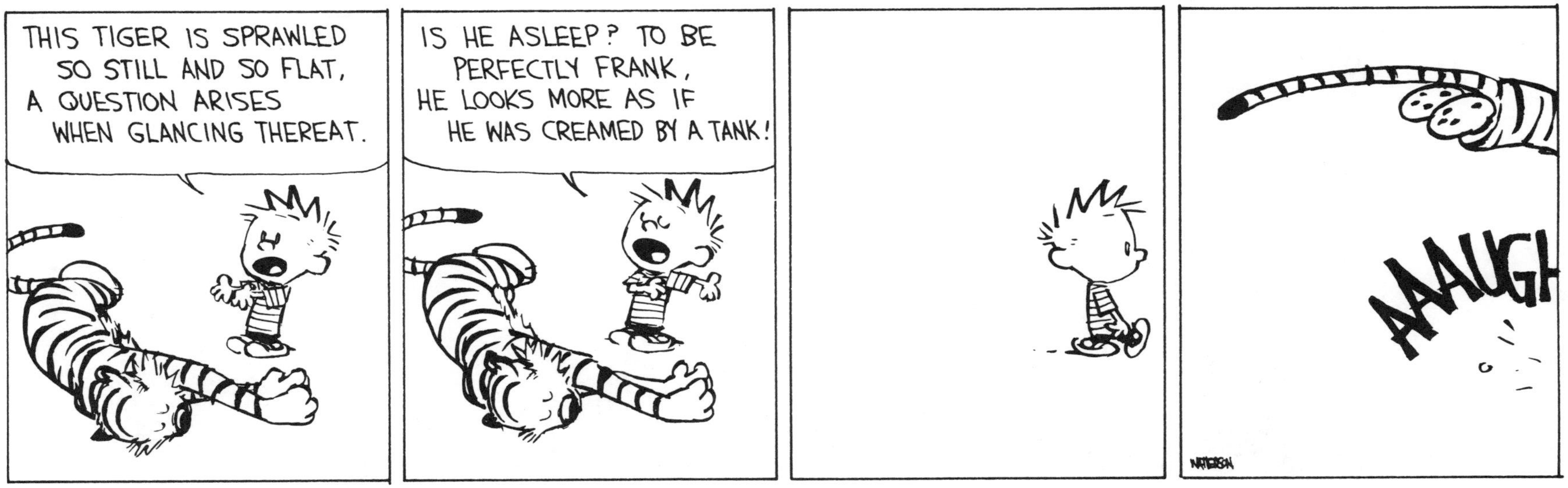
THIS TIGER IS SPRAWLED SO STILL AND SO FLAT, A QUESTION ARISES WHEN GLANCING THEREAT.
IS HE ASLEEP? TO BE PERFECTLY FRANK, HE LOOKS MORE AS IF HE WAS CREAMED BY A TANK!
AAAUGH

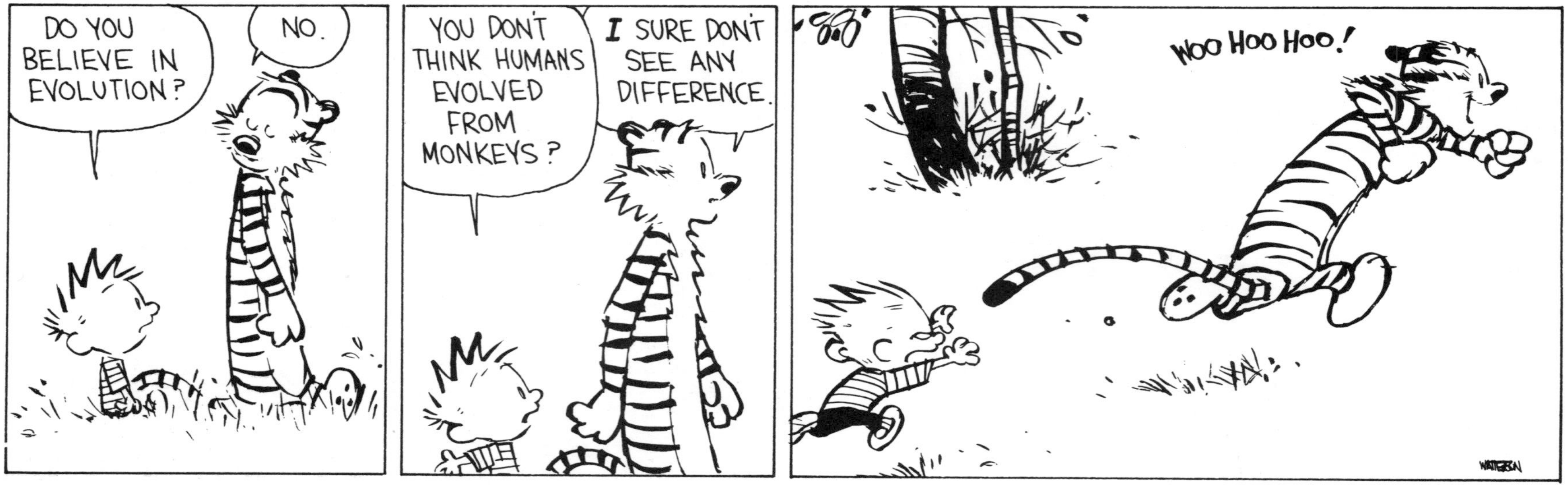
DO YOU BELIEVE IN EVOLUTION?
NO.
YOU DON'T THINK HUMANS EVOLVED FROM MONKEYS?
I SURE DON'T SEE ANY DIFFERENCE.
WOO HOO HOO!
WATTERSON

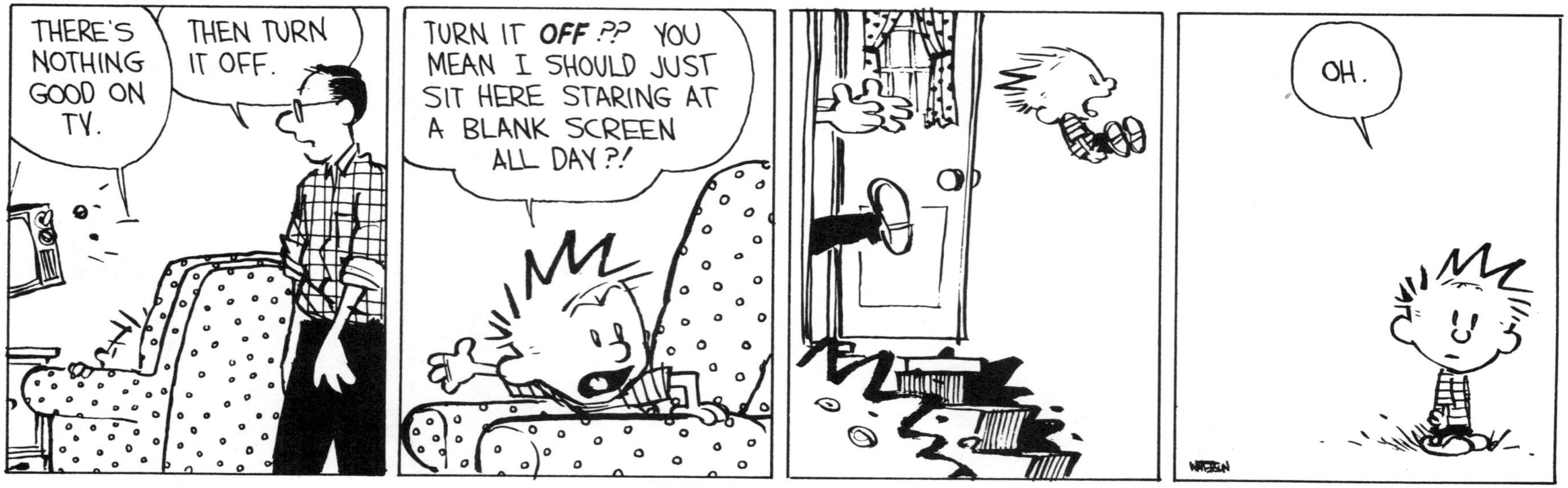
THERE'S NOTHING GOOD ON TV.
THEN TURN IT OFF.
TURN IT **OFF**?? YOU MEAN I SHOULD JUST SIT HERE STARING AT A BLANK SCREEN ALL DAY?!
OH.
WATTERSON

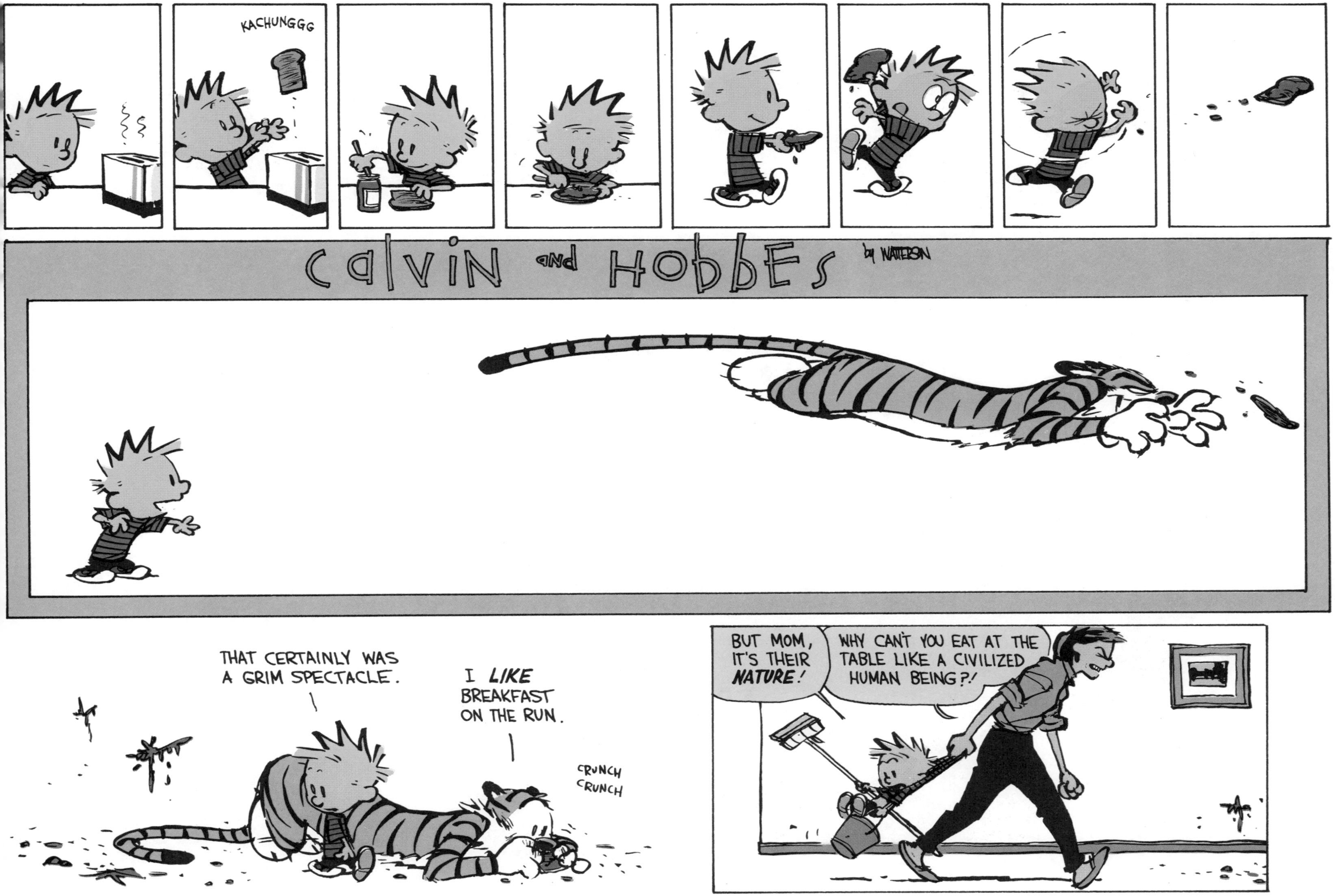
KACHUNGGG
Calvin and HobbEs
by WATTERSON
THAT CERTAINLY WAS A GRIM SPECTACLE.
I LIKE BREAKFAST ON THE RUN.
CRUNCH CRUNCH
WHY CAN'T YOU EAT AT THE TABLE LIKE A CIVILIZED HUMAN BEING?!
BUT MOM, IT'S THEIR NATURE!

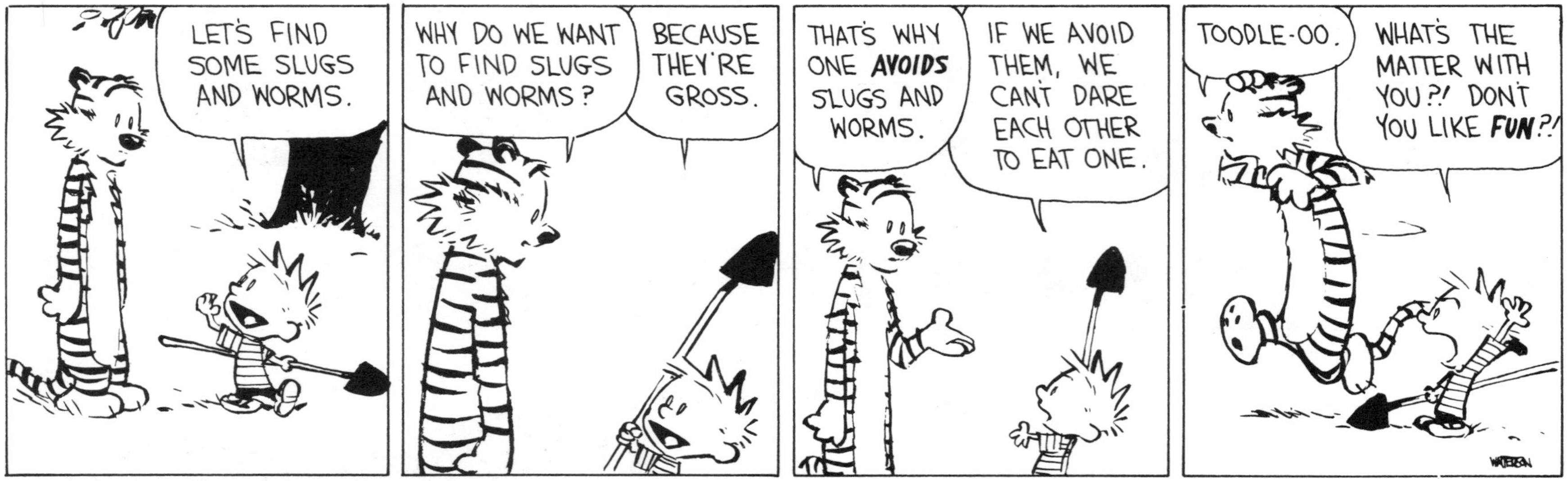
LET'S FIND SOME SLUGS AND WORMS.
WHY DO WE WANT TO FIND SLUGS AND WORMS?
BECAUSE THEY'RE GROSS.
THAT'S WHY ONE **AVOIDS** SLUGS AND WORMS.
IF WE AVOID THEM, WE CAN'T DARE EACH OTHER TO EAT ONE.
TOODLE-OO.
WHAT'S THE MATTER WITH YOU?! DON'T YOU LIKE **FUN**?!

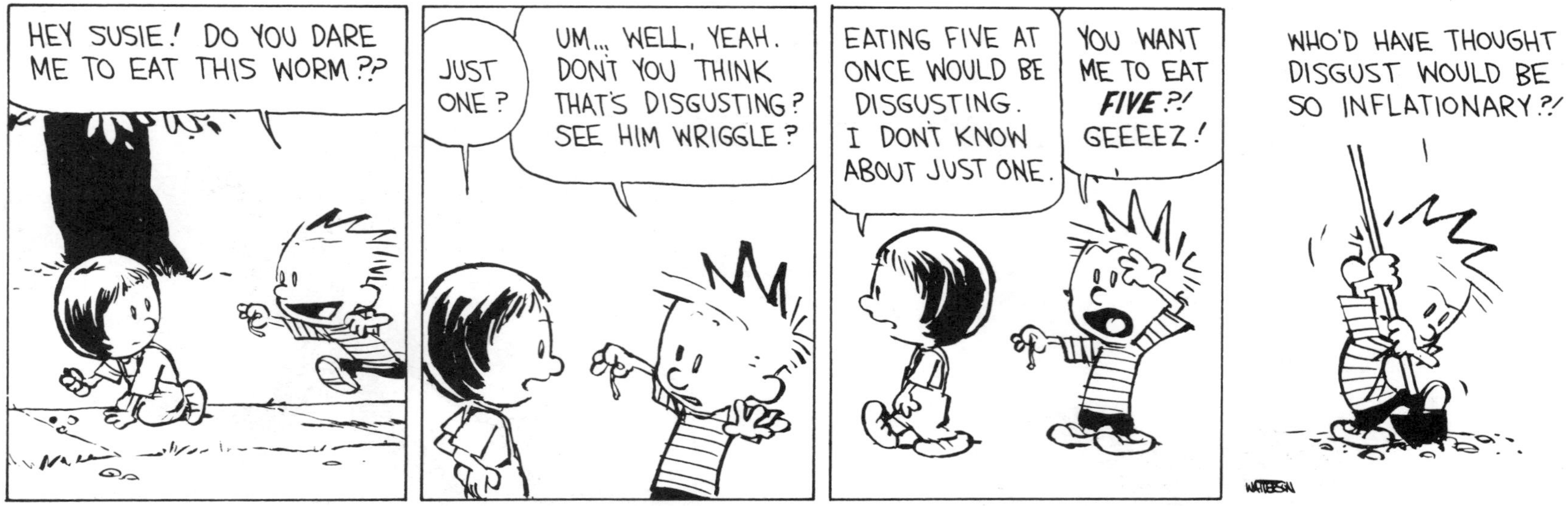
HEY SUSIE! DO YOU DARE ME TO EAT THIS WORM??
JUST ONE?
UM... WELL, YEAH. DON'T YOU THINK THAT'S DISGUSTING? SEE HIM WRIGGLE?
EATING FIVE AT ONCE WOULD BE DISGUSTING. I DON'T KNOW ABOUT JUST ONE.
YOU WANT ME TO EAT **FIVE**?! GEEEEZ!
WHO'D HAVE THOUGHT DISGUST WOULD BE SO INFLATIONARY?!

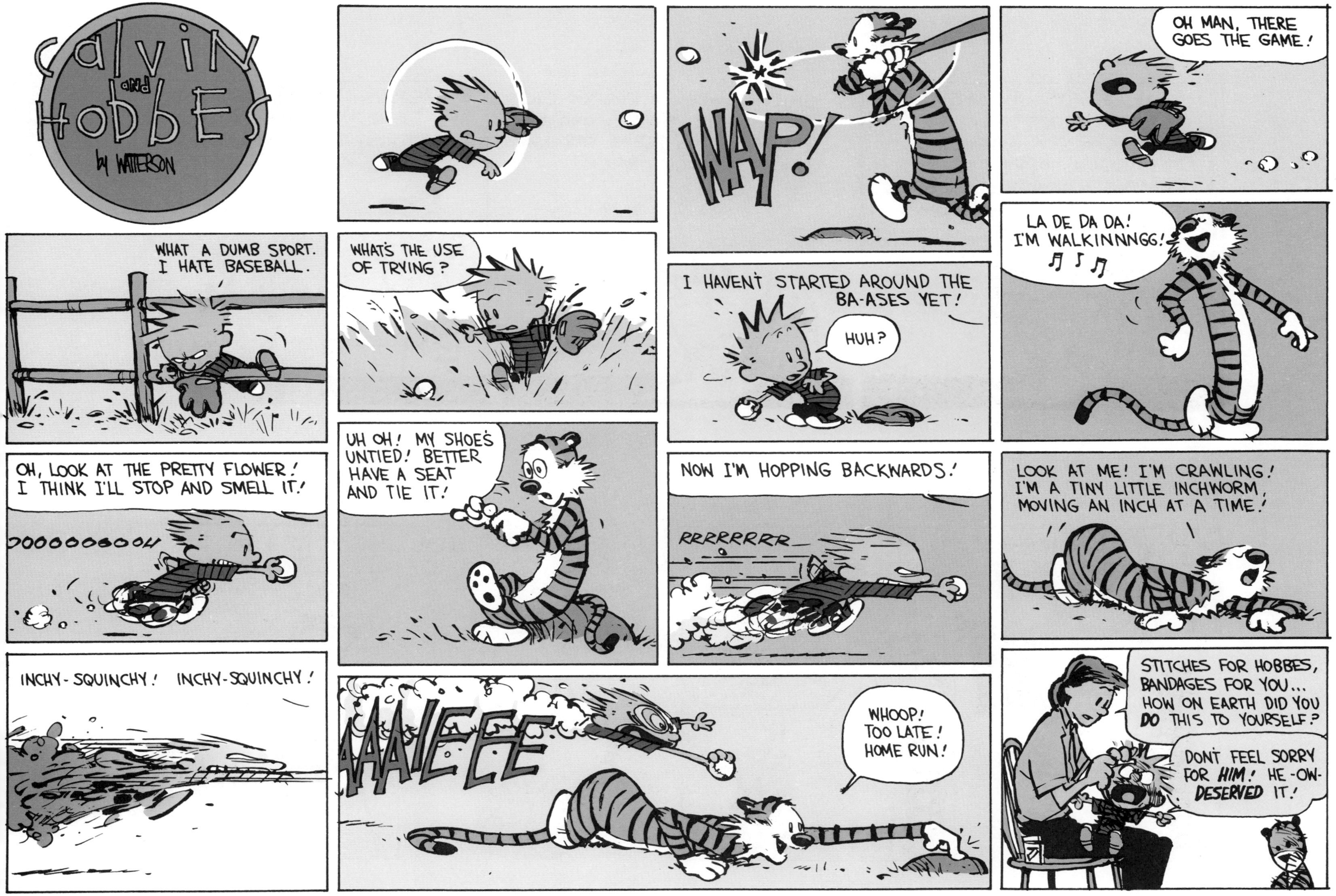

Calvin and Hobbes
by WATTERSON
WAP!
OH MAN, THERE GOES THE GAME!
WHAT A DUMB SPORT. I HATE BASEBALL.
WHAT'S THE USE OF TRYING?
I HAVEN'T STARTED AROUND THE BA-ASES YET!
HUH?
LA DE DA DA! I'M WALKINNNGG!
OH, LOOK AT THE PRETTY FLOWER! I THINK I'LL STOP AND SMELL IT!
UH OH! MY SHOE'S UNTIED! BETTER HAVE A SEAT AND TIE IT!
NOW I'M HOPPING BACKWARDS!
RRRRRRRR
LOOK AT ME! I'M CRAWLING! I'M A TINY LITTLE INCHWORM, MOVING AN INCH AT A TIME!
INCHY-SQUINCHY! INCHY-SQUINCHY!
AAAIEEE
WHOOP! TOO LATE! HOME RUN!
STITCHES FOR HOBBES, BANDAGES FOR YOU... HOW ON EARTH DID YOU DO THIS TO YOURSELF?
DON'T FEEL SORRY FOR HIM! HE-OW-DESERVED IT!

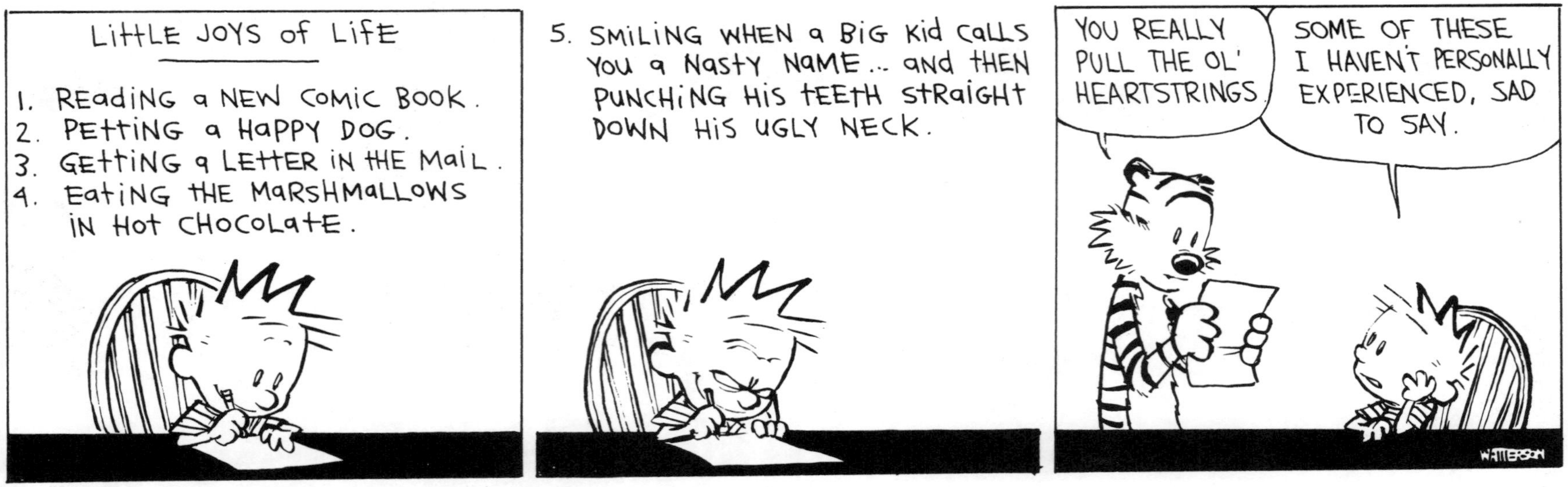
LITTLE JOYS OF LIFE
1. READING A NEW COMIC BOOK.
2. PETTING A HAPPY DOG.
3. GETTING A LETTER IN THE MAIL.
4. EATING THE MARSHMALLOWS IN HOT CHOCOLATE.
5. SMILING WHEN A BIG KID CALLS YOU A NASTY NAME... AND THEN PUNCHING HIS TEETH STRAIGHT DOWN HIS UGLY NECK.
YOU REALLY PULL THE OL' HEARTSTRINGS.
SOME OF THESE I HAVEN'T PERSONALLY EXPERIENCED, SAD TO SAY.
WATTERSON

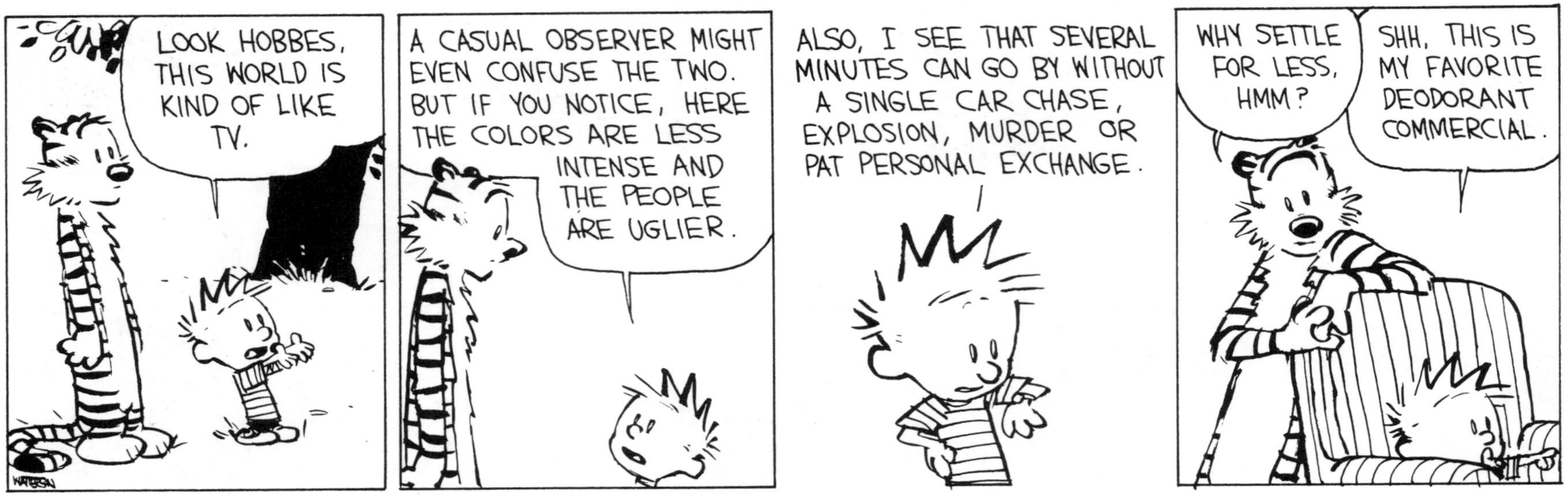
LOOK HOBBES, THIS WORLD IS KIND OF LIKE TV.
A CASUAL OBSERVER MIGHT EVEN CONFUSE THE TWO. BUT IF YOU NOTICE, HERE THE COLORS ARE LESS INTENSE AND THE PEOPLE ARE UGLIER.
ALSO, I SEE THAT SEVERAL MINUTES CAN GO BY WITHOUT A SINGLE CAR CHASE, EXPLOSION, MURDER OR PAT PERSONAL EXCHANGE.
WHY SETTLE FOR LESS, HMM?
SHH, THIS IS MY FAVORITE DEODORANT COMMERCIAL.
WATTERSON

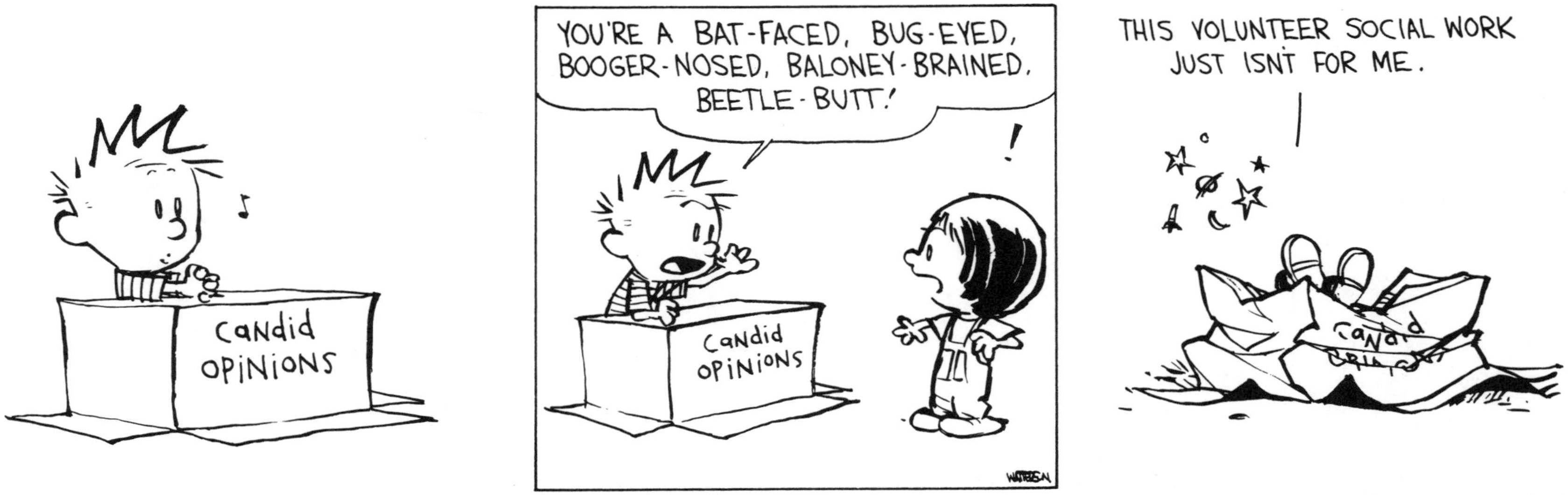
CANDID OPINIONS
YOU'RE A BAT-FACED, BUG-EYED, BOOGER-NOSED, BALONEY-BRAINED, BEETLE-BUTT!
!
THIS VOLUNTEER SOCIAL WORK JUST ISN'T FOR ME.

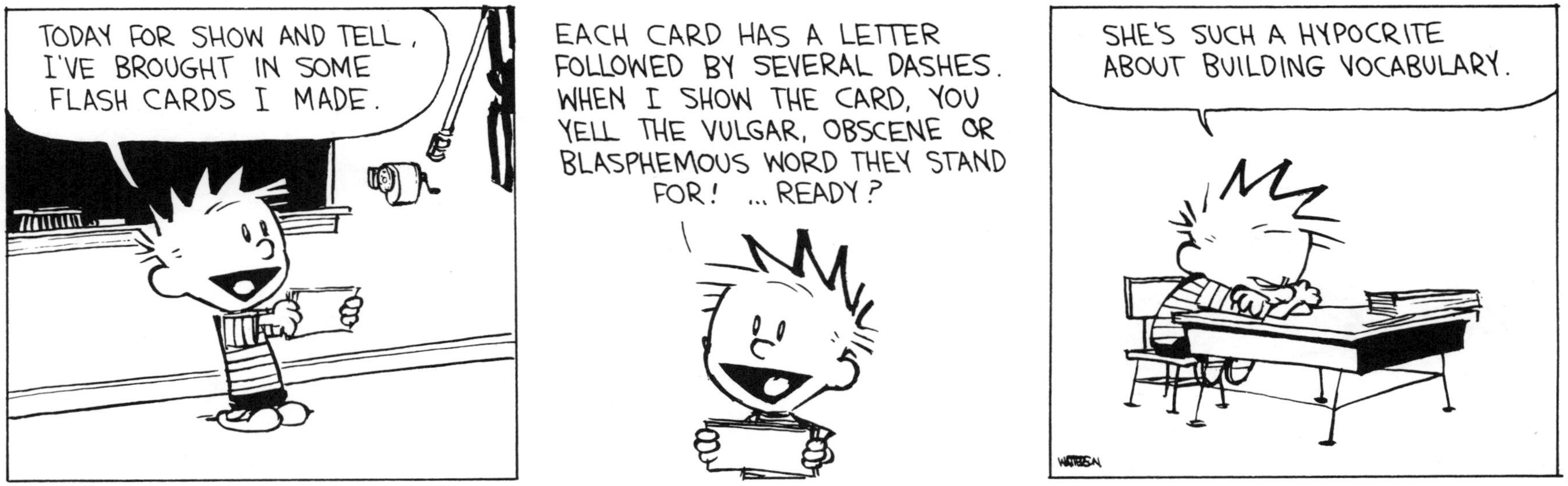
TODAY FOR SHOW AND TELL, I'VE BROUGHT IN SOME FLASH CARDS I MADE.
EACH CARD HAS A LETTER FOLLOWED BY SEVERAL DASHES. WHEN I SHOW THE CARD, YOU YELL THE VULGAR, OBSCENE OR BLASPHEMOUS WORD THEY STAND FOR! ... READY?
SHE'S SUCH A HYPOCRITE ABOUT BUILDING VOCABULARY.

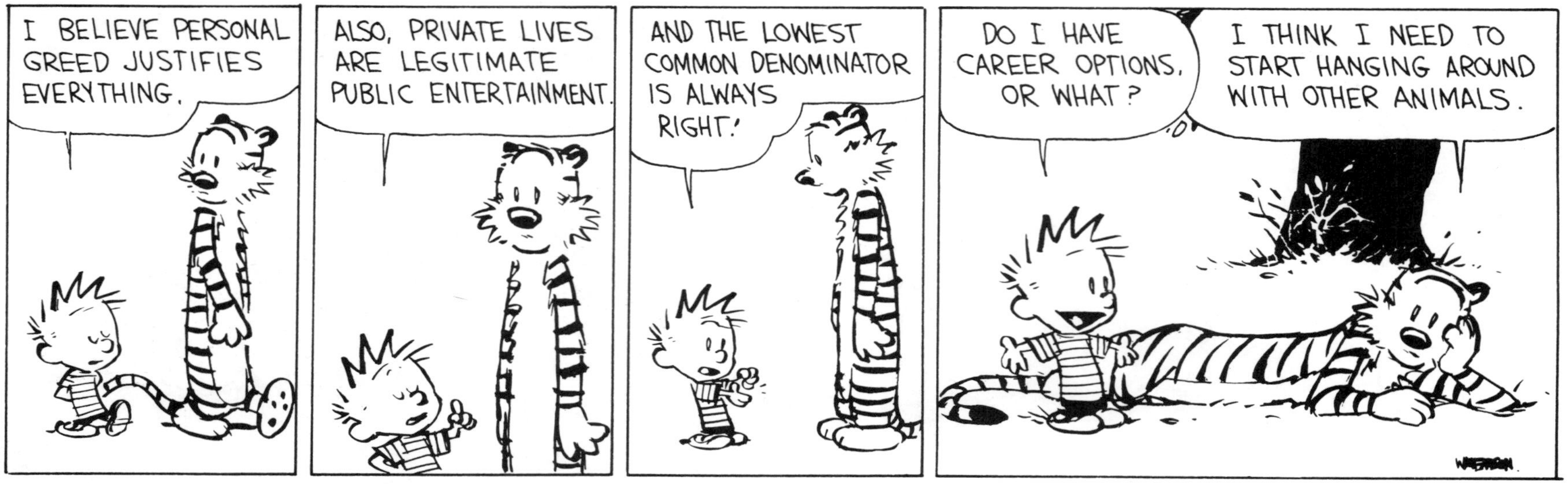
I BELIEVE PERSONAL GREED JUSTIFIES EVERYTHING.
ALSO, PRIVATE LIVES ARE LEGITIMATE PUBLIC ENTERTAINMENT.
AND THE LOWEST COMMON DENOMINATOR IS ALWAYS RIGHT!
DO I HAVE CAREER OPTIONS, OR WHAT?
I THINK I NEED TO START HANGING AROUND WITH OTHER ANIMALS.

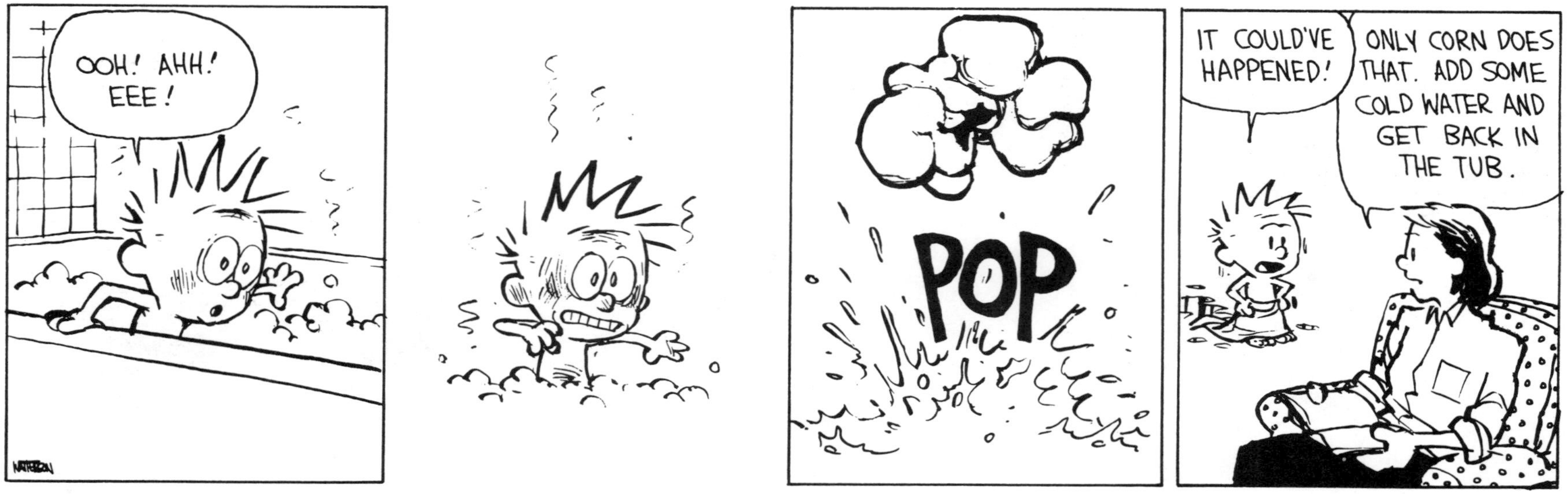
OOH! AHH! EEE!
POP
IT COULD'VE HAPPENED!
ONLY CORN DOES THAT. ADD SOME COLD WATER AND GET BACK IN THE TUB.

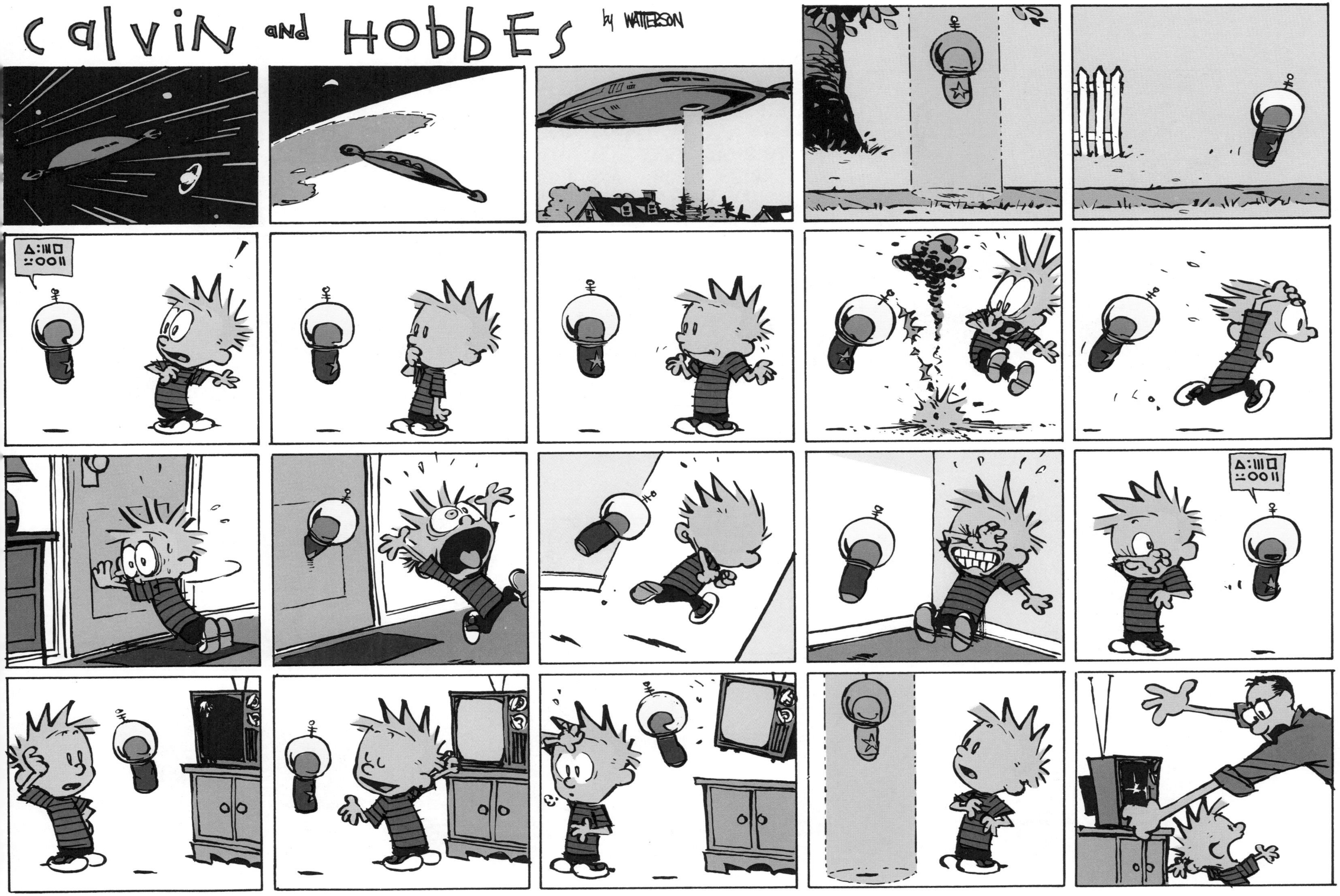
Calvin and Hobbes
by WATTERSON

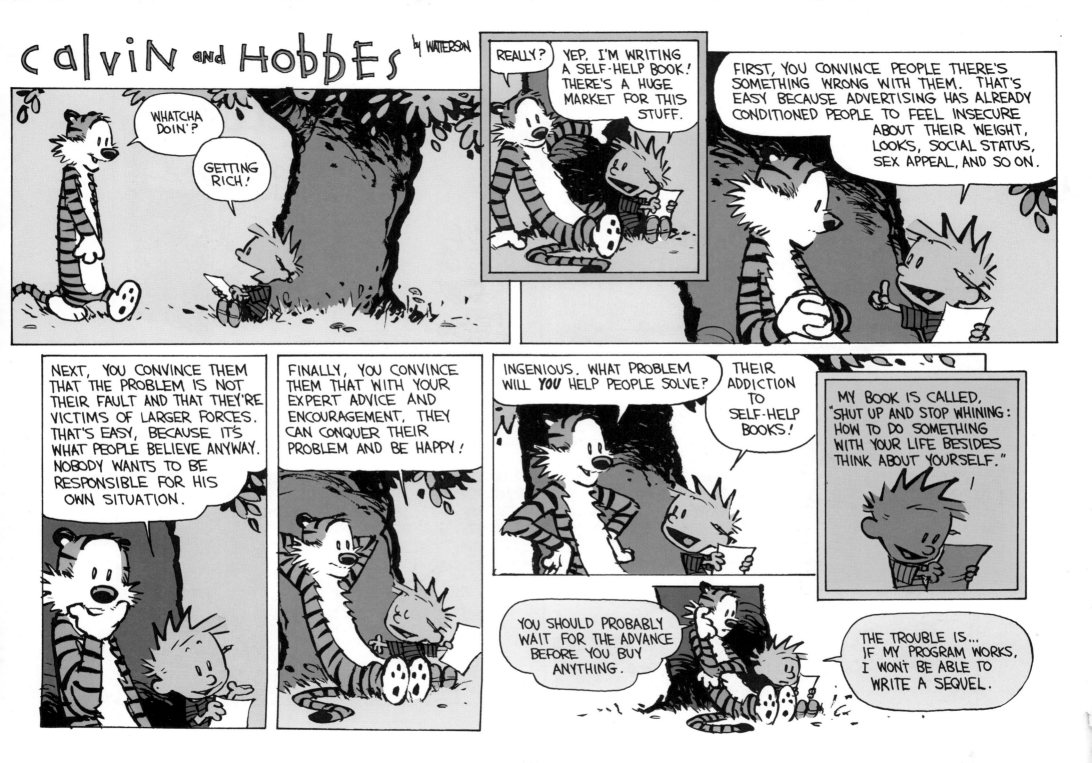

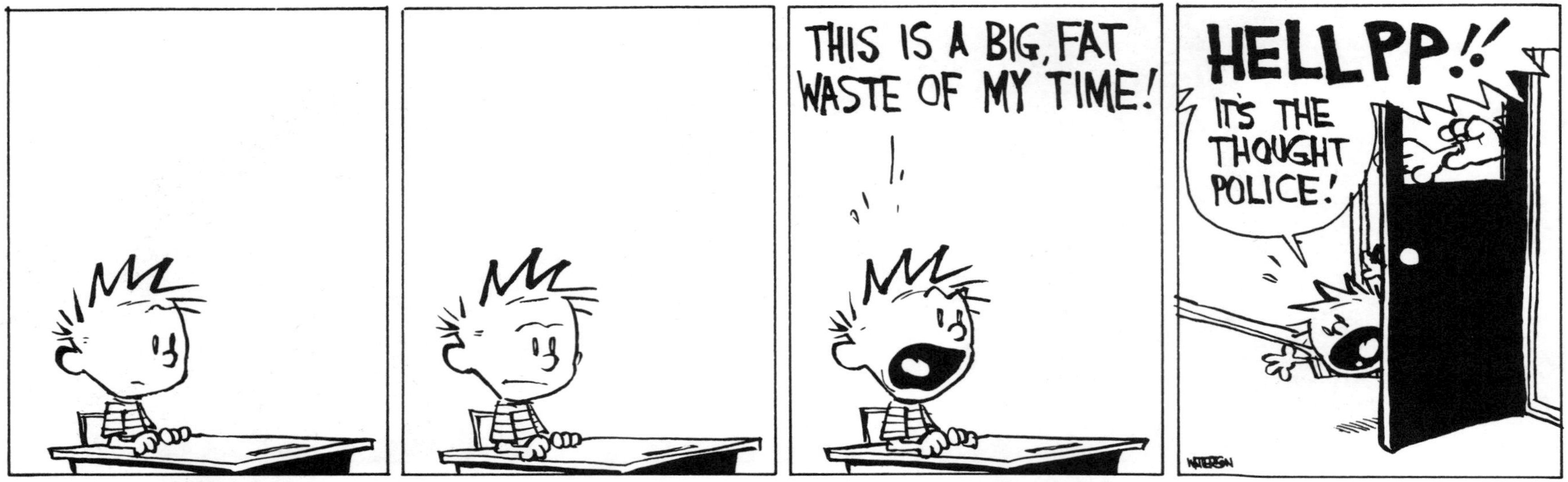
THIS IS A BIG, FAT WASTE OF MY TIME!
HELLPP!!
IT'S THE THOUGHT POLICE!

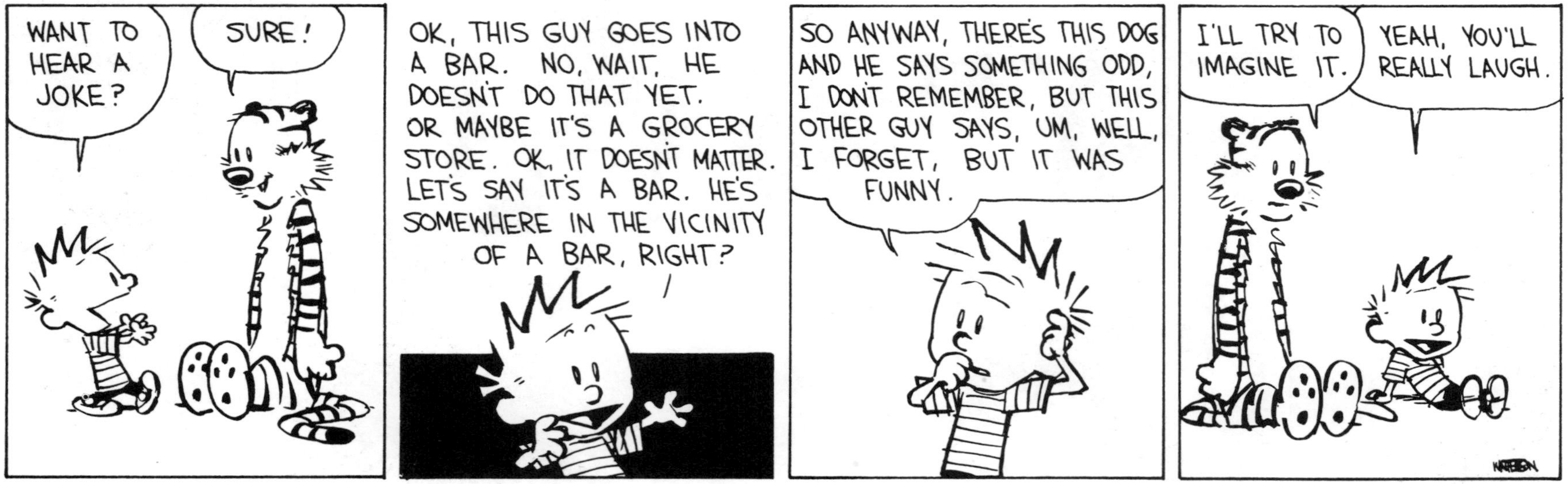
WANT TO HEAR A JOKE?
SURE!
OK, THIS GUY GOES INTO A BAR. NO, WAIT, HE DOESN'T DO THAT YET. OR MAYBE IT'S A GROCERY STORE. OK, IT DOESN'T MATTER. LET'S SAY IT'S A BAR. HE'S SOMEWHERE IN THE VICINITY OF A BAR, RIGHT?
SO ANYWAY, THERE'S THIS DOG AND HE SAYS SOMETHING ODD, I DON'T REMEMBER, BUT THIS OTHER GUY SAYS, UM, WELL, I FORGET, BUT IT WAS FUNNY.
I'LL TRY TO IMAGINE IT.
YEAH, YOU'LL REALLY LAUGH.

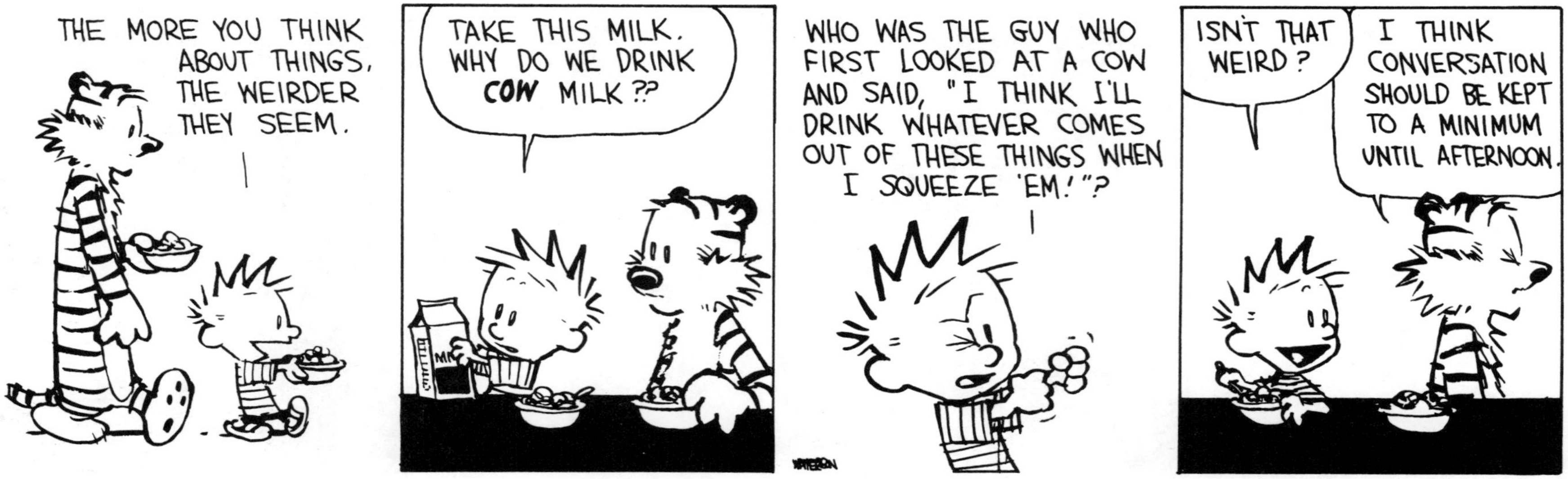
THE MORE YOU THINK ABOUT THINGS, THE WEIRDER THEY SEEM.
TAKE THIS MILK. WHY DO WE DRINK COW MILK ??
WHO WAS THE GUY WHO FIRST LOOKED AT A COW AND SAID, "I THINK I'LL DRINK WHATEVER COMES OUT OF THESE THINGS WHEN I SQUEEZE 'EM!"?
ISN'T THAT WEIRD?
I THINK CONVERSATION SHOULD BE KEPT TO A MINIMUM UNTIL AFTERNOON.

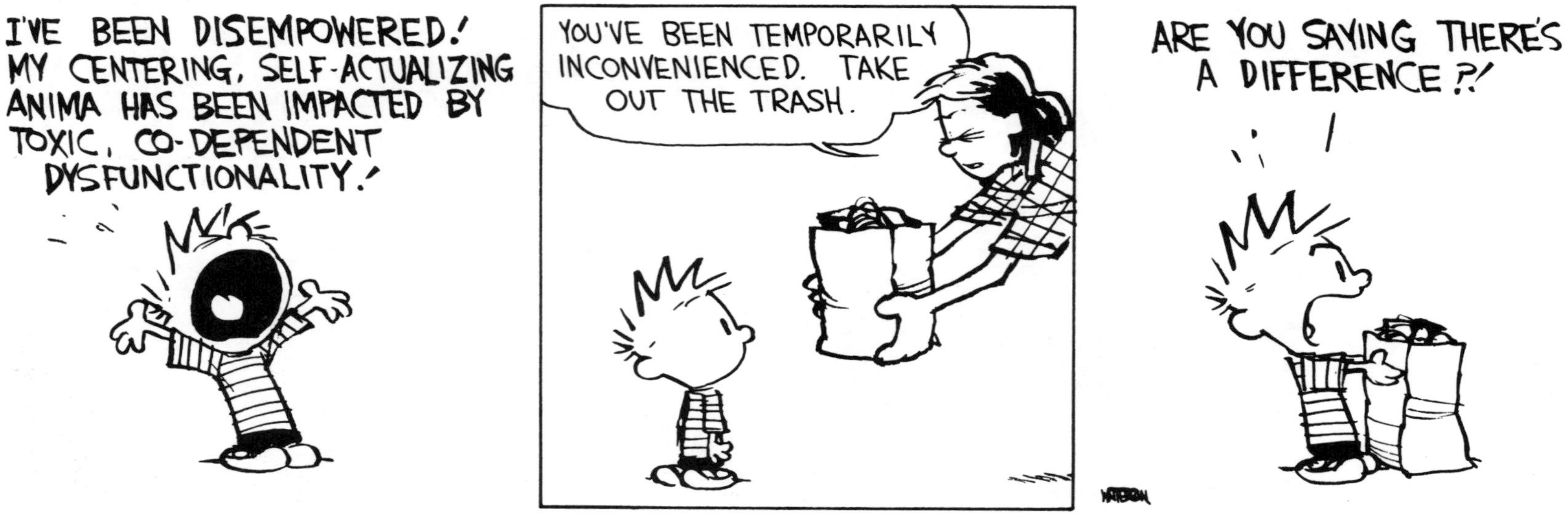
I'VE BEEN DISEMPOWERED! MY CENTERING, SELF-ACTUALIZING ANIMA HAS BEEN IMPACTED BY TOXIC, CO-DEPENDENT DYSFUNCTIONALITY!
YOU'VE BEEN TEMPORARILY INCONVENIENCED. TAKE OUT THE TRASH.
ARE YOU SAYING THERE'S A DIFFERENCE ?!

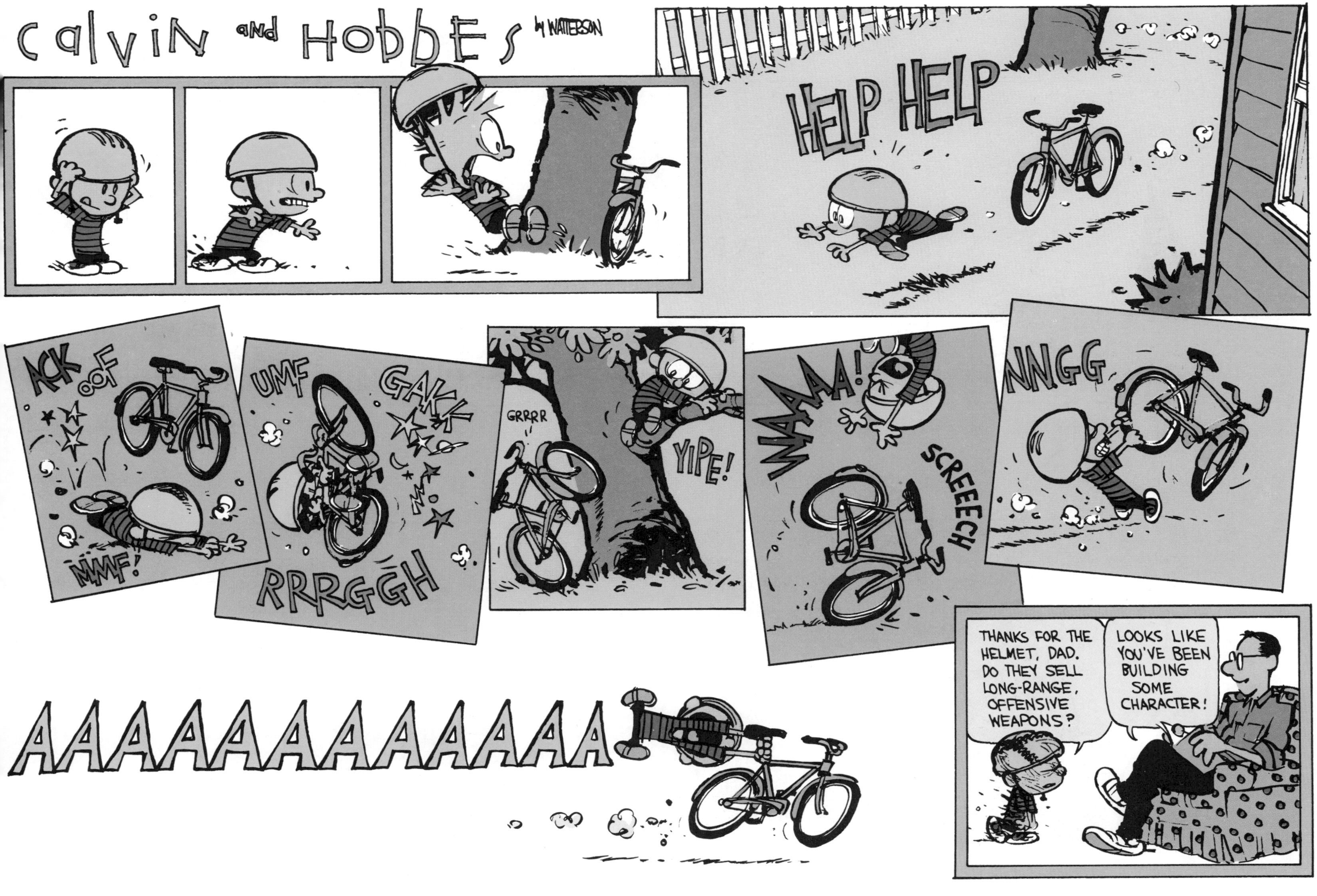
Calvin and HobbEs by WATTERSON
HELP HELP
ACK
OOF
MMF!
UMF
GAKK
RRRGGH
GRRRR
YIPE!
WAAAA!
SCREEECH
NNGG
AAAAAAAAAAAAA
THANKS FOR THE HELMET, DAD. DO THEY SELL LONG-RANGE, OFFENSIVE WEAPONS?
LOOKS LIKE YOU'VE BEEN BUILDING SOME CHARACTER!

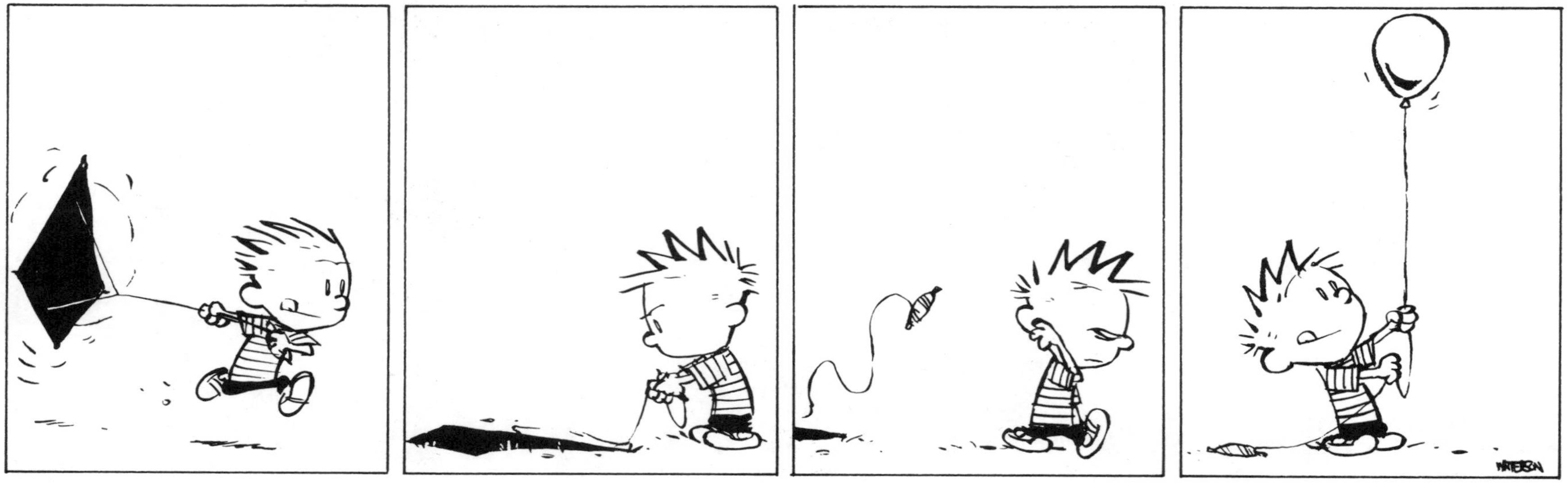
WATTERSON

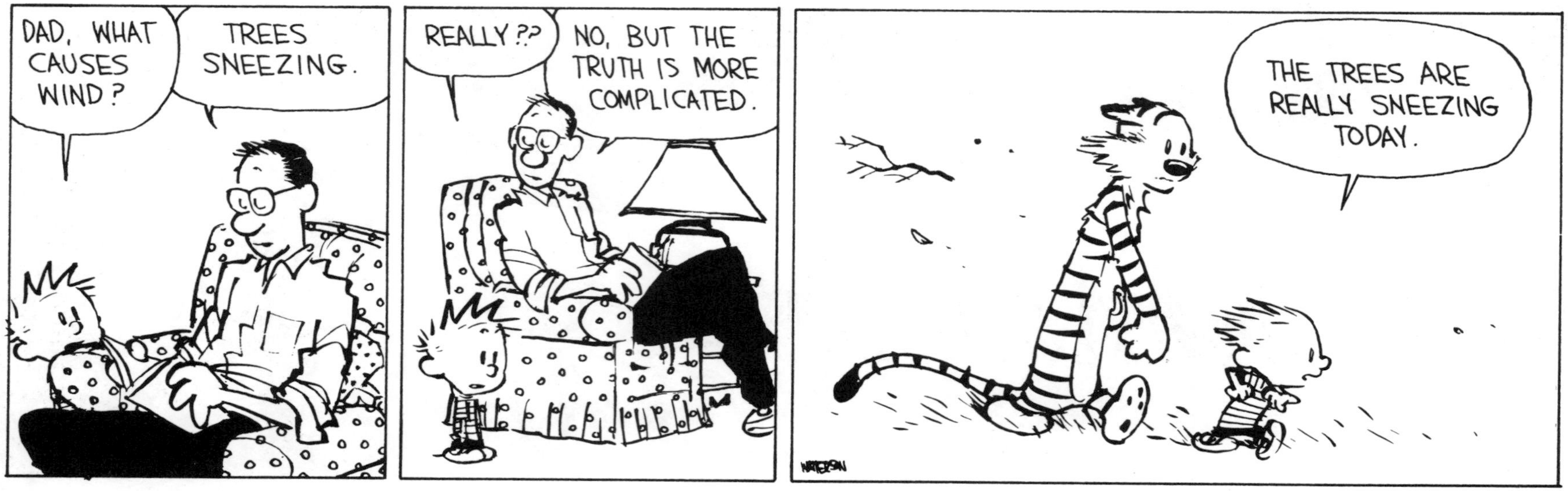
DAD, WHAT CAUSES WIND?
TREES SNEEZING.
REALLY??
NO, BUT THE TRUTH IS MORE COMPLICATED.
THE TREES ARE REALLY SNEEZING TODAY.
WATTERSON

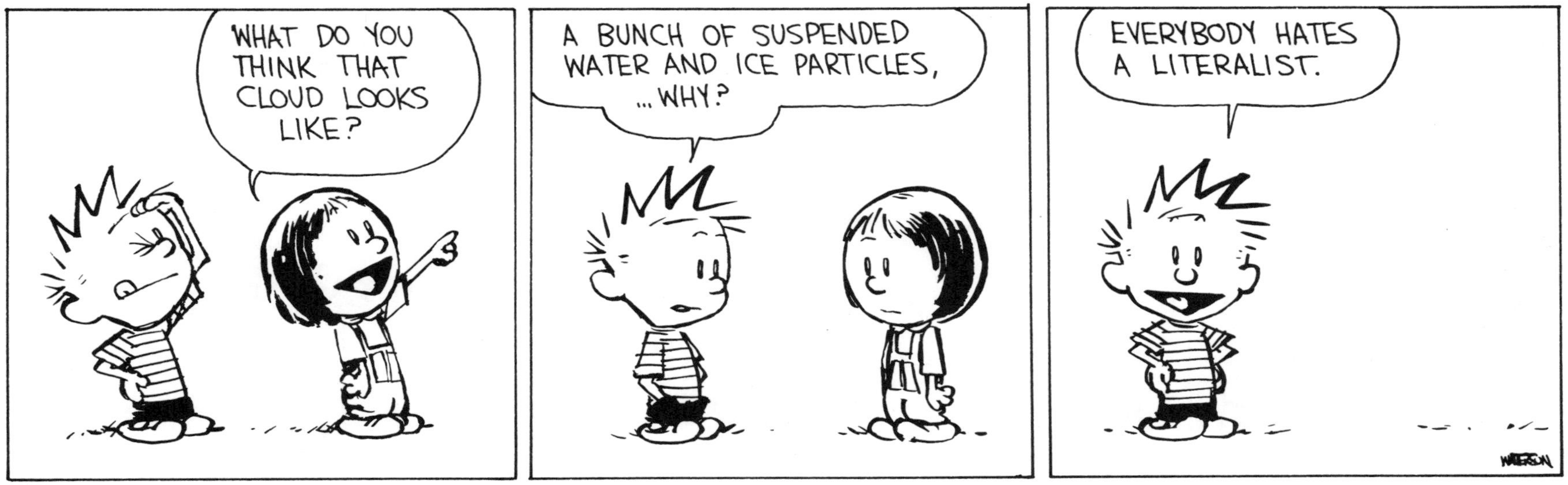
WHAT DO YOU THINK THAT CLOUD LOOKS LIKE?
A BUNCH OF SUSPENDED WATER AND ICE PARTICLES, ... WHY?
EVERYBODY HATES A LITERALIST.

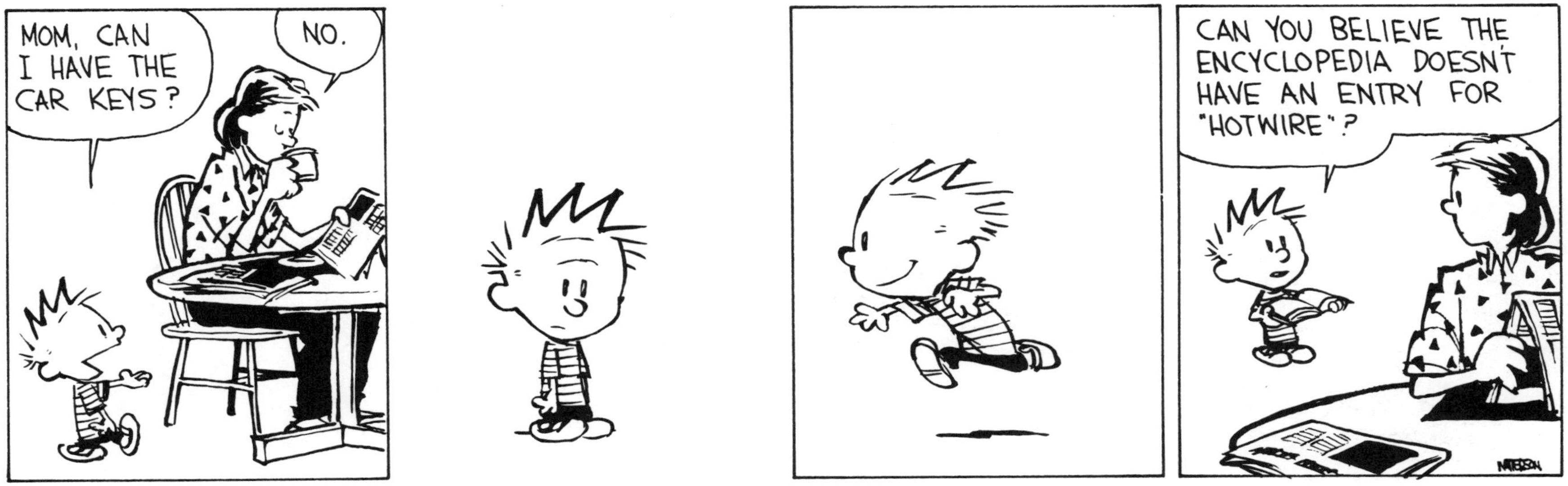
MOM, CAN I HAVE THE CAR KEYS?
NO.
CAN YOU BELIEVE THE ENCYCLOPEDIA DOESN'T HAVE AN ENTRY FOR "HOTWIRE"?

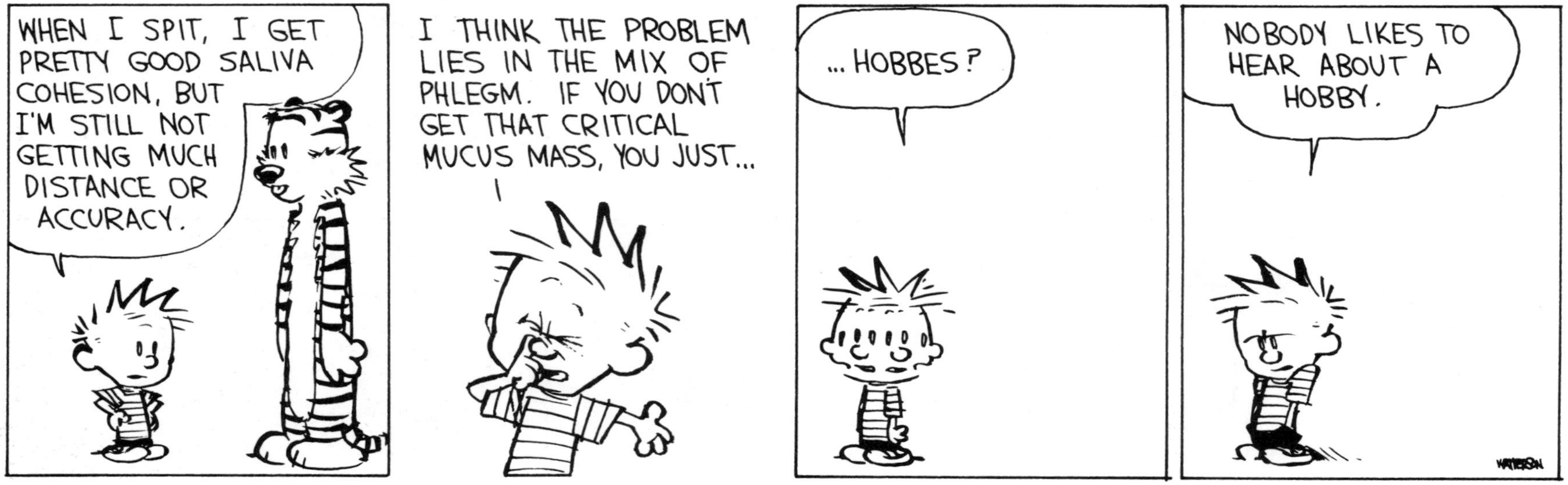
WHEN I SPIT, I GET PRETTY GOOD SALIVA COHESION, BUT I'M STILL NOT GETTING MUCH DISTANCE OR ACCURACY.
I THINK THE PROBLEM LIES IN THE MIX OF PHLEGM. IF YOU DON'T GET THAT CRITICAL MUCUS MASS, YOU JUST...
... HOBBES?
NOBODY LIKES TO HEAR ABOUT A HOBBY.

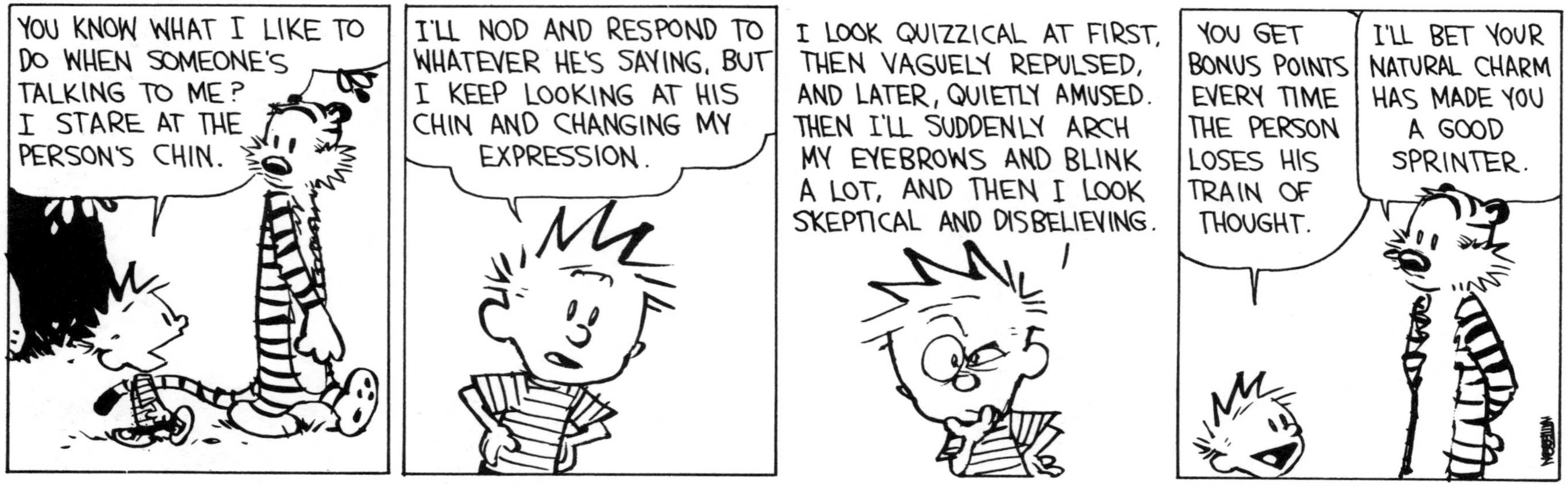
YOU KNOW WHAT I LIKE TO DO WHEN SOMEONE'S TALKING TO ME? I STARE AT THE PERSON'S CHIN.
I'LL NOD AND RESPOND TO WHATEVER HE'S SAYING, BUT I KEEP LOOKING AT HIS CHIN AND CHANGING MY EXPRESSION.
I LOOK QUIZZICAL AT FIRST, THEN VAGUELY REPULSED, AND LATER, QUIETLY AMUSED. THEN I'LL SUDDENLY ARCH MY EYEBROWS AND BLINK A LOT, AND THEN I LOOK SKEPTICAL AND DISBELIEVING.
YOU GET BONUS POINTS EVERY TIME THE PERSON LOSES HIS TRAIN OF THOUGHT.
I'LL BET YOUR NATURAL CHARM HAS MADE YOU A GOOD SPRINTER.

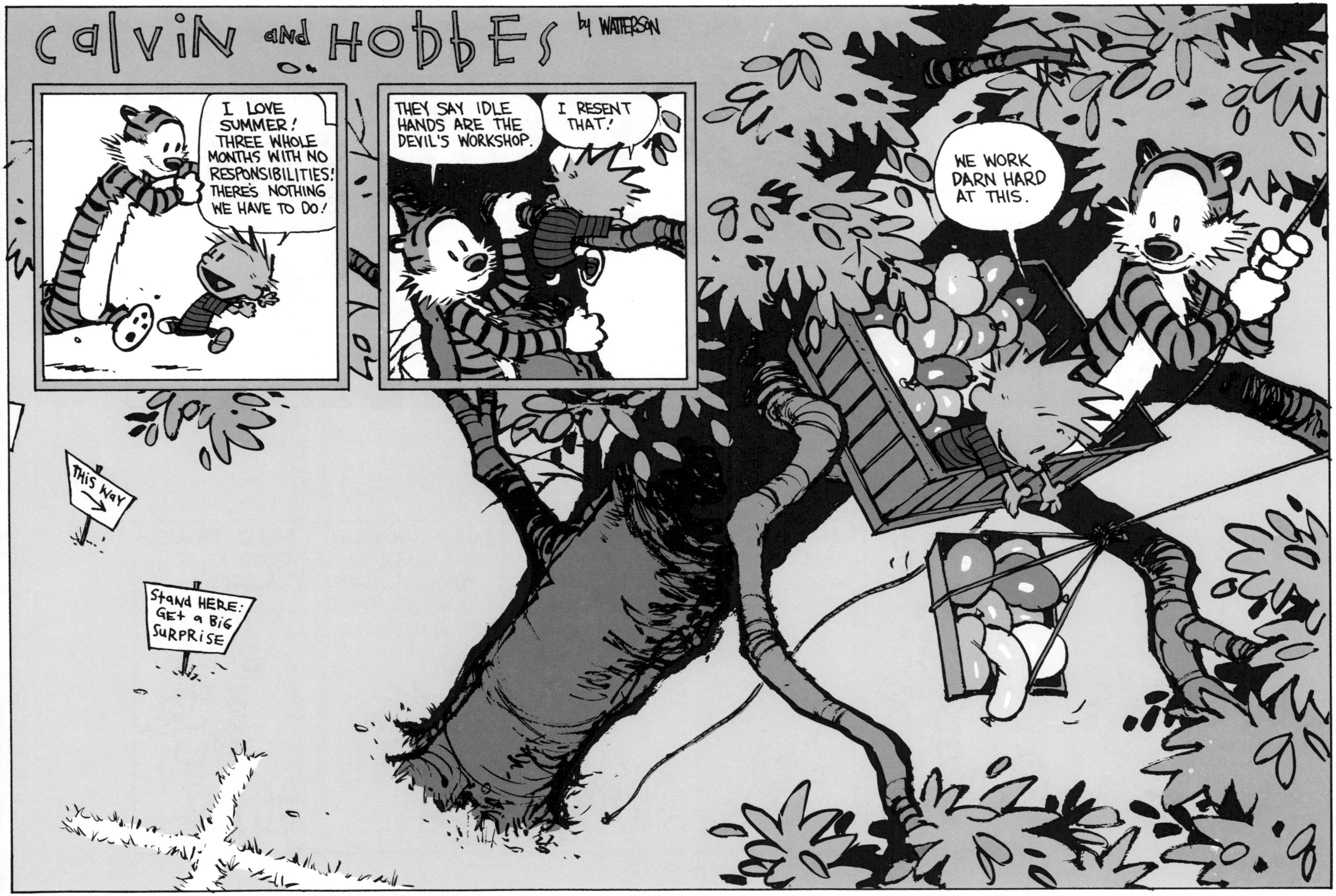

Calvin and HobbEs
by WATTERSON
I LOVE SUMMER! THREE WHOLE MONTHS WITH NO RESPONSIBILITIES! THERE'S NOTHING WE HAVE TO DO!
THEY SAY IDLE HANDS ARE THE DEVIL'S WORKSHOP.
I RESENT THAT!
WE WORK DARN HARD AT THIS.
THIS WAY
Stand HERE: Get a BiG SURPRiSE

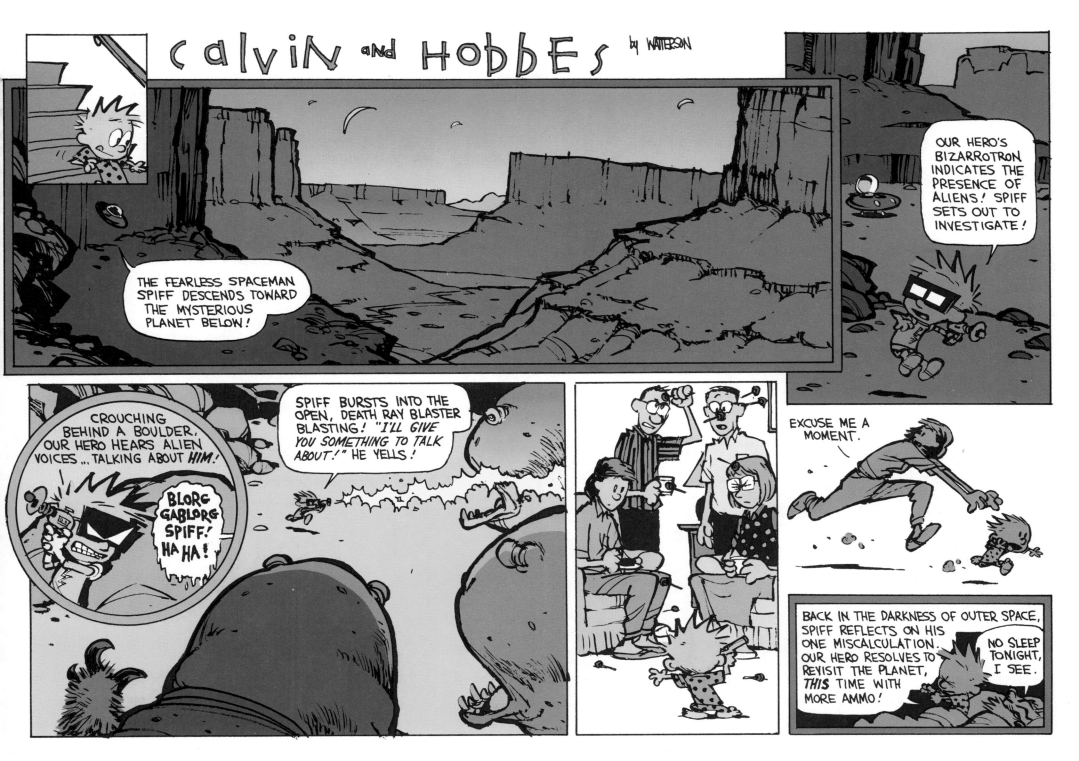

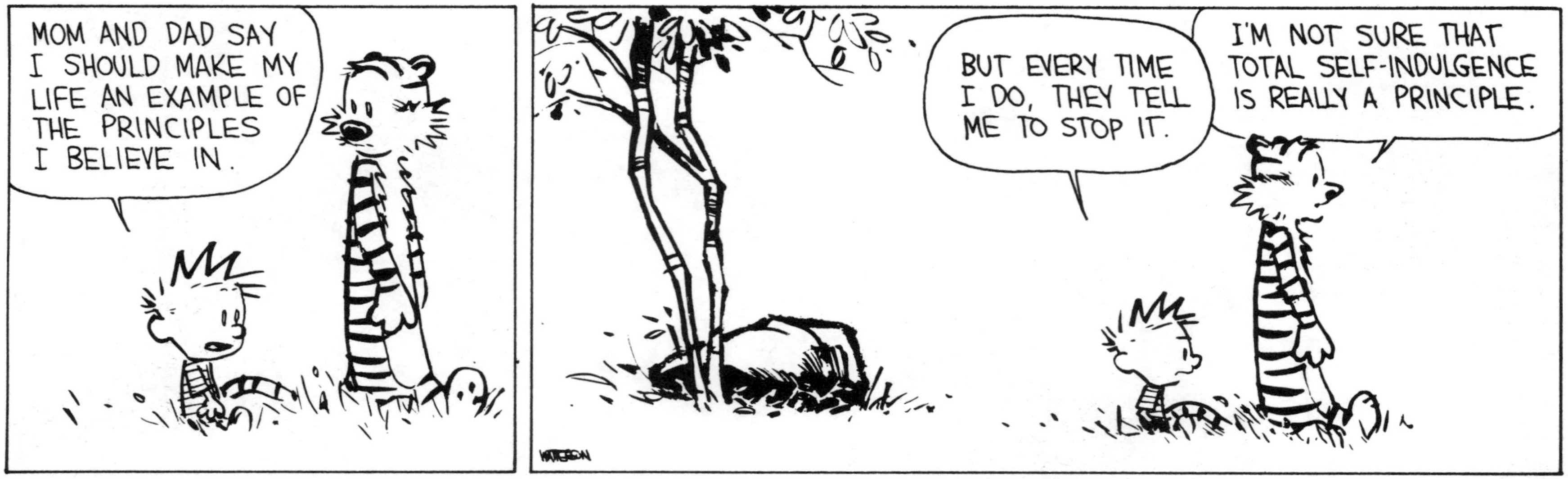
MOM AND DAD SAY I SHOULD MAKE MY LIFE AN EXAMPLE OF THE PRINCIPLES I BELIEVE IN.
BUT EVERY TIME I DO, THEY TELL ME TO STOP IT.
I'M NOT SURE THAT TOTAL SELF-INDULGENCE IS REALLY A PRINCIPLE.

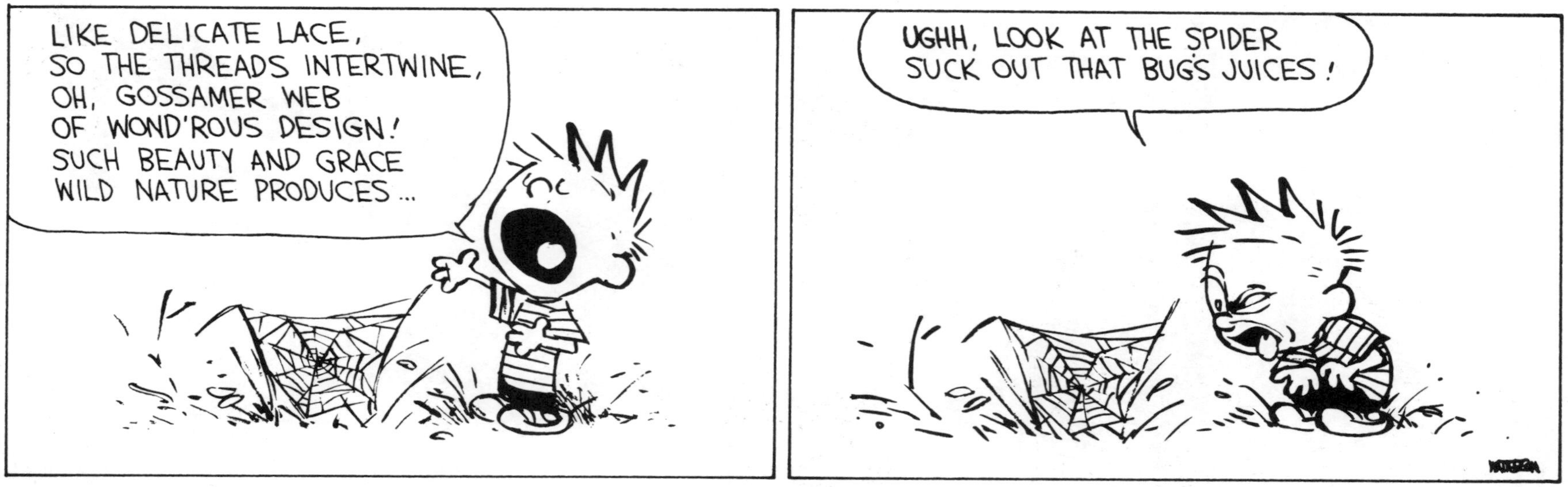
LIKE DELICATE LACE, SO THE THREADS INTERTWINE, OH, GOSSAMER WEB OF WOND'ROUS DESIGN! SUCH BEAUTY AND GRACE WILD NATURE PRODUCES...
UGHH, LOOK AT THE SPIDER SUCK OUT THAT BUG'S JUICES!

157

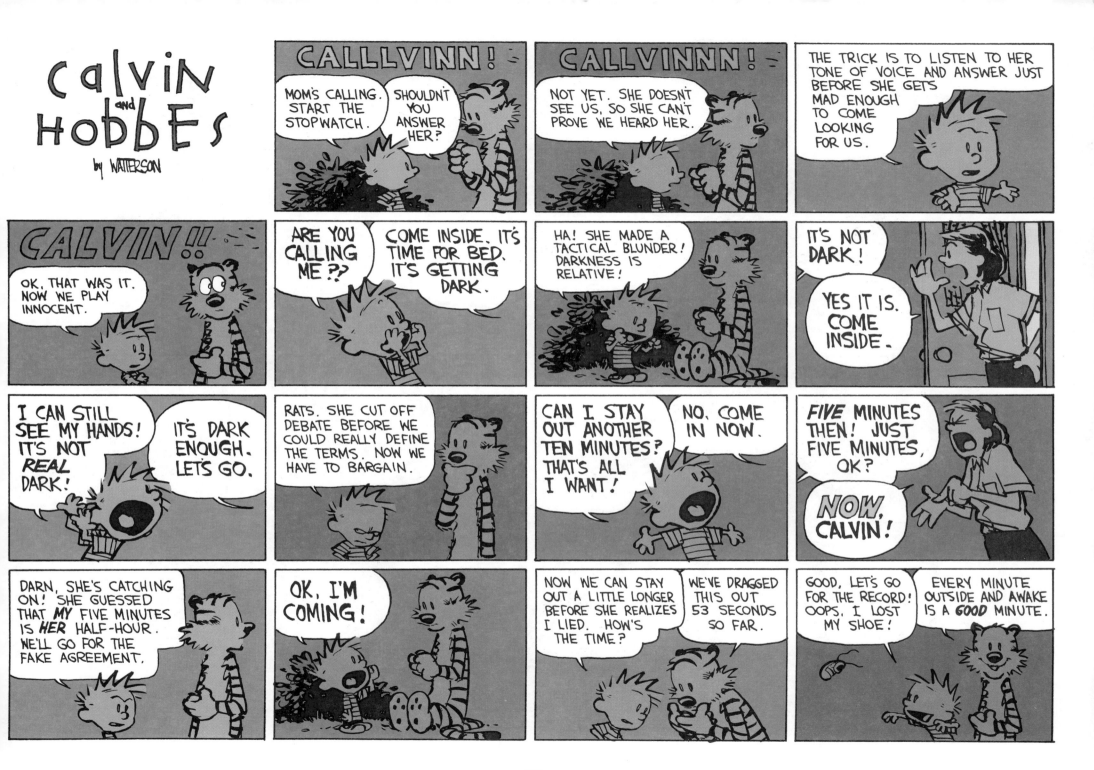

162

164

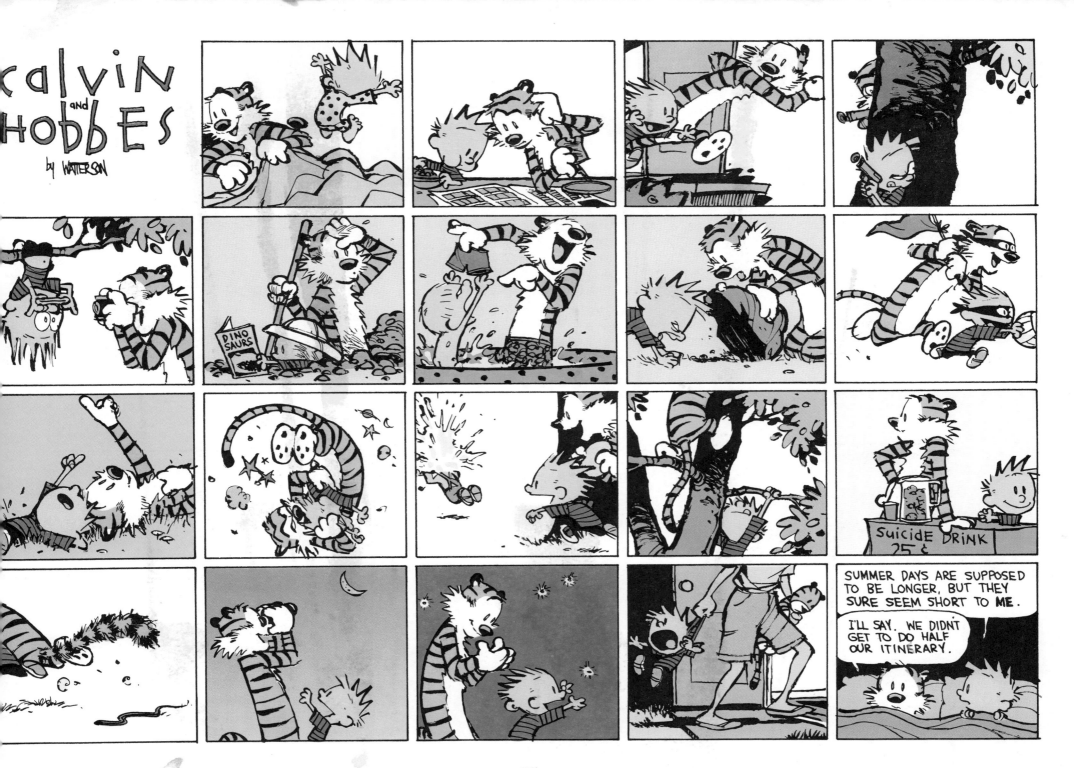